THE JAZZ SINGER'S GUIDEBOOK

A Course in Jazz Harmony and Scat Singing for the Serious Jazz Vocalist

by

David Berkman

Includes CD

Editor and Publisher - Chuck Sher
Cover Art - Daniel Boccato
Cover Type and Book Design - Attila Nagy
Text Editor - Bonnie Allen
CD Recorded by Peter Karl at Peter Karl Studio, Brooklyn, NY
Vocals - Abigail Riccards

© 2009 SHER MUSIC CO., P.O. Box 445, Petaluma, CA 94953
All Rights Reserved. International Copyright Secured. Made in the USA.
ISBN 1-883217-62-8

Table of Contents

INTRODUCTION i

CHAPTER 1 Becoming a Functional Pianist 1

CHAPTER 2 Lead Sheet Basics 31

CHAPTER 3 The Melody of Songs 55

CHAPTER 4 Practicing Scatting 1
The Chord Tones and Tensions of Progressions 67

CHAPTER 5 Practicing Scatting 2
Chord Scales, Friend or Foe? (Friend!) 73

CHAPTER 6 Practicing Scatting 3
Applying Chord Scales to a Tune 80

CHAPTER 7 Practicing Scatting 4
A Tetrachord Approach to Chord Scales 87

CHAPTER 8 Practicing Scatting 5
Chromatic Approach Note Patterns and Bebop Vocabulary 96

CHAPTER 9 Practicing Scatting 6
Guide Tone Lines 105

CHAPTER 10 Practicing Scatting 7
The Blues 110

CHAPTER 11 Practicing Scatting 8
Technical Drill of Intervals 119

CHAPTER 12 Conclusion 128

CONCLUSION 133

CD Examples

TRACK			PAGE
TRACK 1	CHAPTER 3	EXAMPLE 1	58
TRACK 2	CHAPTER 3	EXAMPLE 2	59
TRACK 3	CHAPTER 3	EXAMPLE 3	64
TRACK 4	CHAPTER 3	EXAMPLE 4	64
TRACK 5	CHAPTER 3	EXAMPLE 5	65
TRACK 6	CHAPTER 3	EXAMPLE 6	68
TRACK 7	CHAPTER 4	EXAMPLE 7	68
TRACK 8	CHAPTER 4	EXAMPLE 8	68
TRACK 9	CHAPTER 4	EXAMPLE 9	68
TRACK 10	CHAPTER 6	EXAMPLE 10	81
TRACK 11	CHAPTER 6	EXAMPLE 11	82
TRACK 12	CHAPTER 6	EXAMPLE 12	82
TRACK 13	CHAPTER 6	EXAMPLE 13	82
TRACK 14	CHAPTER 6	EXAMPLE 14	83
TRACK 15	CHAPTER 7	EXAMPLE 15	88
TRACK 16	CHAPTER 7	EXAMPLE 16	88
TRACK 17	CHAPTER 7	EXAMPLE 17	89
TRACK 18	CHAPTER 7	EXAMPLE 18	89
TRACK 19	CHAPTER 7	EXAMPLE 19	91
TRACK 20	CHAPTER 7	EXAMPLE 20	93
TRACK 21	CHAPTER 7	EXAMPLE 21	93
TRACK 22	CHAPTER 7	EXAMPLE 22	94
TRACK 23	CHAPTER 7	EXAMPLE 23	94
TRACK 24	CHAPTER 7	EXAMPLE 24	94
TRACK 25	CHAPTER 7	EXAMPLE 25	94
TRACK 26	CHAPTER 8	EXAMPLE 26	100
TRACK 27	CHAPTER 8	EXAMPLE 27	102
TRACK 28	CHAPTER 9	EXAMPLE 28	106
TRACK 29	CHAPTER 9	EXAMPLE 29	108
TRACK 30	CHAPTER 9	EXAMPLE 30	108
TRACK 31	CHAPTER 9	EXAMPLE 31	109
TRACK 32	CHAPTER 10	EXAMPLE 32	111
TRACK 33	CHAPTER 10	EXAMPLE 33	112
TRACK 34	CHAPTER 10	EXAMPLE 34	113
TRACK 35	CHAPTER 11	EXAMPLE 35	121
TRACK 36	CHAPTER 11	EXAMPLE 36	121
TRACK 37	CHAPTER 11	EXAMPLE 37	122
TRACK 38	CHAPTER 11	EXAMPLE 38	123
TRACK 39	CHAPTER 11	EXAMPLE 39	124
TRACK 40	CHAPTER 11	EXAMPLE 40	125
TRACK 41	CHAPTER 11	EXAMPLE 40	126

Introduction

Well, here is a book I never expected to write.

And if you ever heard me sing, you wouldn't expect me to write it either. (So, I guess we'd better avoid having you hear me sing.)

I started working on this book because of a need I saw. As jazz has moved more and more into academia, we've had a growth in the number of vocalists studying harmony, chord scales and jazz improvisation. Whether this is a good thing or a bad thing, I can't really say. It is a thing—a thing that is happening more and more.

It raises questions about what "jazz singing" is, what the role of scatting is in the world of vocal jazz, what skills are important for vocalists to master and what we want singers to do when they perform. This question gets raised because a lot of our most cherished vocal performances in jazz (and, of course, even more so outside the world of jazz) are not scat solos but versions of the melody (and lyric) of a song. Johnny Hartman with John Coltrane, Nancy Wilson with Cannonball Adderley and Billie Holliday to name but a few—a lot of the performances that these singers are most known for are performances of the melody, in which phrasing the lyrics, feeling, sound and timing are the primary considerations, not complex soloing over changes.

To state the obvious, most vocal performances (even by jazz singers) aren't scat solos.

And yet, being able to scat well means you've internalized the chord changes of songs in a deep way. It also means you understand something about jazz melodicism, swing feel, alterations to chords, and the vocabulary of bebop and blues. Understanding how to scat helps you understand chords and harmony and it allows you to be an improvising musician, composer and arranger.

How you use your skills (for good or evil) is up to you. It is very fashionable for instrumentalists to attack scat solos as inept and out of date. Why do instrumentalists "diss" singers when they scat?

One reason is that many singers venture into scatting with little knowledge of what a jazz solo is. Some singers are more concerned with getting attention than with deepening their musical expression. These are the divas. If they scat, they will do attention-getting things and probably not spend hours studying solos and harmony. If you are this kind of singer, then this book is probably not for you. (But feel free to buy it anyway!)

Another reason for antipathy to scatting is the instrumentalist's preoccupation with musical virtuosity and facility (in the same way that trombonists are the butt of jokes because the trombone tends to be hard to play with the extreme facility that sax players more commonly display). (On that score a personal favorite has always been: What's the difference between a trombone and a chainsaw? A chainsaw sounds better in a small group. And while I am at it, what do drummers get on their college entrance exams? Drool!) There can also be an element of sexism in some male jazz players attitudes toward the "chick singer."

More substantively, though, instrumentalists tend to dislike scatting because scatting is so hard to do well, and often instrumentalists scat better (not in terms of vocal technique but in terms of note choice) than singers do. Singers who attempt to scat with only the most rudimentary awareness of chord changes are often not worth listening to. Some singers who aren't really hearing the chord changes of the song ape the mannerisms of great jazz singers—the syllables, the gravelly voice of Louis, the superficial "vibe" of scat singing, without developing their sense of harmony and their understanding of what goes on in a jazz instrumental solo. For these reasons, often the instrumentalist's dislike of scatting is justified—why should a jazz player who has practiced and studied the harmonic and rhythmic foundation of soloing over chord changes (who has honed his craft as an improviser emulating the players who inspire him) respect singers who are winging it? (Conversely, instrumentalists have a GREAT respect for scatting when done by masters such as Louis Armstrong, Jon Hendricks, Bobby McFerrin, Ella Fitzgerald or Sarah Vaughn.) Most singers ARE winging it because they don't know of a way to practice improving their awareness of the harmony of tunes. They don't know a way to practice improvising.

I started thinking about this issue when I was a guest at a workshop for singers. I suggested to one of them that she try and scat on the tune that she had just sung. She replied that she couldn't do that because she hadn't been singing the tune long enough. I asked what her method was for becoming familiar enough with a tune to begin scatting on it and she told me that she had to spend a long, long time with the melody, singing the song many times so that she would know it well enough to start deviating from it.

This is not an entirely stupid approach, of course. There is a lot to be gained by repetition, and knowing the melody well will help you scat better. But, I would say it isn't a terribly focused approach. Learning the harmonic structure of a song can be practiced much more directly.

This is one of the skills I am hoping you can improve with this book. The more you are able to pinpoint what you wish to work on when you are practicing, the more successful you are likely to be. If you want to learn the harmony of a song to be able to deviate from the melody, you need to find a focused way of practicing THAT. You want to find a way of practicing that is more helpful than singing the melody over and over.

To begin exploring the song's harmony, we'll start by analyzing the melody to see how it fits with the harmonic structure of the song. We'll work on ways to "loosen up" the melody, using the lyric of the song. The most direct way of working on the underlying harmony of a song is to sing pieces of that harmony, free from the melodic choices of the composer. That is, essentially, what the process of working on scatting is.

Understanding and hearing harmony better will help you sing the melody better, with a greater sense of freedom. This last point is important. Learning the harmony better makes you a better singer. Learning to scat gives you the ability to create interesting melodies over the harmony of a song. Being able to make melodies over the harmony of the song will allow you to deviate from the melody in the first or second chorus of a tune in interesting "instrumental" ways, and this will have a big effect on your singing whether or not you choose to scat when you perform.

All these things can be practiced using many different approaches to explore the problem of harmony in songs. Some of what vocalists need to practice are the same things that instrumentalists need to work on. I wrote a book called "The Jazz Musician's Guide to Creative Practicing" and that book was about helping (primarily) instrumentalists practice better. In my experience singers practice much less efficiently than instrumentalists do.

Of course, we don't give singers much help. I think that a lot of jazz schools teach vocal technique fairly well (if they teach technique). Often this is because they have a classical technique teacher that handles that end of things. But as far as teaching vocalists to practice the harmonic fundamentals of tunes, we either put them in the same improvisation classes that instrumentalists take, or we ignore this aspect of their vocal development. Most jazz schools do both of these things, alternating between them in different classes.

Some of the things that vocalists need to study are quite different from the things instrumentalists need to study. It's easier to send someone to the practice room to do something complicated than to think of a way to work on the same thing in a simpler way, more connected to the nature of the voice. Ultimately, singers can't push any button on their body to make a sound—it all has to be conjured out of the air. So, with that in mind, a group of approaches specifically tailored to vocalists is needed. To name one example among many, instrumentalists often play a long continuous line of 8th notes moving straight up and down their instruments changing scales as the chords change. While I wouldn't discourage singers who wish to work on long chord scales, this long scale exercise is so challenging vocally that the technical demands of this exercise become a distraction from the real point of it. If you can't internalize the exercise in a simple way, it isn't really doing you much good. In other words, if you are practicing singing scales in 3 octaves going up and down, or even in 2 octaves, the exercise is going to revolve around the vocal technique required to do this rather challenging thing, when the point of the exercise (on instruments) is to help you find chord scales anywhere on your instrument. It is a lot more useful for singers to work on tetrachords rather than whole scales (to hear the chord changes better) and guide tone lines are even more useful. In short, smaller pieces of scales tend to be more vocalistic.

But as I said, this is one example among many. One of the main goals of this book is to find easy, vocally accessible ways for you to work on harmony and scatting.

Of course, there are also many things that vocalists need to know about music that aren't directly connected to scatting. These things include basic piano skills, understanding the theory concerning chord progressions and substitutions, ear training relating to the intervals of the melody and other intervallic studies, to name a few. Part of this book is about these things, about ways to practice that will have a big impact on your singing, again, whether or not you choose to scat.

Everyone can be a functional pianist and many great singers are. The amount of piano skills that you need to accompany yourself adequately is within the range of every musical person. Although many vocal students are piano-phobic, it is my hope that if you follow the mostly painless approach to working on the piano outlined in this book, that you will be able to accompany yourself adequately at the piano.

It is my hope that you will be able to use this book to learn how to practice. In my experience, most singers are at a loss when it comes to practicing improvising. You CAN develop a greater sense of how to go about practicing on your very difficult instrument, the voice.

Instrumentalists will also gain from practicing exactly these same things. Perhaps, along with technique on your instrument, this is all you really need to practice, since learning to sing something is essentially learning to hear something and if you can hear it and sing it, then you can teach yourself to play it.

Finally, let me say that a lot of jazz vocal instruction is a sort of performance coaching: knowing the lyric well and understanding the story telling aspect of singing, smiling and having a pleasant, relaxed demeanor while you deliver the lyrics, having a good working relationship with other musicians, counting off tunes, focusing your energy as a performer, etc. This book is not about those things. I'm not a singer and can't really teach you about that, useful as that kind of coaching may be. Instead, this book is about what you need to do every day in a practice room with a piano. This book is about understanding the harmony of tunes in a deeper way to enhance your understanding of the music you sing. This book will help you practice better, and hopefully become a vocal musician, making progressive steps to improve your ability to improvise, instead of just a vocal performer.

When I first moved to New York, I was lucky to work on and off for several years with a great singer named Dakota Staton. When people referred to her as a jazz singer, she always said, "I'm not a jazz singer, I'm a song stylist." If you have the kind of storytelling ability, phrasing and soulfulness of a Dakota Staton, maybe you don't need to develop your piano skills and learn to hear and understand more of the harmony of songs. But why wouldn't you want to? If an instrumentalists' understanding of singing contributed to the vocal artistry of Louis Armstrong, Shirley Horn, Carmen McCrae, Sarah Vaughn, Ray Charles, Chet Baker, Nat "King" Cole, Rosa Passos, Andy Bey, Diana Krall, Dena DeRose and countless others, maybe it will help you too.

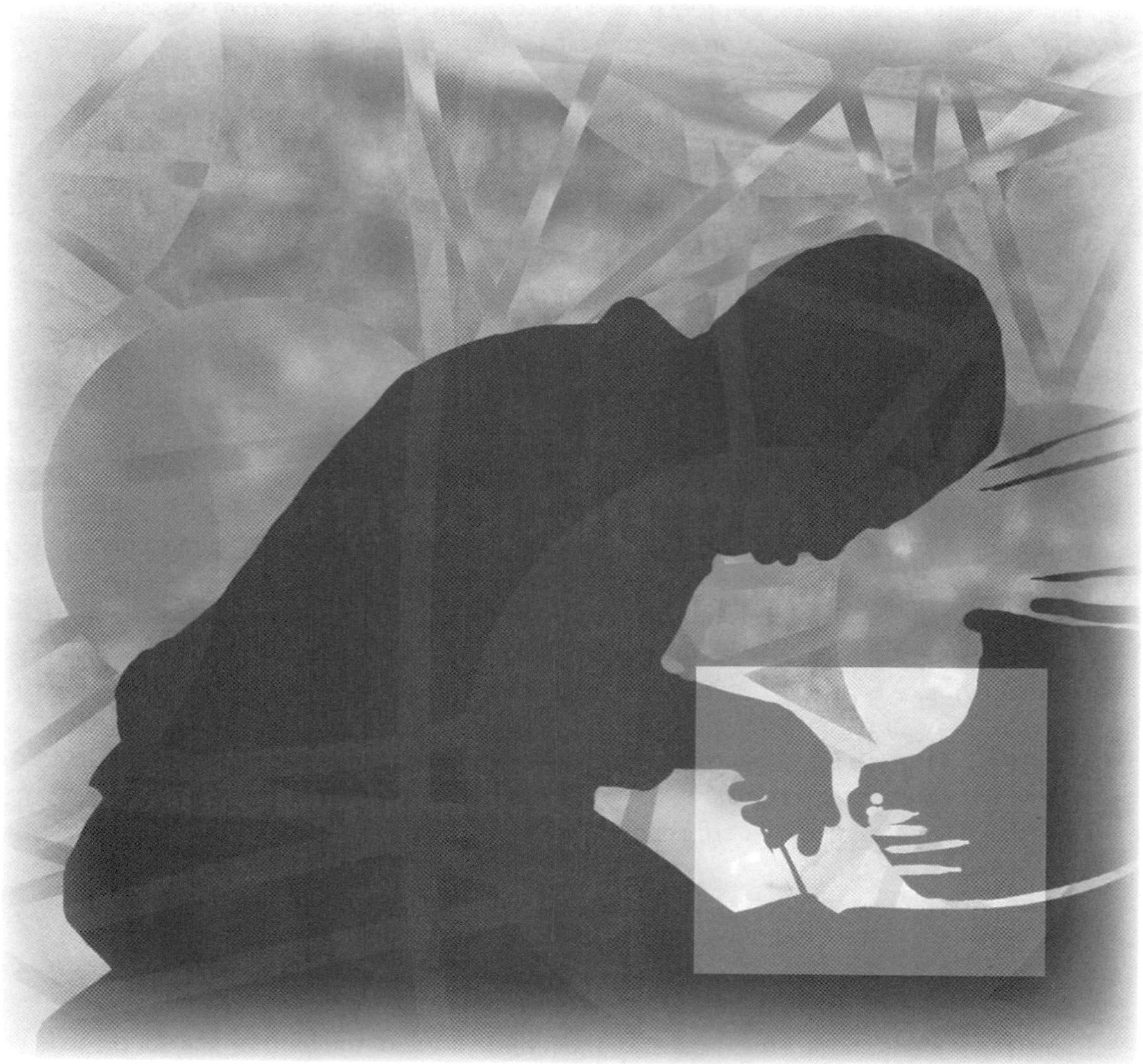

CHAPTER 1

Becoming a Functional Pianist

Let's look at the piano. Don't be scared. It is essential that singers who are looking for ways to improve their ability to improvise have a good knowledge of the piano. This is because your instrument (the voice) is essentially an ear-activated slide whistle. You can't push a button to find a note when you are singing. Fortunately, when you are playing the piano, that is exactly what you do.

Keep in mind, for starters, that you don't need great technique at the keyboard to begin. What you need first and foremost is to be able to find notes on the keyboard, and this leads to finding harmony on the keyboard and perhaps even finding melody, scales and interesting material to sing over progressions at the keyboard. You need to become a functional pianist in the style that used to be called "arranger's piano."

Some of you may have experienced a wave of fear, or a feeling of self-loathing (or perhaps "piano-loathing") when I mentioned that you need to become functional as a pianist. One thing that many singing students have in common is a bad past experience with theory classes or piano study. I remember talking to a good working singer and something related to theory came up in the conversation and she said, "I should remember that—we talked about that in theory class and I thought I had it memorized." It was as if she was trying to remember a formula, how to do quadratic equations, or the combination of a locker. If you have not integrated theory basics into something that you can do at the piano (or guitar, although this is somewhat less desirable due to the complexities of the guitar fingerboard and the simplicity of the piano keyboard) then you might as well not study theory at all.

I had another student once—an opera singer who wanted to study piano—but confessed that she had an extreme mental block concerning the piano. She couldn't even remember the pattern of white and black keys, and she hoped I could help her overcome this mental block. So we spent a lot of time concocting different tools she could use, writing the note names on the keys, drilling different aspects of note finding, using a drawing of a keyboard and other ideas. Finally, since she was improving so little, I asked her to keep a diary of her work. When she returned three weeks later, she had recorded a total of 20 minutes of piano practice since I had last seen her. "Aha," I said, "I have discovered the nature of your mental block. You aren't practicing." Learning the piano does take time and effort. But by taking minimal steps and focusing on the music, you can improve steadily and I think somewhat painlessly. Thirty minutes a day should lead to massive improvement within a few months. (It should also give you six-pack abs and buns of steel, but I'm not promising anything there.)

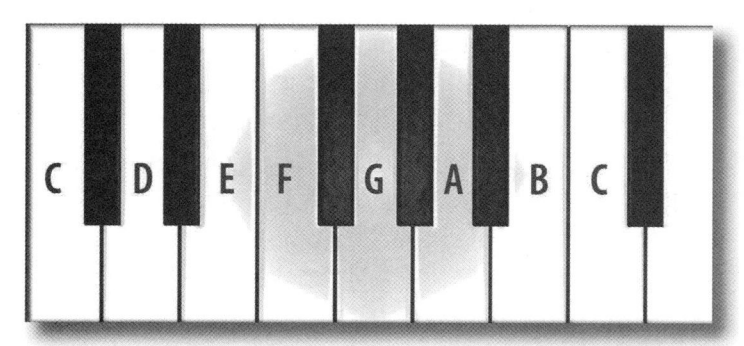

CHAPTER 1

If you have had a bad experience with studying the piano, I think I can help. In almost every case, people (who are musical, as I am assuming all of you are) who have had a hard time learning the piano have been asked to do too much, too quickly, or have asked themselves to do too much too quickly. The level of piano playing that I have in mind for you is pretty much obtainable by every vocalist. It's important to work on this because you will get practice at that most basic of practice processes—namely, breaking large difficult problems down into smaller more manageable ones. This is the primary skill that you will need for everything else that we will cover, so why not begin now with the piano?

So where should a piano neophyte begin? Let's start with the most basic skill, finding notes on the piano keyboard. Probably most of you know how to find the notes on the piano and if you do feel free to skip this paragraph. If you haven't mastered this, it's not difficult to do so. It's all a question of orienting yourself to the basic pattern of black keys (grouped 2,3,2,3...) and then recognizing this relationship over and over in different parts of the piano. (For example, C is the white note that is to the immediate left of the first (or left-most) of the two black keys in a two-black-key group. The D is the white note that falls between the two black keys in a two-black-key group. The E is the white key to the right of the 2nd black note (or right-most black note) in a two-black-key group, etc. These locations are fairly easy to memorize and you should do so for all of the white keys. The black key immediately to the right of the white key is a sharp (the key immediately to the right of D is D#.) The black key immediately to the left of a white key is a flat. (The key immediately to the left of D is Db). Every black note has two names (D# = Eb). Begin looking for notes by orienting yourself to middle C, the C just about in the middle of the piano (it's right under the "e" in the Steinway decal—or the "o" in the Story and Clark decal if you aren't so favorably endowed.)

For most of you, the above information isn't new. I assume most of you can name pitches on a keyboard. The skill that you really need to practice is locating these notes in different octaves and finding them quickly. Eventually, we want this knowledge of the keyboard to be instant and instinctual, requiring no thought.

This raises an important point. If you are like any one of the hundreds, possibly thousands, of people who have come up to me on a gig to let me know that they used to play piano as a child and are kicking themselves for having let it go as they got older and moved on with their lives, I have a message for you. In your adult life, you will only play things on the piano that are really easy (and fun) for you. If you practice something and you get most of it, meaning you can sort of play it, or you can get

CHAPTER 1

through it with effort, well—that's not good enough. You are going to quit because you haven't internalized whatever you are playing completely. Even if you practice a lot as a child and can play some fairly hard pieces pretty well, you will find that as an adult, watching reality television is easier and, if not equally fulfilling, at least filled with a sort of grim fascination that is less painful than working on "Für Elise." So you really need to spend some time, when you work on the piano, on fully internalizing the things you want to practice. You can do that by practicing everything in small pieces—only that part of the puzzle that is manageable and no more.

Of course, there is a real up-side to this sort of practice (apart from the fact that it works better than practicing things that are too hard). If you practice what's easy, you aren't practicing things that are difficult. (Okay, that sounds obvious, I'll grant you, but so does velcro after someone else came up with it.) What I mean by this is, if you are reluctant to work on the piano, when it is probably the simplest and most powerful tool a singer can employ to improve his or her musicianship, it is because you ARE PRACTICING THINGS THAT ARE TOO HARD. (Of course, you might have been led down that path by an old teacher, but those days are long gone. Visualize your happy place with a piano in it and move on.)

Okay, so let's try to improve our grasp of where the notes are on the piano. **Open a fake book and pick any tune at random.** That's right, any tune. Even a really hard one, even "Colors of Chloe"—anything that has chord symbols above the staff. **Your job is to find the bass notes of the chords in your left hand on the piano.** You don't have to do this in time. All we are practicing is finding notes in the left hand. If you see an AbMaj7, play Ab. Play the roots in the octave that is about two octaves below middle C. That's it.

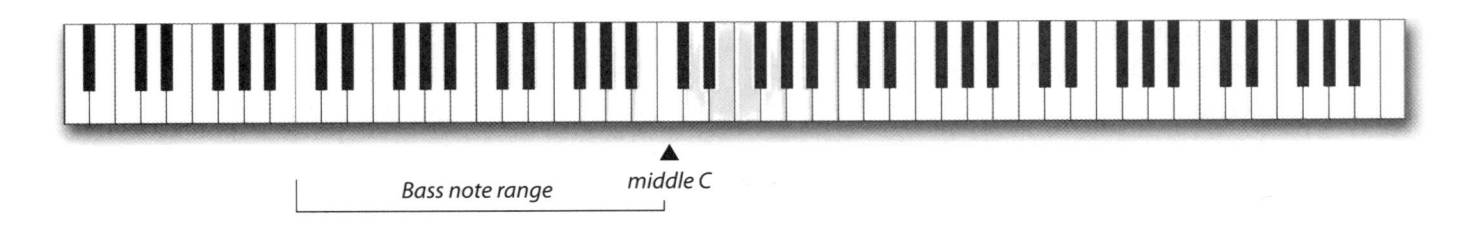

Bass note range — *middle C*

DESIRABLE BASS NOTE RANGE

What do you get out of doing something that is SOOO easy? You get practice at the one thing that we are trying to develop: finding notes on the instrument.

CHAPTER 1

Okay, now let's try this with the right hand, play all of the roots with your right hand in the octave above middle C.

middle C

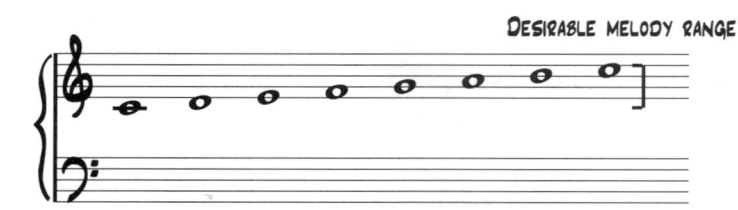

DESIRABLE MELODY RANGE

Now let's try it with both hands simultaneously, playing the roots of the chords about three octaves apart, the right hand an octave or so above middle C and the left hand two octaves below middle C. Again, there is no time pressure here, the emphasis is on finding the right notes and not making mistakes, rather than playing the song in metronomic time. Try this with some of the tunes that you sing, your lead sheets or arrangements in the keys that you sing them in, again, with no thought about doing this in time.

Monitoring Your Progress

I am giving you a process of moving very slowly step by step to get greater familiarity and comfort playing the piano. I am moving this slowly because, as I said above, many singers have had bad experiences attempting to play the piano in the past, and the way to avoid this negative experience is to move slowly, only doing what is easy. For some of you, playing the roots of the chords of the song is already something that you can do without effort and so you needn't spend any time on this step. However, for those of you that can't do this step immediately, there is much to be gained by moving at a slow pace. (That reminds me, Q: what did the snail riding on the turtle's back say? A: Wheeeee!) For one thing, playing the roots is usually enough, especially on songs that you know, to get a sense of the harmony of the tune and so you can use the roots alone to accompany yourself. Singers in a band situation often like singing with just the bass player, the rest of the band laying out, because the harmony is implied but there is a lot of space. In a sense, when you play the roots of the chords at the piano and sing the melody of the song, you are singing over a bass, albeit a simpler bass line than most bassists play. Also, playing the roots is something that, even if you haven't done it before, you can usually master relatively quickly. Doing this helps you find notes quickly, learning the location of the notes on the piano.

DON'T ASSUME YOU CAN DO THIS STEP EASILY (OR ANY OTHER STEP YOU ENCOUNTER IN THIS BOOK) UNTIL YOU'VE TRIED IT. You may find that even though you understand how simple playing the roots is, you stumble a bit or make a mistake here and there. Don't accept imperfect performance of any of these easy steps. You need to fully internalize the process and if it is not too hard for you, so much the better.

My point here is that you have to constantly monitor what you are capable of doing easily in your practice. Try to practice that thing that is only slightly difficult, slowing it down or repeating it a few times to move it from the "slightly or minimally difficult" column to the "easy" column. With each repetition you want to reduce the effort, doing the same thing in a simpler, easier way. If you are practicing something that is TOO easy, you will be able to do it perfectly the first few times and you can move on. Anything more difficult than that needs more practicing.

To return to our gradual descent into piano playing, keep working with just the roots, either doubled or in the left hand only. Make sure that you keep the roots in the right range of the piano, 1 to 2 octaves below middle C because this is where the roots sound like they are functioning as bass notes—up higher they sound like they might be somewhere in the middle of the chord instead of at the bottom of the chord defining what the root is. This quality of the piano is important; what you play (what part of the chord, the root, the 3rd, the 7th or tensions: 9ths, 11ths and 13ths) depends to some extent on where you are on the piano—what range of the instrument (or in other words how far to the left or right your hand is). In the range we are talking about, 2 octaves below middle C, notes sound like the roots of each chord.

Students using keyboards often lose the sense of where they are on the piano since many keyboards have less than 88 keys and so don't exactly look like a piano keyboard. Find middle C and ALWAYS orient yourself, whatever instrument you are using.

Go through many (all?) of your charts, singing the melody as you play the roots of the chords. Is this enough accompaniment for you to hear the harmony of the song? Are some of the roots that you are playing obscuring the harmony for you? Perhaps you have some changes that are not so good. Eventually we will be analyzing chord changes to try to improve (or at least simplify) your chord changes to make your charts easier to play, but for now, you might want to notice which chords seem to be helping—which bass notes help make the harmony clearer for you—and which bass notes make the harmony less clear.

One last time, before we move on, I want to emphasize that if you cannot do this step easily (playing the roots and singing) you will benefit a lot from repeating it with many tunes until it becomes easy. Keep in mind that if something is just a little difficult but mostly doable, that is precisely the feeling you want to have ALL THE TIME as you practice. Most students think that if they "get it" more or less it's time to move on. It isn't. Repeat the step many times until it is REALLY easy, and THEN move on. If something resists becoming easy, meaning that you are repeating it but not seeing any change in the amount of effort required to do it (it's in the "slightly difficult" column or even the

CHAPTER 1

"almost easy" column and no matter how many times you play it, it doesn't get into the "really easy" column), then you are doing too much or doing something that is too difficult. Find a way to simplify what you are working on by practicing the piece in 4-bar units, by doing it at a slower tempo, by practicing with one hand or by some other way that is appropriate for what you are practicing. Repeat THAT until it is easy, and gradually build back up in stages to the thing that resisted becoming easy in the beginning.

Of course, eventually you WILL need to move on. One thing that might be helpful would be to **try to play some melodies with your right hand WHILE you play roots with the left.** Look for simple melodies without lots of 8th notes. Tunes like Tune Up, Blue and Green, But Not for Me, Cherokee, Here's that Rainy Day and countless others have relatively simple melodies and are good tunes to begin with. When playing melodies with your right hand, again, try to break down the process into easy-to-accomplish steps. Perhaps a first step would be just finding all of the right pitches out of time with one finger, playing only the melody in the right hand, leaving out the left hand roots. Next, you might try to find a fingering that is a little more efficient than the one finger approach. (Or not. Again, if this isn't easy for you, you would probably benefit greatly from playing through some standards using only one finger. You'd be practicing finding pitches and gaining greater familiarity with distances on the keyboard. Some people, however, would find this awkward and uncomfortable and so they wouldn't realize the potential benefit that could come from a little one-finger practice. Remember: always monitor yourself, the level of difficulty and your interest level in what you are doing, and try to be creative about ways to break down complex problems into something simple.)

There are a few simple rules that help you to come up with a logical fingering. First, avoid putting the thumb (otherwise know as the first finger in piano lingo) on a black note. This rule probably holds true about 95 percent of the time when you are playing single note lines. (When you are playing chords this rule doesn't apply). Second, try to move your hand position as little as possible. You are trying to find groups of notes that will sit underneath your hand and won't require you to change position often. A piano teacher of mine referred to this as reading "for groups of notes" instead of individual notes. Sometimes there is nothing you can do, and you must move your hand, but whenever possible, you want to move it to a position where it will be able to play all of the notes for the next phrase, or large part of the next phrase.

And that's it for fingering. Eventually, it is useful to work a bit on scale fingering, or try some simple Bach pieces to get some fingering ideas for dealing with melodies and moving your hand up and down the piano, but for now don't worry too much about that. (Unless that seems interesting to you. Remember: Monitor your level of interest!) Just try to find reasonable fingering in an intuitive way, doing the best you can.

When you are comfortable playing one of these easy melodies with the right hand only, you are ready for the next step, mentioned above, playing the

melodies and bass notes simultaneously. Try practicing the song in four bar units at a slow tempo. Again, try to keep the left hand about 2 to 3 octaves below the right. There is a tendency to want to put the two hands closer together so you can keep an eye on both of them at the same time. Try to avoid this tendency. Now you are playing something that sounds a little more like the song, like music. Hopefully, this is fairly enjoyable and not too painful. If so, try this with many tunes and you will start to get comfortable with playing two things at once, a task that is specific to the piano.

One more time, let me repeat myself here. You don't need to move past this level of playing right away. You will get a lot of benefit from working through all of your tunes like this. You'll reinforce your sense of the melody and hear the chord changes, at least to the extent that you can derive the chord changes from the root motion of these tunes. You may even find that you are starting to enjoy playing the piano a bit. (There, I said it, but I am not going to push you. This is the mistake your parents made and you didn't become a doctor anyway.)

Let's look at some chords. Chords are combinations of more than two notes struck at the same time. A particular vertical arrangement of the notes of a chord is called a "voicing". The most basic voicing of a particular chord is a "root position" voicing. Root position usually means stacking the chord tones in 3rds from the root, so for a CMaj7: C, E, G, B would be the chord in root position.

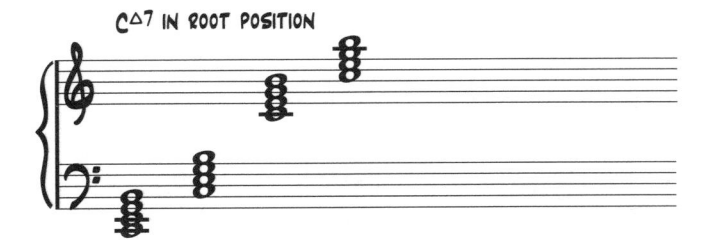

C△7 IN ROOT POSITION

Practicing chords in root position is useful as a way of becoming familiar with chords on the piano but root position is not a particularly interesting voicing. Root position chords are not especially pianistic for reasons which we'll discuss below. Still, knowing the chord tones for all seventh chords is important and spending time with root position voicings is a good way to learn them. One reasonable way to practice this is to **play the root position chord in both hands, in the octave below middle C in your left hand and one octave higher in your right hand. You should practice all chord qualities this way:** major 7, a major triad with the natural 7th, the "ti" of the major scale; minor major 7, a minor triad with the natural 7th, the "ti" of the major scale; dominant seventh, a major triad with the flatted 7th; minor seventh, a minor triad with the flatted 7th; minor seventh flat five, a diminished triad with a flatted 7th, and the diminished seventh, a diminished triad with a double flatted 7th (the same note as the 6th). In addition to this, you should practice finding these chords in all keys. (Below, find all the different chord qualities in C major and F major. **Keep transposing around the circle of fifths** {Bb, Eb, Ab, Db, Gb, B, E, A, D, G} **until you've played every chord quality in all keys.**)

CHAPTER 1

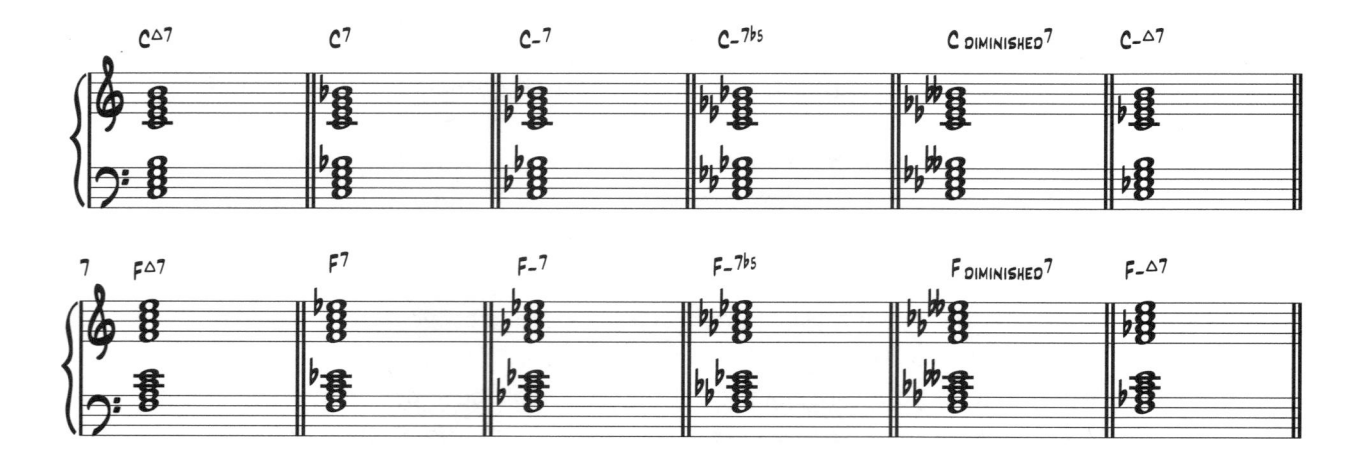

[Musical notation: Two rows of seventh chord voicings in root position. First row in C: C△7, C7, C-7, C-7b5, C diminished7, C-△7. Second row in F: F△7, F7, F-7, F-7b5, F diminished7, F-△7.]

You can now combine the last two approaches and play the melody of a song in your right hand and the root position chords in your left. Do this with a few of the simple songs that you played earlier with the melody in the right hand, roots in the left hand, such as "Blue in Green," "Cherokee" or "All the Things You Are."

[Musical notation: Four-bar example in 4/4 with chord symbols F-7, B♭-7, E♭7, A♭△7, melody in treble clef and root position chord voicings in bass clef.]

As you played the root position chords underneath the melody, you might have had problems deciding which octave to put the left hand in. Sometimes, the root is a little too high up on the piano and doesn't really sound like a bass note (because it's getting close to middle C, as happens in the first bar) but if the root is in the correct register to sound like a bass note one octave lower, the rest of the chord sounds muddy (as in the fourth bar). The chord sounds muddy because in the bass range of the piano, larger intervals (octaves, fifths, sixths and sevenths) tend to sound better, not the stacked 3rds that occur in a root position voicing. This is one of the difficulties of the root position voicing.

Of the four chord tones, the root is the most important (as we've seen) since that identifies the bass note of the chord. The 3rd is the next most important note, because that defines whether the chord is a major or minor chord. Finally, the seventh tells what kind of seventh chord this is. These three notes are said to "define" most chords (with the exception of the minor 7th flat five chord—or half diminished 7th—and diminished 7th chord). Stated more simply: 1, 3 and 7 are very important notes in most seventh chords and the 5th is not a very important note. For that reason, one way to improve on this root position voicing as you play the melody in your right hand is to leave the 5th out of the voicing while still keeping the most important notes: 1, 3 and 7 for all of the chords.

CHAPTER 1

So let's try this next step: play 1, 3 and 7 in your left hand for all of the chords of a tune. Let's try this with a ballad popular with singers, "We'll be Together Again."

We'll Be Together Again

Medium Ballad

Carl Fischer, Frankie Laine

No tears, no fears, Re-mem-ber there's al-ways to-mor-row, So what if we have to part, We'll be to-geth-er a-gain. Your kiss, your smile, Are mem-'ries I'll treas-ure for-ev-er, So try think-ing with your heart, We'll be to-geth-er a-gain. Times when I know you'll be lone-some, Times when I know you'll be sad; Don't let temp-ta-tion sur-round you, Don't let the blues make you bad. Some day, some way, we both have a life-time be-fore us, For part-ing is not good-bye, We'll be to-geth-er a-gain.

Two changes in a bar get two beats apiece.

©1945 (Renewed) by Music Sales Corporation, Cares Music Co. and Fischer Music Co.
All Rights for Cares Music Co. Administered by Music Sales Corporation (ASCAP).
International Copyright Secured. All Rights Reserved. Used by Permission

9

CHAPTER 1

Play 1, 3 and 7 for the first chord, with the root a fifth below middle C. Actually we have a little bit of a choice here, should the root of the chord be the G below middle C or a G an octave below that? Try playing both of these 1,3,7 voicings and see which one you think is better. Depending on the quality of piano you are playing, chords low on the instrument will sound more or less muddy, but I would say that probably the lower voicing of the two is too muddy to use in this context. **Go through all of the left hand voicings in this way, playing 1,3,7 for each chord in a range that is suitable. See if you can add the melody in your right hand,** practicing it in pieces, doing only what is easy. Be flexible with the rhythm of the song at first, or try it at a very slow tempo.

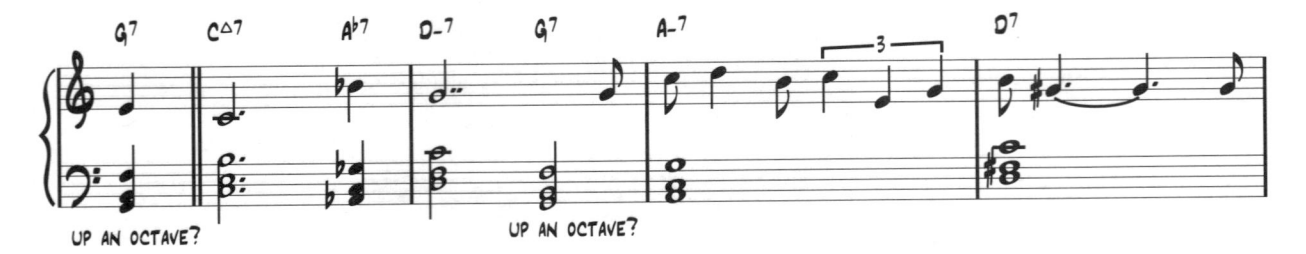

Now, you could play a lot of songs this way and really see an improvement in your piano playing, both from the standpoint of finding chords (or the important notes of the chords) with your left hand and playing melodies in your right. Some problems will probably come up, and perhaps the most obvious (especially if you are an alto and reading your own charts in your key) is that when the left hand seems to be in an effective range, sometimes the melody (right hand) will be in the same range as the left, so the two hands interfere with each other a bit. You can solve this by raising the melody an octave, or just try to bear with it by occasionally leaving the 7th off in the left hand to make more room for the melody. The next step in creating voicings will deal with this problem in another way, so remember there is always another voicing coming down the line that will help problems as they come up (and perhaps create new problems to solve.)

This is an important point. Whenever students get a new voicing, they tend to try use it in a lot of situations, some of which will work and some of which won't. For example, take the root position voicing we were looking at earlier. If a student tries this voicing, he or she gets to hear more harmony and that's good, but maybe they are frustrated by the way the chord tends to sound either too muddy or too wimpy, depending on the register. Also, the melody may sound disconnected from the chord voicing, because the best sounding voicings often have an even distribution of notes across the range of the voicing, whereas root position voicings concentrate a lot of notes in a moderately low range of the piano, with the melody pretty far above those roots. So this voicing has some good qualities and some built-in problems associated with it. The 1,3,7 voicing improves somewhat on this, but still has a lot of the same difficulties. In the end, you will need to have many voicing options so that you can use the voicing that works best in each situation, changing voicings when you run into difficulties arising from range considerations, interference with the melody or other issues.

Still, using the 1,3,7 voicing under the melody is effective in its way. You can hear the whole chord and it's not as thick sounding as 1,3,5,7. (Whenever you have to play a minor seventh flat 5 or diminished seventh, for now, play them as 4-note 1,3,5,7 chords.) When we get to playing scales in the right hand (oh, we're going to get to that, don't you worry) this 1,3,7 voicing is very handy because it is so complete sounding.

The down-side of this voicing is that it still tends to get muddy a bit in lower registers. Of course, the part that makes it muddy is the 3rd of the chord. As I said above, muddiness comes from small intervals low on the instrument, so if we were to get rid of the 3rd of the chord from the left hand, things would get a little cleaner sounding down low. Unfortunately, we really need this 3rd to tell us whether the chord is major or minor. The obvious answer is to put the 3rd up an octave. Let's leave the melody out of things for a moment. **Play through all of the chords for "We'll Be Together Again" using this voicing, 1 and 7 in the left hand and the 3rd of the chord in the right hand.**

In general, this voicing has a tremendous number of applications. This is because with 1 and 7 in the left hand and the 3rd of the chord played in the right hand a 10th above the root (or in the left if your left hand is large enough to manage it) the important notes of the chord are there, and any notes that we add above the 3rd will fill out the sound of the chord. It's worth noting now that when we start to add more colorful notes to the chord voicing (9ths, 11ths, 13ths) these notes tend to sound better above the important chord tones than below them, so this voicing functions well as the foundation or bottom half of most chords.

Please notice how in the above example, the G7's in the first and third bar, the Ab7 in the second bar and the A7 in the fourth bar are particularly improved by these voicings with the 3rds up an octave. Wherever the 1,3,7 voicings you were using before sounded muddy, raising the 3rd an octave is especially helpful. Now these same chords sound strong, because they have roots that are low on the instrument, so they sound like bass notes and 3rds a 10th above, clear and not muddy.

It this is not easy for you to do, practice this voicing on any (or perhaps all?) of your charts. Work on being able to play 1 and 7 in the left hand and the 3rd in the right hand for any tune or chord progression. Once you can find this voicing on any of your charts, sing the melody over the voicing as you play through each one of your tunes, slowly.

CHAPTER 1

Once you are starting to feel comfortable finding 1,7 and 3, let's return to "We'll Be Together Again." **One more time, play through the chords using the 1, 7 and 3 voicing, playing the 3rd with the thumb of your right hand. Now let's add the melody.** This means playing two notes in your right hand, the 3rd below and then melody above it. (Unless the melody IS the 3rd of the chord, then there will be only one note in your right hand.) The melody must always be the top note in your voicing, because the top voice sticks out. If I play a note above the melody, then that new note sounds like the melody (or it just sounds wrong). We tend to hear from the extremes, the top note first, then the bass and what's inside the voicing last. This voicing might be a little harder for me to find than 1,3,5,7 in my left hand and the melody in my right hand, since I have to find the root and 7th in the left hand and both the melody and the 3rd of the chord underneath the melody in my right hand, but it is a voicing that is more suited to the piano overall. This voicing takes advantage of some of the strengths of the piano: it has a large interval between the bass note and the next voice (the 7th) to avoid muddiness. It has the important note (the 3rd) in a good strong place near middle C, so not too low, and finally, the melody is on top of the voicing. The other good thing about this voicing is its SPACING. The notes are evenly spaced (this does depend somewhat on the range of the melody, but at least compared to the previous version—with the left hand playing either 1,3,5,7 or 1,3,7 and the melody in the right hand—the notes are MORE evenly spaced). With the notes spaced fairly evenly with no gaping holes in the middle of the voicing, with larger intervals on the bottom of the chord between the root and the next note up and with smaller intervals above that, these voicings tend to sound clear and resonant.

There are a lot of other spacings that pianists like to use, including notes spaced very close together (called clusters) or voicings that have big holes in them (for effect), but these more unusual voicings tend to sound edgier or slightly unusual. Evenly spaced notes in a voicing tend to make the piano sound full and rich, making normal (in the positive sense of the word: consonant, clear-sounding) voicings. To return to "We'll Be Together Again," the first chord underneath the pickup note has the fifth finger of the left hand on a low G, the left hand thumb plays the F (dominant 7th), the right hand thumb plays the B (3rd) and the melody note, E is on top, played with third or fourth finger. (There are other fingerings that work as well, so if you are using different fingers in your right hand, that's fine as long as you are comfortable.) The next melody note is a C, low in the range for the melody. If we want to play the 1,7 in the left hand and the 3rd beneath the melody in the right hand, we have to put the voicing down an octave. This is a little low, possibly too muddy. Our other option is to use the left hand voicing of 1,3 and 7 that we used earlier. (This is an example of how knowing more than one voicing can help you find the appropriate voicing in situations where range plays a factor) Going on this way, you can play the whole tune using these 1,7,3 + melody voicings.

CHAPTER 1

This is a very complete sound for each chord and a big improvement on all of the previous voicings we've used to harmonize the melody. **Try using this voicing (left hand 1 and 7, right hand 3 and melody) to play versions of the melody for some of your simpler charts where the melody doesn't move around too much.**

Whew! That's a lot of piano, especially if you are coming to this as a complete beginner. Let's take a breather and review the steps that we've used so far in our conquest of the piano and keyboard harmony.

1. Find the roots of chords (using songs of your choosing from a fake book or set of lead sheets. Play them in your left hand out of time. Repeat with many tunes.
2. Play them in your right hand.
3. Play them in both hands.
4. Use your lead sheets or arrangements of songs in your keys. Again, play them in both hands out of time.
5. Play the roots in a slow tempo while you sing the melody of the tune. Repeat with many or all of your lead sheets.
6. Play the root in your left hand while you play the melody in your right hand. Repeat with many tunes.
7. Play all chord qualities, all keys with the root position voicing 1,3,5,7 in both hands in octaves.
8. Play "We'll Be Together Again," melody in right hand, 1,3,5,7 in the left.
9. Play "We'll Be Together Again," 1,3,7 in left hand for all of the chords of the song
10. Play "We'll Be Together Again," melody in right hand, 1,3,7 in left.
    Play 1,7 in the left hand, 3 in the right hand a 10th above the root for all the chords of "We'll Be Together Again." Sing the melody.

Repeat with all of your charts, singing the melody of each. Play "We'll Be Together Again," melody and 3rd in the right hand, 1,7 in the left. Repeat with many tunes.

THE SINGER VOICING

Let's continue working on the harmony of "We'll Be Together Again" without playing the melody. In step 10 above, we played 1 and 7 in the left hand and the 3rd of each chord in the right hand. If we add the 5th above the 3rd in the right hand, we have all of the chord tones for each chord.

13

CHAPTER 1

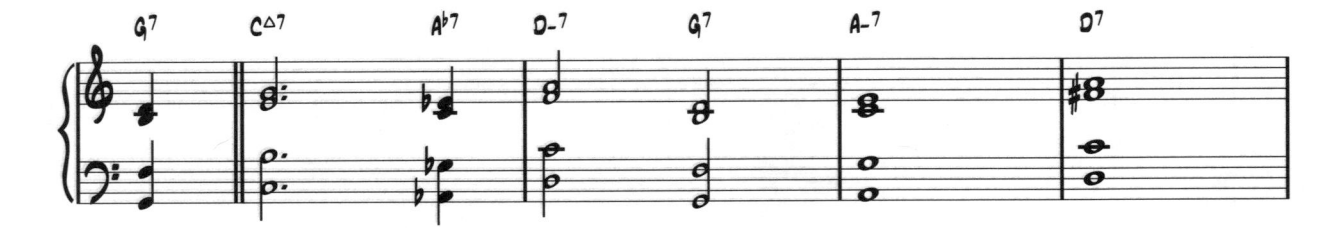

[Musical notation: G7, C△7, A♭7, D-7, G7, A-7, D7]

This voicing is more versatile and pianistic than my root position 1,3,5,7 voicing. Sometimes this voicing is referred to as the singer voicing because it is often learned by vocalists (as well as horn players and others, of course) so that they can play chord progressions to accompany themselves. **Try this voicing on one of your tunes, playing it for every chord change. Also, drill this voicing for all chord qualities and in all keys as we did with the root position voicing.**

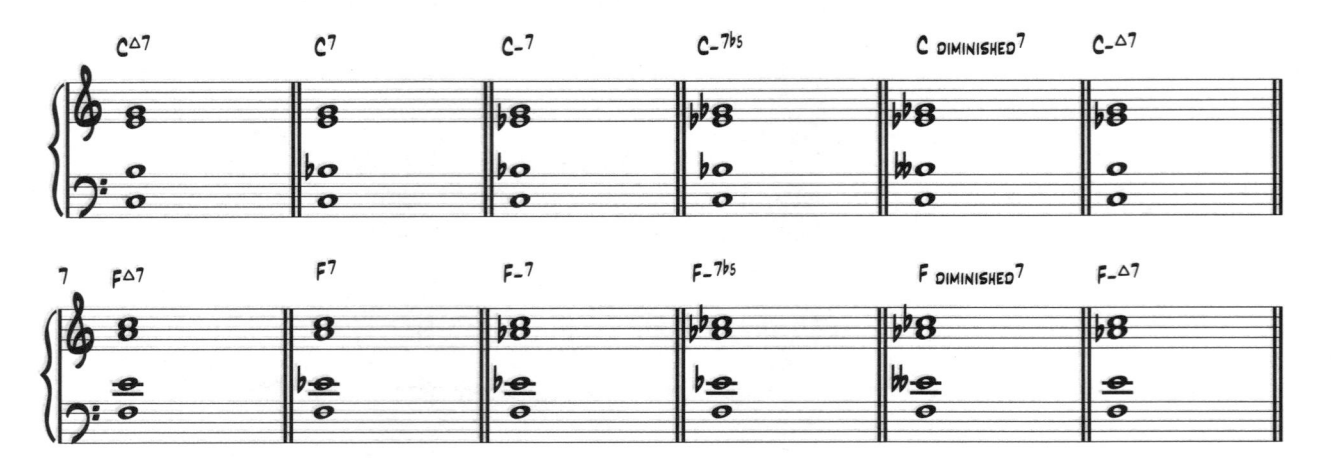

[Musical notation: C△7, C7, C-7, C-7♭5, C diminished 7, C-△7]

[Musical notation: F△7, F7, F-7, F-7♭5, F diminished 7, F-△7]

As I said above, one of the great things about this voicing is its versatility. If I want to add a colorful note to this voicing I can make it more interesting. I'm referring here to tensions. Tensions are the notes above 7 (9, 11 and 13) that we can add to chord tones to create more color in the chord voicings we choose. I'm going to go through these possibilities now. For those of you who are not so experienced with harmony, this may be the last step on our whirlwind tour of piano comping, so hang in there!

Probably the easiest color note to add is the 9th. The 9th is located a whole step and an octave above the root (although it can appear in any octave up or down, depending on what sort of voicing you are making). So two simple variations of the singer voicing add a 9th in the right hand, either below (and next to) the 3rd in the right hand or above the 5th (an interval of a 5th above the 5th it turns out). **Try adding 9ths to your voicings as you play through one of your charts.** Below are the possibilities for the harmony of the first 5 bars of "We'll Be Together Again."

CHAPTER 1

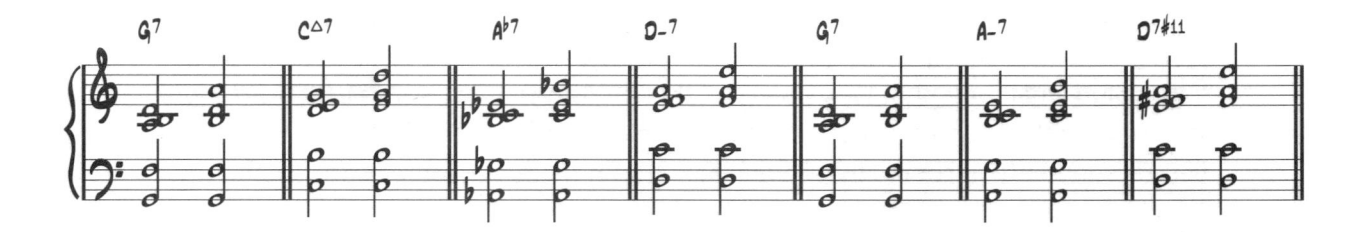

Try to play these voicings, either with the 9th below the 3rd in the right hand, above the 5th in the right hand, or varying the position of the 9th in the chord, for all the chords in the progression. Once you can manage this, sing the melody over these voicings.

One thing to keep in mind is that whenever we are adding colors to a chord, we risk coming into conflict with the melody. Did any of the 9ths sound wrong against the melody as you sang through the tune over your comping? This could happen. In such a situation, the simplest thing to do is just leave out the color that doesn't belong. In general, when I look at a C-7, C7, Cmaj7, C-7b5 or Cdim7, the 9th is an available note for me to add. That means, I can add it if I want, I don't have to wait until I see a Cmaj9. The 9 comes with the minor seventh, the major seventh, etc, if I want it. (Like all those cupholders in an SUV). The 9th of these chords is referred to as an available tension, because it's there for me to use if I want. Still, just because something is available, it doesn't mean it's right for every situation. Pepper is available to me on cottage cheese (and my mother eats it every day for lunch like that) but I'm not crazy about it. Although I am quite fond of pepper in general. Go figure. (Don't get me started on mustard.)

However, if you are going to add something, the 9th is a pretty easy note to add. If tensions are spicy notes, then the 9th is parsley. It goes almost everywhere. (Or maybe olive oil, but that isn't really a spice. Salt is a little too common. Salt would have to be the root. Except the chord tones are really the meat of the chord, so salt couldn't really be a chord tone. Hmmm...let's just stick with the 9th being parsley.)

To get another variation of the singer voicing, try adding the 6th (13th)—the note a whole step above the 5th (so in our "We'll Be Together Again" example, you would add an E above the D for the first G7 voicing so you'd have B, D and E in your right hand)—or replacing the 5th with the 6th (so you'd have B and E in your right hand.) In my spice analogy, the 13th is...um...maybe basil—it shows up in a lot of places and won't freak anybody out most of the time.

CHAPTER 1

(To be completely honest here—and have you known me ever to be anything other than that?—I'm oversimplifying a little. How unusual—or how colorful, or how spicy, depending what metaphor we use—all of these tensions sound varies a bit from chord to chord. Ninths are pretty neutral sounding on every chord quality; 13ths are pretty neutral sounding on chords that have major 3rds in them, but more exotic sounding on chords that have minor 3rds in them.)

A slightly more unusual sounding note would be the 11th. The available 11th is located one whole step above the 3rd. This means that if you are working with a major or dominant seventh, the whole step up from the 3rd would be the #11th, and that's the note you get to add to the chord. (These numbers refer to a major scale. Numbers larger than 8 are displaced up an octave, so the 11th is the same as the 4th note of the scale. All of this sounds a little more complicated than it really is. Play a C major scale. Stop on the 3rd (E). The next note of the major scale (the 4th note) is a half step up (F). This would be the 11th. But I told you that the available tension for major chords is located one **whole** step above the major 3rd. So you have to make the F an F#. This tension is called the #11.) For minor chords, minor seventh flat5 chords and diminished chords, the 3rd is minor, so the tension that is one whole step above the minor 3rd is the (natural) 11th (or 4). It all boils down to this: if a chord has a major 3rd in it, play the #11, if the chord has a minor 3rd in it, play the natural 11.

Okay, so now we have **another** set of variations that we can use adding the 11th a whole step above the 3rd. (In our spice analogy, the #11th is...let's say cumin.) Since the 11th is (arguably) a more colorful note than the 9th or the 6th (13th), chords that have this color in them have even more potential to interfere with the melody, so they should be used with care. In the end, you are choosing a sound and you have to pick the sounds that you want. The #11 is a beautiful sound, but you might not want it everywhere. (Or you might.) But for now, if these sounds are a little unfamiliar to you, make sure you check them out so that you can start to integrate them into your harmonic vocabulary. **So go through the tune you've been working on and replace all of the 5ths in the singer voicing with 11ths and #11ths.**

(To be exact, the #11 tends to be the more colorful note. The natural 11 (found on minor chords) is a more neutral sound, potentially easier to add to your voicings.)

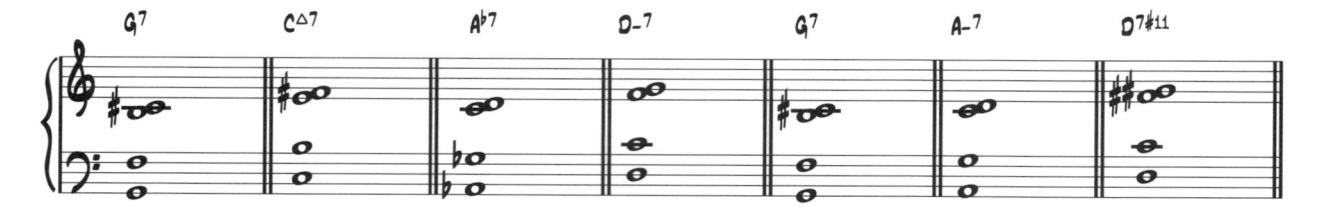

Of course, these aren't the only possibilities of variations for this voicing. You could add more than one tension to your singer voicings, adding 13ths to the above chords with 11ths in them, or add 9ths to the 13ths in the previous example. Also, if you wish to

CHAPTER 1

have a more "clustery" sound, you could add fifths to these chords. Sometimes adding notes that are very close to each other creates an interesting, sort of "misty" impressionistic effect. In addition to that, you might even want to leave out a 3rd from time to time. This also creates a more ambiguous chord sound that might be appropriate in certain situations.

So, you can use 9ths, 11ths and 13ths; that must be it, right? Nope. We still have to consider **altered tensions.** Altered tensions are only available to you on the dominant seventh chord, but they are very important for bringing a lot of the colorful sounds we most associate with jazz to your comping. (In our somewhat labored spice analogy, this is the rest of the spice rack and you can assign whatever spices you want to the different altered tensions, although #9 is definitely cayenne or something hot like that. This is a favorite tension in pop culture—you hear it when a dancer in a broadway show pantomimes licking her finger and then touches her hip and makes a steam hissing sound indicating her "hotness," or played by a guitar through a wa-wa pedal when a bunch of hippy-looking types are dancing in a psychedelic disco scene from 80s television shows.) The basic rule here is that you can use the 9th, #11th and 13th (or 6th) that we have been using, but you can replace the 9th with b9th or #9th and you can replace the 13th with b13. Below are some of the possibilities for comping a C7.

So here is a quick review to sum up all of the available tensions for each type of chord.

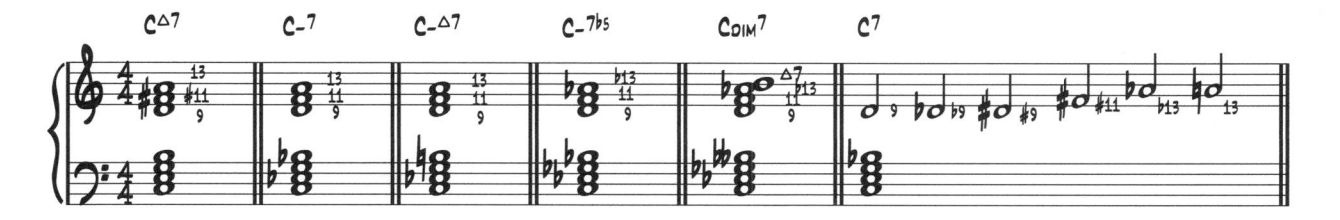

Using just the options listed above, **on the next page is a comping version of the chord changes to "We'll Be Together Again." Sing the melody over this.** Do you like all of the voicings below? Change the ones that you don't like and come up with your own comping arrangement for this tune.

We'll Be Together Again

Carl Fischer, Frankie Laine

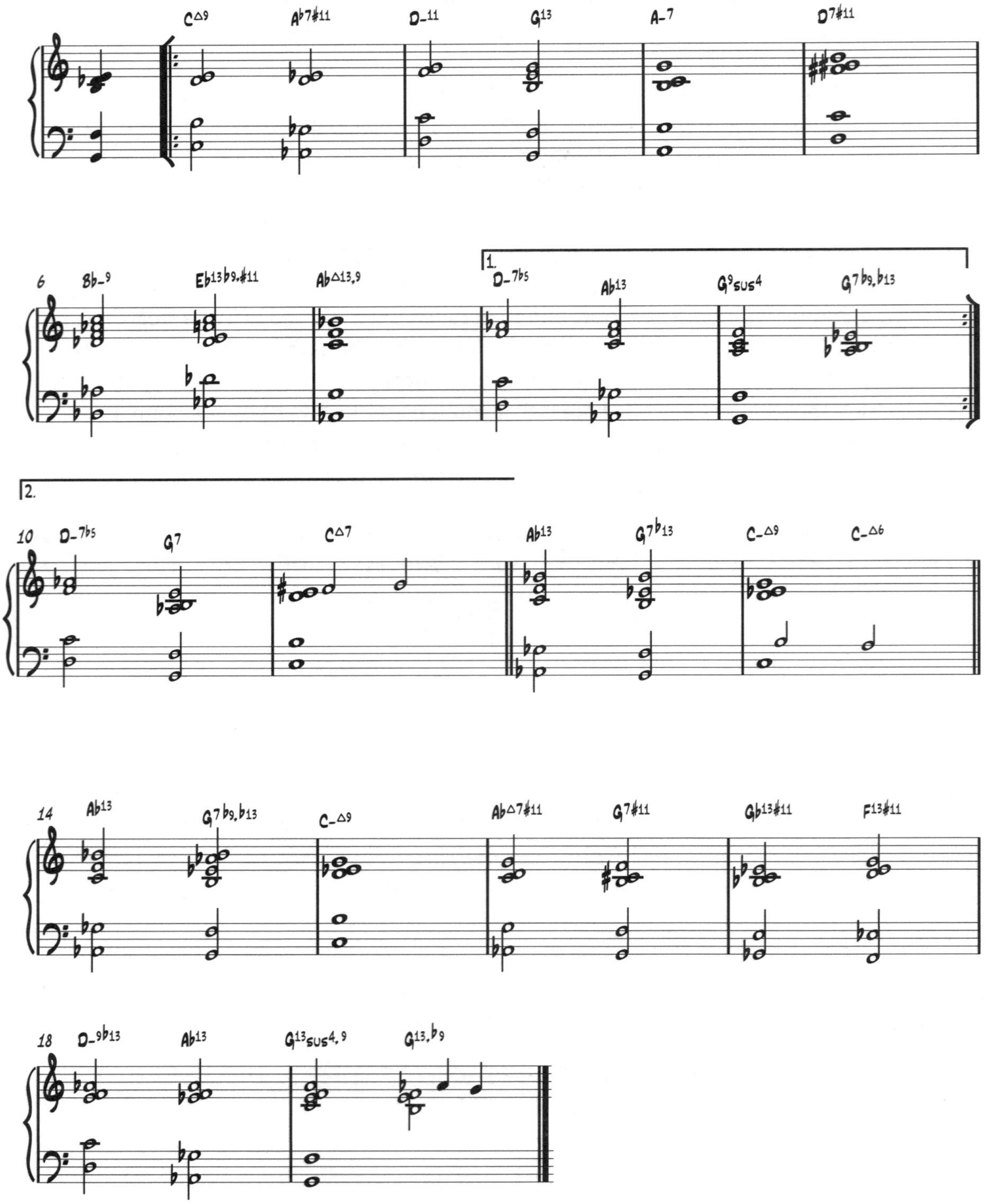

 18

(There are a couple of things in this arrangement that need just a bit of explaining. I mentioned above that a C minor 6 can replace a C minor major 7 chord, and sure enough it does in bar 11. Also, we haven't really discussed dominant seventh sus4 chords. These are chords that don't have a 3rd—instead they have a 4th, so the chord tones of a dominant 7 sus4 chord are 1,4,5 and7. Also, occasionally a note in the left hand is repeated in order to create more rhythmic momentum. One last thing, a tension on a dominant chord can be natural and then altered within the course of a measure as happens in bars 3 and 17).

Look how far you've come. You are already comping for yourself and using some pretty nifty voicings. As I mentioned above, **if you want to fixate on this step for a while, coming up with many variations of these singer voicings for all of your tunes, go ahead.** Think of it as a kind of victory lap. (No, you don't have to thank me. Okay, if you insist…)

Having reached this step, those of you who have had enough piano playing for now, feel free to leave this chapter and go on to more vocally-oriented sections of this book. You have acquired the basic skills to play a competent version of the melody and harmony of a tune, as well as to comp through the tune using two-handed voicings with tensions. You can always come back and take on more piano challenges at a later time.

To underline this point, let's give you a clue here…

I mean it. You can go if you want.

For those of you who are still here, thanks for sticking around. Now let's return to the melody of the song. We are going to leave the left hand alone and just keep playing roots and 7ths in it. The right hand still has the melody on top, and the 3rd of the chord below the melody. What I am interested in now is, what notes can I add to this voicing? For now, I won't be adding anything to the left hand (after all, it took us 10 steps to get all the junk out of the left hand!) Let's add notes to the right hand. What notes should I add? Or to put it another way, are there any notes (chord tones or tensions) that I shouldn't I add? One note I don't need to add is the root. Doubling the root higher up in the chord just tends to add weight to a voicing without adding interesting color. Doubling the 3rd or the 7th is fine, as is adding the 5th, especially if that note is in the melody, but I wouldn't suggest doubling chord tones as the first choice. The first choice is to look for a 9th, 11th or 13th that will add more color to the chord.

CHAPTER 1

So for the first chord change, the 13th is in the melody.

You can add any of the following notes in any combination that appeals to you: the b9, 9, #9, #11, and 5. The number of possible combinations of these available notes is a really big number. (Of course, these things are relative. It's not like a "number of grains of sand on a beach" sort of number. It's more of a "number of marbles in a tin can" sort of number).

So try all of these combinations and come up with a voicing you like. A couple things to keep in mind—while you do have many possible combinations, certain combinations make a lot more sense than others. For example, an altered tension and a natural tension don't usually get played together so b9 and natural 9, #9 and natural 9 and 13 and b13 almost never get played simultaneously in the same voicing. (As we saw above, though, natural 9 sometimes LEADS to b9.) Also, for a similar reason although it's not as hard and fast a rule, 5 and b13 don't share space in a voicing too often. But you don't have to memorize these as "voicing rules". Try all of the different combinations and your ears ought to tell you which of the available tensions sound good with each other. Here are a few possibilities to get you started:

After the first note of the melody, the pickup, there is a long note on middle C over a Cmajor chord. This note is a little problematic, as we discussed earlier. Either we can put the root and 7th in the left hand very low or we have no possibility of filling in notes around this chord. Below are these two possibilities. (I did mention that you might break our prohibition on putting anything in the left hand between 1 and 7 and use the 1,3,7 voicing, since the first voicing below sounds a little empty.) Notice that for the lower voicing, I have tried to keep relatively large spaces between the notes to keep the voicing from becoming muddy sounding, at least, as non-muddy sounding as possible, given that the voicing is low to begin with.

CHAPTER 1

[Musical notation: Cmaj7, Cmaj7]

For the next chord, the melody jumps up, giving me a lot more room to create a voicing underneath it.

[Musical notation: Ab7]

Now, there is a rule of thumb that is good to consider when you are making voicings of dominant seventh chords. Dominant seventh chords tend to come in two basic varieties: ones that have altered tensions in them, and ones that don't. In the above case, we know that the 9th (Bb) is natural, because that is the melody note. For that reason, the 13th is more likely to be natural than altered. Of course, these are decisions that you can make best by trying out all of the possibilities, and there are a lot of good exceptions to this (a chord based on the whole tone scale will have a b13th and a natural 9th) but as a general rule, if the 9th is natural, the 13th often is too.

Another clue that the above chord might be a dominant 7th that has natural tensions is where the chord is leading. In general, dominant seventh chords that take altered tensions are usually those dominants that lead to a chord a 4th up (or a 5th down). We'll talk more about this in later chapters, but the bottom line is this: dominant seventh chords that resolve up a 4th (like the first chord of the tune, the G7 that leads to C major 7th) are more likely to have altered tensions, especially if the chord that the dominant leads to is a minor chord.

So, on the strength of these considerations, you can add any of the following notes, in any combination to the above voicing (below the melody in the right hand): Bb, D, Eb, F and Gb. Below are a few of the possible voicings.

[Musical notation: Ab13, Ab13#11, Ab9]

CHAPTER 1

Deciding between these possible voicings is what you need to do as you work on coming up with your piano arrangement of this tune. **Working chord to chord, decide on the rest of the voicings for this tune. After you have settled on all of the voicings, learn to play your arrangement fluently.**

At this point there is one last step that I suggest you try. Play through your arrangement of the song. Are there any chords that you are still not satisfied with? Sometimes no matter how hard you try, certain voicings don't sound good to you. Perhaps this is because of the limitation of 1 and 7 in the left hand for each chord. While this is a good left-hand voicing that is often on the bottom of many chords in successful arrangements of tunes, there may be places where this limitation is preventing you from finding the voicing you want. **Circle a few of the problematic voicings (if you feel there are any) and try replacing 1 and 7 in your left hand with any of the following root based voicings:**

1,3; 1,3,7; 1,3,6; 1,5; 1,5,7; 1,5,9; 1,5,10 (3); 1,7,10 (3) or anything that sounds good to you and has the root on the bottom of the chord.

Did changing a few of the left hand voicings help? Using 1 and 7 is a good way to start your arrangement, but you don't need to be chained to this approach.

Now you can repeat this process with other songs arranging them by building interesting voicings under the melody in the same way you did on "We'll Be Together Again." Good tunes to try this approach on include "Cherokee," "Tune Up," "Blue in Green" and "All the Things You Are." Look for songs to work on where the melody doesn't move around too much, meaning melodies that aren't comprised mostly of 8th notes.

Probably by now you can see some of the benefits of working on creating voicings with the melody on top. It allows you to hear the chords, the harmony and the melody at the same time. But even more importantly, working in this way allows you to discover voicings that you might not find otherwise. For example, the voicing that you eventually settled on for the G7 with the G on top that the song begins with is yours to keep. You can use it on another tune. It goes into your mental library of chord voicings and you can whip it out when you want that particular color.

This is one of my favorite methods for discovering voicings at the piano and becoming a better comper. I like it because you can begin at a simple starting place (1,7 in the left hand, 3 and the melody in the right hand) and add notes, picking the colors you like and using your ears.

This is another extremely logical place to stop if you'd like to get off the piano train and get started on singing. If you want to leave this chapter right now, I wouldn't blame you one bit. Hence the footsteps of departure:

CHAPTER 1

For those of you who decided to stick around, let's reward you with something easy and useful. Far and away the most beneficial way to work on piano comping (in my opinion) is to create your own voicings in the manner that you have been doing. Of course, there ARE a few stock voicings that are helpful to know. King among these voicings are the non-root voicings called "A" and "B" voicings (a terminology that goes back to John Mehegan's jazz piano books of the late 50s and early 60s).

To hear these voicings in context, listen to any Bill Evans recording. At some point in the record, he will play a repeated chord sound in his left hand while he solos with his right hand, often with a left-hand punctuation for every (or most of) the notes in his right hand. That sound is what we associate with non-root A and B voicings (although, in fairness, Bill Evans played a lot of different things in his left hand, and of course many, many pianists besides Bill Evans use these voicings—I dare say all of them at one time or another. Maybe not Cecil Taylor, come to think of it.)

Anyway, without further ado, here they are.

Now at the heart of these A and B voicings is a very simple and powerful thing, the 3rds and 7ths of the chord. Lets go back to our 1,3,7 voicing. If I play a D-7 to G7 to C major 7th progression and I leave off the roots, I will be playing the 3rd and 7th on each of these chords. In the key of C that would be F and C for the D-7, B and F for the G7, and E and B for the CMaj7. However, if I reverse the two notes of the G7, I get F and C for the D-7, F and B for the G7 and E and B for the Cmaj7. This kind of reversing of notes is called an **inversion.** When I use a particular inversion to create less leaping around in the middle of a voicing, this is called **smooth voice leading.** This voicing with the F on the bottom of the first two chords and the E on the bottom of the last chord is found in the middle of the "A" voicing above. Of course, I could also start with the 7th on the bottom of the voicing for the first chord, so that the bottom notes would be C, B, B. This is what is going on inside the "B" voicings above.

So, the A and B voicings are inversions of each other. Same notes, different order. We'll see why that's important a bit further on.

CHAPTER 1

Let's talk a little bit about this D-7 to G7 to Cmaj7 progression. This is the most important progression in jazz, called ii-7 V7 I Maj7. We will talk a lot more about chord progressions in the next chapter, but I just want to point out that this progression is what defines a key, meaning that if you hear this progression you know where "Do" or 1 in the key is. You can demonstrate this to yourself by playing the above progression (let's use our smooth voice leading for practice) with roots.

Play the above progression and then sing C. C sounds like Do, like 1, like home base for the key we are in. Most standard songs use this chord progression, along with modulations (visits to keys other than the main key that the tune is in) as some of the main building blocks to create the chord progression that each song is based on.

So, returning to the A and B voicings above and summing up, these are completely self-contained versions of the chords. They have chord tones and tensions and they lead well from one to the next, so they are easy to play and you don't have to move your hand much. They are inversions of each other, inversions that differ by placing either the 3rd or the 7th at the bottom of the voicing. This raises two questions: 1) How do we use these voicings? and 2) why is it important to know them in two different inversions?

If you listened to the Bill Evans recording, you heard one important use of these voicings: as left hand, non-root voicings. Every voicing we have examined up until now has had the root on the bottom of the chord. This is important because we need to hear the root to know what key we are in or what sort of chord is being played. The root defines the harmony of the tune and gives us a context to hear the other notes of the chord. However, in a typical jazz rhythm section, the bass player has the primary responsibility for this job of playing the roots of the chords, freeing the pianist from playing them all of the time. A pianist who plays left hand voicings that contain the root of the chord in a heavy sustained manner will get in the way of the bassist and interfere with the lines the bass is creating.

Sometime this point is over-stressed, it seems to me. Just because a bass player is present doesn't mean that you should NEVER play the roots of the chord. Here's another listening assignment: listen to Bud Powell, preferably on something from The Genius of Bud Powell, such as "Celia." Even though he is playing with a rhythm section (and for that matter, a great one, Ray Brown and Max Roach) he often plays the root of the chord. Playing root-based voicings if they aren't accented too heavily or sustained too long, is fine and, if you are using A and B voicings a lot, it's often nice to add a few root based voicings to create some variety in your left hand.

Okay, this lengthy aside notwithstanding, some of you are probably asking yourself just how often (at this point in your piano playing career) you are going to be playing in situations with bassists. This brings us to the second use of these voicings, as right hand voicings to which you can add roots in your left hand.

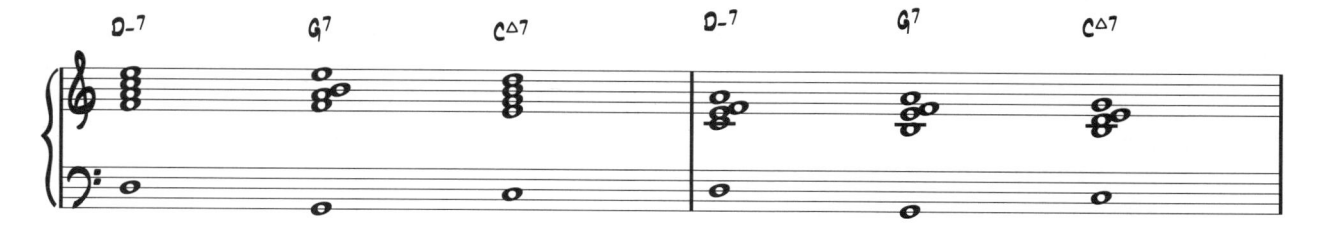

Used this way, the piano functions a bit more like an organ, with the roots in the left hand and the rest of the chord in the right. Again, these voicings are clear, have good voice leading and define the harmony well. You can add them to your other comping options. **Try playing these voicings, first in all keys and then for some of the tunes you sing, singing the melody over them.** When you are using these voicings in your right hand with the roots in your left hand, use either the A voicing or the B voicing, whichever you think sounds better, switching as you feel is appropriate.

By switching between the A and B versions of these voicings, you can keep the chords in the same range of the piano. For example, let's say you have the following chord progression in one of your tunes:

A-7 D7/ D-7 G7/ Cmaj7   —   I can play the A-7 and D7 using a B voicing

and the D-7 G7 and CMaj7 using an A voicing

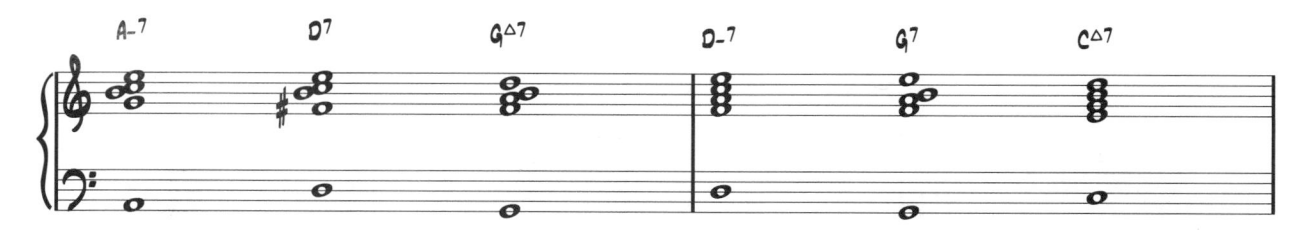

for particularly smooth voice leading. As you play through your tunes using these

CHAPTER 1

voicings, try to switch from the A inversion to the B inversion and vice versa in order to keep your voice-leading smooth. **Practice playing these voicings on your tunes and singing the melody over them.**

Of course, if we can have a ii V I progression in a major key, we can have it in a minor key as well, so we need one more set of A and B voicings, this time for a minor key:

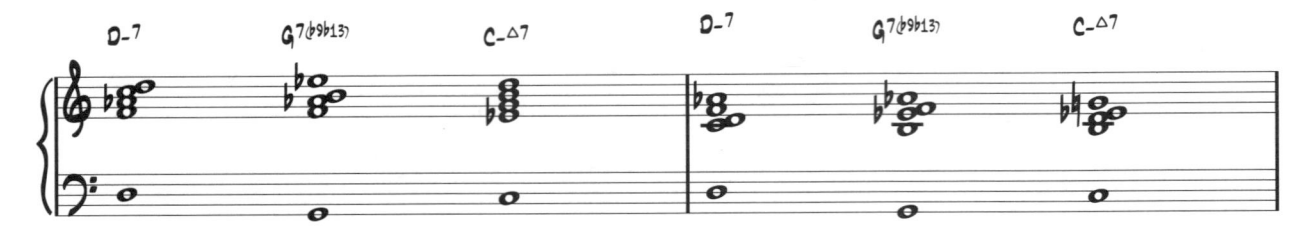

You'll notice that the first chord of each of these "non-root" based voicings has a root in it, albeit at the top of the voicing rather than the bottom. The reason for this is a little complicated and has to do with the fact that the 9th on this chord (the note that the root is replacing) is a coloristic choice that doesn't always work in minor situations. You can use the 9th on a minor seventh flat 5 chord, but it doesn't work well as the default option for this progression, since there are a number of situations where this is more color than you want. Enough said. **Practice these minor voicings in the same way you did the major voicings, first in all keys and second on some of your minor tunes, as you sing the melody over them.**

Now let's practice these voicings as left hand voicings. When we use these voicings in this way, we have to consider the second question I asked earlier, namely, why do we place so much stress on two different voicings that are inversions of each other? For those of you who said "because of range considerations," pour yourself a hearty beverage of some kind. When I am playing these voicings in my left hand, I don't want them to be either too low (where they sound like root position chords because the bottom note sounds like a bass note) or too high (where they interfere with whatever my right hand is doing, such as playing the melody.) This means there is a sweet spot on the piano where these voicings sound not too low, not too high, just right. This sweet spot is roughly from the low extreme of C below middle C to G or so above middle C. Of course, the upper limit of this sweet spot moves depending on where my right hand is, higher if I am playing higher up on the piano, lower if I am playing lower.

Still, certain keys favor A voicings, and others favor B voicings. I can make a chart for which ii V I progressions will more likely make use of the A or B form:

MORE OFTEN SEEN AS A VOICINGS	MORE OFTEN SEEN AS B VOICINGS	COULD BE EITHER
Db, C, B, Bb,	G, Gb, F, E,	Ab, A, Eb, D

CHAPTER 1

Again, none of these rules are hard and fast and you should let your ears determine which inversion works best in different situations.

Even if you aren't playing with bassists very much right now, you can use these voicings for variations in your left hand. Also, if the song doesn't move very quickly, you can use these voicings on the second or third beat in the bar after playing the root in the octave below them on the first beat of the chord change.

Wow. That's a lot of piano stuff. I have just one more voicing I want you to consider before we move on to the next chapter to talk about the construction of lead sheets.

This voicing takes advantage of the line that is created by the 7th of the ii-7 chord moving to the 3rd of the dominant seventh in a ii-7 V7 situation, the same line we saw buried in the A and B voicings above.

This is a fast way of playing ii-7 V7s with the left hand only. Any time you see a ii-7 V7 in a tune you can play, use this left hand voicing.

If you have this voicing in your left hand, it gives you more voicing possibilities for the right hand. For example, let's use the A voicing for the ii-7 V7 in the right hand over this left hand.

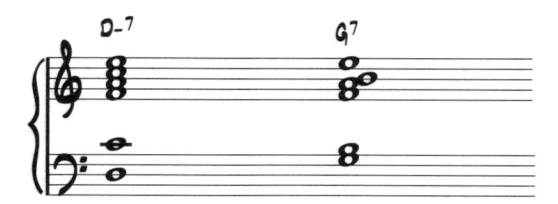

The ii-7 chord sounds great, but in the right hand V7 has a 3rd in it that doubles the 3rd in the left hand. I can replace this 3rd with the #11th, and I'll get a more colorful voicing without doubling.

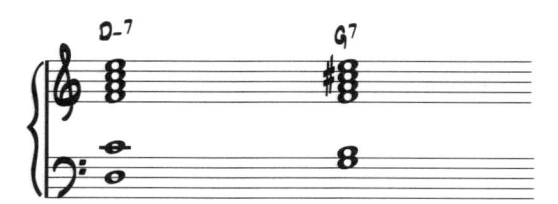

Since the second voicing is a dominant seventh, I can have all of these interesting variations of this basic voicing by altering the 9ths and 13ths.

CHAPTER 1

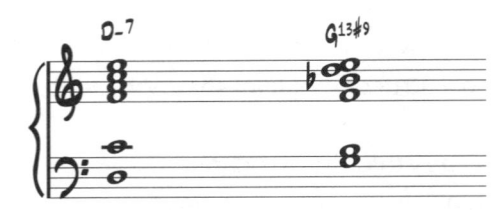

Practice these voicings in all keys and integrate them into your comping on tunes.

Okay, that's it. Enough piano already. Either you guys are gluttons for punishment or it wasn't all that bad after all, or perhaps a little of both.

Let's recap everything we've done at the piano. Those of you who didn't pour yourself a refreshing beverage earlier are commanded to do so now. You've earned it, soldier.

PIANO COMPING AND VOICING BASICS RECAP

1. Find the roots of chords (using songs of your choosing from a fake book or set of lead sheets). Play them in your left hand out of time. Repeat with many tunes.
2. Play them in your right hand.
3. Play them in both hands.
4. Use your lead sheets or arrangements of songs in your keys. Again, play them in both hands out of time.
5. Play the roots in a slow tempo while you sing the melody of the tune. Repeat with many or all of your lead sheets.
6. Play the root in your left hand while you play the melody in your right hand. Repeat with many tunes.
7. Play all chord qualities, all keys with the root position voicing 1,3,5,7 in both hands in octaves.
8. Play "We'll Be Together Again" in C, melody in right hand, 1,3,5,7 in the left.
9. Play "We'll Be Together Again," 1,3,7 in left hand for all of the chords of the song
10. Play "We'll Be Together Again," melody in right hand, 1,3,7 in left.
11. Play "We'll Be Together Again," 1 and 7 in left hand, 3 in the right hand a tenth above the root for all of the chords of the song
12. Play "We'll Be Together Again," melody and 3rd in the right hand, 1,7 in the left.
13. Repeat with many tunes.
14. Play 1,7 in the left hand, 3 in the right for all the chords of "We'll Be Together Again." Sing the melody.
15. Repeat with all of your charts, singing the melody of each.
16. Play the singer voicing (1,7,3,5) for all chords in all keys
17. Play the singer voicing for "We'll Be Together Again," all chords; sing the melody
18. Play the singer voicing for any (all?) of your charts; sing the melody
19. Go back to "We'll Be Together Again." Try adding 9ths to each chord, either below the 3rd of the chord or at the top of the voicing, whichever sounds better to you.
20. On "We'll Be Together Again," add 13ths to all chords, either above the 5th or in stead of it.
21. On "We'll Be Together Again," add 11ths and #11ths to all chords, as appropriate.
22. On "We'll Be Together Again," add altered tensions (b9, #9, b13) on dominant chords wherever appropriate.
23. Pick your favorite voicings from steps 19 through 22 and make a complete arrangement of piano comping for this tune.
24. Repeat steps 19 to 23 for other tunes in your repertoire, as many as you find inter esting and fun to do.
25. Return to playing "We'll Be Together Again" with 1 and 7 in the left hand and the melody and the 3rd of the chord below it in the right hand. Add notes to the right hand as you wish, trying all available tensions, natural and altered, until you have created an arrangement of this tune that you are (moderately) happy with.

CHAPTER 1

26. Go back over the arrangement and see if there are any voicings that you still don't really like. For these voicings try changing the left hand voicing to another root-based voicing, such as 1,3; 1,3,7; 1,5; 1,5,7; 1,5,6; 1,3,6; 1,5,9; 1,5,10 (3); or some thing of your own devising.
27. Repeat this song arranging process with many songs.
28. Play A and B non-root voicings, ii V I major, in all keys in right hand with roots in left hand
29. Play 3,7 for ii; 7,3 for V; and 3,7 for I in right hand, roots in left, all keys.
30. Play 7,3 for ii; 3,7 for V; and 7, 3 for I in right hand, roots in left, all keys.
31. Try some of your charts using these voicings. Sing the melody.
32. Play A and B non-root voicings, ii V I MINOR, in all keys in right hand with roots in left hand.
33. Try some of your charts that are in minor keys with A and B voicings in the right hand, roots in the left.
34. Play left hand A and B voicings for ii V I in all keys. Use the appropriate voicing (either the A or B form) to put the chord in the proper register of the piano.
35. Try some of your charts with these left hand voicings. Play the melody in the right hand. On slow ballads with a long time on each chord, try playing the root with your left hand on the downbeat of the measure and go to the A or B voicing on the second or third beat of the bar.
36. Play 1,7 in LH for ii-7 chords, 1,3 for V7 chords. Practice in all keys.
37. Add right hand above LH in 3,6; use A voicings for ii-7 chord, but replace the 3rd in the V7 A voicing with the #11 or 5. Try all variations of altered tensions. Practice in all keys.

There are lots of options for further developing your piano playing. You can get a lot of ideas if you listen to pianists who are great vocal accompanists. Some of the best of these are pianist/singers, for obvious reasons—they know better than anyone what sort of accompaniment a singer needs. Shirley Horn in particular was such a brilliant comper, so subtle and astute in her use of voicings and reharmonization, and at the same time so swinging, that invariably wherever she played, the club was filled with pianists trying to pick up a few ideas. Equally helpful are the many excellent duo recordings by great pianists and singers, including Ella Fitzgerald and Oscar Peterson, Sarah Vaughn and Oscar Peterson, Ella Fitzgerald and Tommy Flanagan, Tony Bennett and Bill Evans, Carmen McCrae and George Shearing, to name but a few.

Now that you have an idea of how to create piano arrangements of lead sheets and how to comp for yourself from lead sheets, let's turn to examining those lead sheets with their diverse chord progressions in greater detail.

Lead Sheet Basics

I was on a gig recently with a singer, playing standards. She had brought charts in her keys and some of the changes were pretty bad so I offered to fix a few of the worst offenders. The singer rolled her eyes and said: "Every pianist says the same thing—the chords are wrong. But if one pianist changes a chord, the next pianist will think the chord the last guy changed is wrong. It never ends." Fine. Sheesh, I was just trying to help. But I can relate to her frustration. If you don't know anything about harmony, your charts assume a kind of untouchable status. "Don't do anything to them," you think. "they seem to be working."

But this approach, unfortunately, removes you from the equation. Actually, it is kind of an old approach, harkening back to a time when the singer showed up at the recording session and put him- or herself into the hands of a competent arranger, who dealt with all of the harmonic and arranging issues. Nowadays, in countless jazz programs, singers are taught that they have to make their own charts for whatever tunes they sing, prepared in their keys.

But how do you write a chart? In some ways, having mediocre charts of standards is worse than having no charts at all. Incidentally, when I first began playing gigs back in the dark old days of the mid 70s (when we didn't have all these crazy new-fangled devices like electric can openers, and licorice whips were just 3 cents a pound, for criminy sakes), it was still pretty common to go on gigs and have to play all the tunes (in the singer's key) without any charts. Knowing the changes of common standards (and not so common ones too, if you were a singer accompaniment specialist) and being able to transpose them into any key was just part of the gig for pianists. It still is, to some extent, (singers usually have charts these days, but a pianist who can't transpose or doesn't know a really common standard—"My Funny Valentine" or something of that sort—will probably still get some nasty looks) although as I said above, that's changing. Nowadays, you are more likely to encounter charts prepared by the singer, although that preparation may just be the changes copied from a fake book transposed into his or her key.

Let's distinguish between two types of charts for standards. The first type are arrangements. These are versions of a standard in which something important has been changed according to the taste of the arranger. (I am differentiating this type of "arrangement" from the piano arrangement you did of "We'll Be Together Again.") As I am using the term here, I mean a version of the tune written by an arranger who makes decisions about the underlying harmony, as opposed to voicing a given set of changes for piano with the melody on top. The type of "piano arrangement" could more accurately be called a "realization" or "harmonization" of the tune because the chord progression was given. The underlying harmony may be changed, bars added to the melody or subtracted, the rhythm altered. There may be "feel" changes or variations in the form, such as interludes, intros and endings. Essentially, arrangements are new ver-

CHAPTER 2

sions of the standard, a recasting of the old material of the tune into something new that reflects the concept of whoever has arranged it. These are not the sort of charts I am likely to take a red pen to on a gig.

The other type of chart is an attempt to put the normal changes of the standard into the key of the singer, for the benefit of the band members (so they don't have to transpose by sight from the "regular" key), especially those who might not know the tune at all. Sounds simple, but unfortunately it isn't.

Where does this second sort of chart come from? And what are the "right" changes for a standard? Is there a set of "right" changes for a standard?

The answer to THAT question has also changed a lot over the years. When I first started playing gigs, I used to hear a lot about the "right" changes. The reason why the "right" changes aren't talked about as much now is because musicians learn standards in different ways today than I did in the early 70s when I first began playing gigs.

When I was growing up, my father, an amateur pianist who put himself through law school playing gigs with dance bands in college was amassing a sizable collection of loose sheet music from the 50s, 60s and 70s. He kept it all in large, unruly 3-ring binders and it covered a lot of show tunes and popular music of the day, much of it what we now refer to as standards.

These sheets were usually about 3 to 6 pages long and had a front cover with either pictures of the star who sang the tune, some scene from the movie or Broadway show that the tune came from, or every so often, the composer of the song. Inside, there was the tune, usually including the verse, the lyric and a piano arrangement of the song, either taken from the Broadway arrangement of the tune, or created expressly for the sheet music. There were even guitar or ukelele chords written in a kind of pictograph representation of the neck of the guitar or ukelele (with the frets and strings that you are supposed to play to produce the particular chord marked on them) above the melody. From these sheets, my father learned standards. I'm not sure if he took them on gigs with him (the books were truly enormous with dog-eared and yellowed pages, so finding anything in a hurry would have been a challenge) but this is the main way he practiced and learned the tunes that he played. I would imagine there were many people like my father, who learned music from the original sheet music versions of the tunes.

When I was in high school, the Real Book appeared. The Real Book was (is) a fake book, which is a book that contains the melody line and chord symbols for each tune. These books were illegal, in that no composer received royalties for the publishing of his tunes. The Real Book was not the first fake book to come along—I have a few from the 50s—but the Real Book received a much wider distribution than any of the earlier fake books. A few years later, when I was in Berklee for a couple of semesters, I met one of the book's creators. He claimed that he and his partner (or co-conspirator) spent a lot of time researching the tunes that they included, both the standards and the musician's tunes (being from Boston, they included tunes from some of the more well-known Boston musicians, such as Gary Burton, as well as players' compositions that reflected their musical tastes.) He also claimed that they got permission from each of the jazz composers to include his tunes in the book. (The writers ultimately received a lot of publicity from having their tunes included, which may have been a worthy trade-off for not receiving publishing royalties for the inclusion of their tunes in the Real Book. I'm not evaluating the truth of this story, just passing it on.) They worked hard on the book for a year or so, printed it on heavy paper stock so it would last and began selling it. Within a few months, someone had copied the book on cheap paper and was selling it for half price across the street from Berklee. Alas, there is no honor among thieves.

The Real Book swept through the world of jazz and pop music. Everyone had one and by the time I was out of college, it was the main source for learning standards for younger players, worldwide. It appeared in legal forms, spawned more real books and fake books, both legal and illegal, many of which improved on the earlier versions of the book. In the late 70s and early 80s, though, a lot of older players disliked the Real Book. They called it the "Unreal Book" and complained that the changes for the standard tunes were wrong. Some of the original changes WERE simply wrong ("Round Midnight" mystifyingly so, if I remember correctly), and some were reharmonized fairly extremely ("Here's That Rainy Day," "My One and Only Love"), but more significantly, on the less controversial tunes, the changes reflected the pared-down way that Boston jazz musicians viewed standard progressions. Gone were a lot of the harmonic details that were present in the Broadway arrangements of the tunes, in favor of a more ii V I-oriented approach to the harmony. (Also gone were the ukelele chords. Sadly, by the mid 70s, the age of the ukelele had passed—Tiny Tim notwithstanding—but there are those of us who hope that she will one day rise again and assume her rightful place in the world.)

Now, here is where things get a little sticky, and also where we find the explanation of what all this history has to do with my singer's frustration with piano players changing her charts, now illegible from their constant bickering about the right chords to a tune. Just how much of the harmonic details (from the original arrangers and composers of standards) you want to keep is a source of contention among different players.

The reason why jazz musicians favor pared-down harmony over the more detail-oriented harmony of Broadway arrangers, is because they use standards in a way that is different from how standards are used in musicals or in pop music. In a show, a standard will usually be sung either one-and-a-half or two times through the form. This is because these tunes are stories, and it doesn't make a lot of dramatic sense to sing the lyric more than twice. Since the lyric has some connection to story telling in the dramatic context of the show, the arrangement that delivers the lyric will also try to make some story-telling connection to the lyric, either with reharmonization or other musical effects. The singing of a standard in a show is also different from the way jazz

CHAPTER 2

singers render the song. For the show singer, the vocal interpretation has to be kept within the parameters prescribed by the arranger. On the jazz side, however, singers want to be able to sing the lyric in a laid-back manner or improvise around the melody. This is something that all jazz arrangers working with singers need to be aware of. When I write for a singer, I try to be careful to have the harmony move slowly enough for the singer to have some choices in how she sings the melody. Old Broadway arrangements of standards tend to be filled with passing chords that dovetail with the melody, as long as you sing the melody in a very straight, as written, sort of way. If you phrase more freely, these harmonic details won't line up with the melody in the way they were intended. Further, if someone is going to improvise many choruses over the harmony of the tune, these harmonic details really get in the way.

However, there is a fine line here. You want to keep the harmonic details that are important. If you streamline the harmony TOO much, it might not even work with the melody any longer! This is another complaint that I used to hear from older players when playing with young, harmonically focused pianists. They would complain that during their solos they played some of the melody and it didn't work with the chords that the (overly hip) piano player was playing.

So, as the cliche goes, the devil is in the details. By the way, my father was NOT one of those older players who complained about the Real Book. He loved it. For a player who came up with ukelele chords, the Real Book changes were very liberating. They were easier to solo over and they made things a lot more fun. Not to mention, the Real Book was a lot less bulky than his old notebooks.

In an interview conducted by pianist and radio host Marian McPartland, Bill Evans talks about the importance of understanding the harmonic structure of a tune. When Marian McPartland asks, "you mean, the chord changes?" Bill replies, "No, the harmonic structure." What I think Bill Evans means here is the underlying deep structure from which come the many possible sets of chord progressions that can be played on a tune.

To get a clearer sense of all of this, let's look at a tune and try to determine what kind of chart would best reflect the deep structure of the tune, and also try to examine some rules for finding chord progressions that spring from that deep structure.

First, let's talk a little bit about chord progressions. In the last chapter, we noted that the main building block of chord progressions is ii-7 V7 IMaj7. This is a kind of musical sentence. The ii-7 chord leads to the V7 chord, which leads to the IMaj7. The dog goes to the store. D-7 G7 CMaj7. Both the sentence, "The dog goes to the store," and D-7 G7 CMaj7 have a sense of completeness to them. Stop anywhere before the end of the sentence and we are left wondering what about that dog? Where's he going? Aha! the store. I get it. The same with the musical sentence. D-7? D-7 to G7? Aha, I get it, D-7 to G7 to CMaj7! This sense of destination is what harmonic progressions are all about.

CHAPTER 2

When we are talking about a ii-7, V7 or IMaj7, the roman numeral refers to the root of the chord relative to a major scale. In each case, when we build a chord on one of the degrees of the major scale, we stack 3rds using notes of that same scale, so the IMaj7 is built on the first note of the major scale and contains the 1,3,5,7 of the scale. In C major, you have C,E,G,and B. The ii-7 is built on the second degree of the scale and contains the 2, 4, 6 and 8 (1) of the scale. In C major, the ii-7 chord is D-7, containing the notes D, F, A and C. In this manner, I can make chords for all seven notes of the scale. These are called "diatonic seventh" chords. (One quick note about the notation below. I use the old system of roman numerals for these chords, where chords with a major 3rd in them are upper case roman numerals and chords with a minor 3rd in them are lower case roman numerals (dominant 7sus4 chords would also be upper case.)

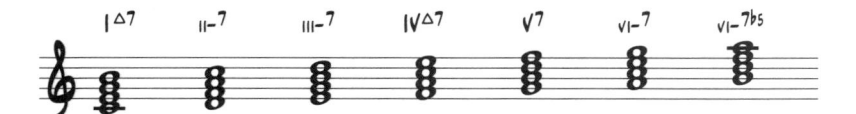

(We have finished the piano chapter, so I hesitate to mention that this is also an excellent thing to practice in all keys. **Play the diatonic sevenths in both hands, doubling the right hand above with the same chords in root position in your left hand, or use the singer voicing: 1,7, 3,5. Go around the circle of fifths,** practicing the diatonic sevenths in F major, then Bb, etc. As you practice in each key, pay attention to what note goes on each scale degree, so that you say to yourself: "Key of C, ii-7 is D-7. iii-7 is E-7, etc." When you are in more difficult keys, this becomes important for drilling yourself. "Key of Gb, ii-7 is Ab-7, iii-7 is Bb-7, etc." This is largely a mental exercise, so go slowly and don't worry about developing a lot of speed in playing these chords. As long as you can move steadily from chord to chord, knowing where everything is in each key, you've accomplished the task.)

Each of the above diatonic sevenths behaves in a certain way in a key. What I mean by this is the I major seventh chord always sounds like home in the key—it is the point of the resolution ii-7 V7 I maj7. The iii-7 and the vi-7 both act like variations of the I maj7 chord. They are kind of like homes away from home, maybe hotels if you wish, each with a different feeling than the I major seventh chord and are referred to as "tonic" functioning chords. The ii-7 chord sounds like a chord that prepares us for the dominant that is coming next and can be replaced by IV major seventh (and often is in other styles of music). These chords are called "subdominant" or "dominant preparation" functioning chords. The V7 chord sounds a bit unstable (we don't want to wait too long on it) and has a strong desire to resolve back to the I major seventh. The vii-7b5 is a relatively uncommon replacement for the V chord and these chords are called "dominant" functioning chords.

So that is what all of these seventh chords "do" in a key. This is called "functional harmony" because each chord has a certain function in the key—each chord has a job.

CHAPTER 2

To understand harmony, you have to realize that chord progressions are all about telling a story. I don't mean "storytelling" in the way the lyrics tell a story. Chord progressions tell a story about movement—about moments of rest and moments of increasing tension. As the song moves from one chord to the next, we feel more of a compulsion to get off of a given chord, or to rest on it. Chords can push us forward to the next point, or wait, they can send us on to the next chord in search of a resolution and then surprise us with a different sound than what the last chord prepared us for. They are about drama, surprise, expectations created and satisfied or denied. That's the story that harmony tells.

To understand how songs work, we need to identify a couple of different components that a lot of standards employ. Even though these rules may seem a bit abstract to you now, try to hang in there and follow them. When we start examining the possibilities available on an actual tune, things get easier to follow.

The first of these components is called a "turnaround." Turnarounds are the ways that songs tread water, just passing time in a particular key. Nothing much is going on dramatically, just the I chord, then a ii-7, V7 that leads back to the I chord again. Here are a couple of common turnarounds in the key of C:

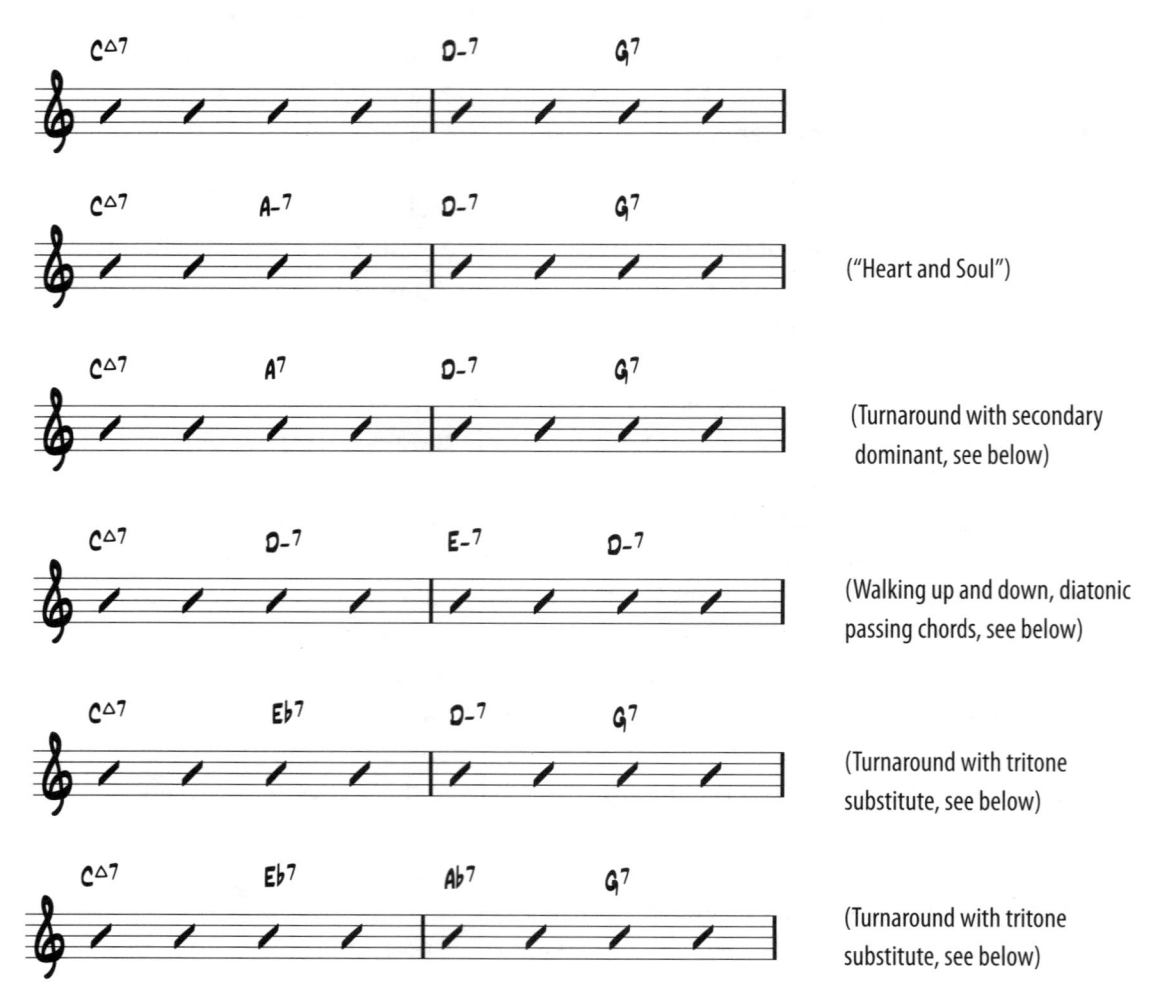

| C△7 | | D-7 | G7 |

| C△7 | A-7 | D-7 | G7 | ("Heart and Soul")

| C△7 | A7 | D-7 | G7 | (Turnaround with secondary dominant, see below)

| C△7 | D-7 | E-7 | D-7 | (Walking up and down, diatonic passing chords, see below)

| C△7 | Eb7 | D-7 | G7 | (Turnaround with tritone substitute, see below)

| C△7 | Eb7 | Ab7 | G7 | (Turnaround with tritone substitute, see below)

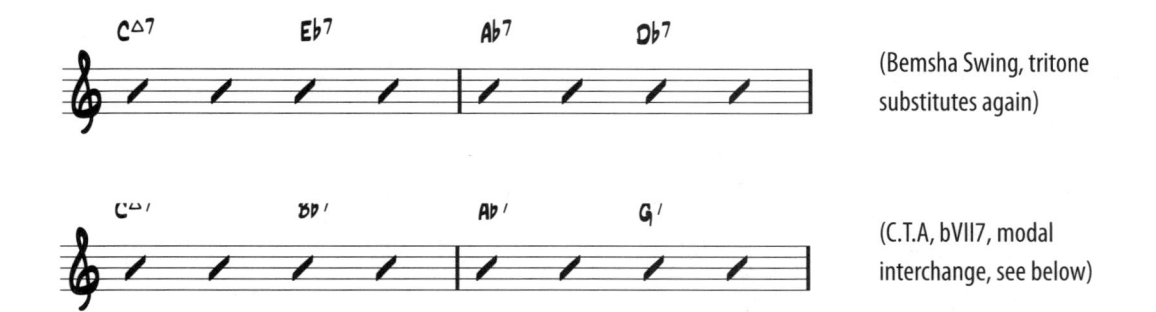

[C△7 Eb7 | Ab7 Db7] (Bemsha Swing, tritone substitutes again)

[C△7 Bb7 | Ab7 G7] (C.T.A, bVII7, modal interchange, see below)

Functionally, these turnarounds all do the same thing. They take you from the I chord to the V7 chord and back. In most situations, these turnarounds are substitutes for this progression:

[C△7]

The difference between sitting on a C chord and playing one of the above turnarounds is a little like waiting for a bus at a bus stop. I could just stand there, or I could walk three paces one way, turn around and walk back six paces the other way and then turn around again and walk back three paces to get back to where I started at the bus stop. The effect is the same, I am waiting for the bus and not going anywhere, but one way I am completely immobile, and the other way I am in a holding pattern.

Don't worry too much about the information in parentheses beside the turnarounds above. This will be explained below. The important point to focus on now is that all of these turnarounds essentially do the same thing in terms of the harmonic story they are telling. They make holding patterns while we circle in one key.

Another important song component is the ii-7, V7. It is a piece of many of the turnarounds above but it can also stand alone as a component of the song, separate from the turnaround. This is a ii-7, V7 progression that is not followed by I. This is called a half cadence. The phrase ends in an unfinished way, pushing us toward the beginning of the next phrase where we often find the I chord (or one of its substitutes) waiting. The effect of a half cadence is one of being left hanging. It's like a sentence that ends in the rising intonation of a question. Typically, half cadences occur at the end of a section of a song, and help to push us forward to the next section. Half cadences usually occur in the last bar of a standard if you are going to play another chorus, but they don't happen if the song is ending. Songs almost never end on half cadences.

Even though a song is in a particular key, it can have chords that are from another key within it. There are five ways that this usually happens in standards.

CHAPTER 2

1. Any of the six diatonic sevenths other than the I chord can be preceded by a dominant seventh a fourth below. These types of chords are called secondary dominants. The addition of a secondary dominant makes the diatonic chord it precedes a little more of a destination point in the music. So, if we're in the key of C and I want to emphasize the D-7 chord as a destination point for some reason, I can play an A7 before it, even though A7 is not found in the key of C (because it has a C# in it). This A7 is called V7 of ii-7. I can add a ii-7 (E-7 in this case) and make the D-7 even more of a destination point. This sort of added ii-7 chord is called the related ii of the V7 of ii-7.

2. I can modulate. Standards modulate all the time. All that means is that I can switch keys and use a ii-7, V7 or any of the other diatonic sevenths in the new key, even though the song begins and ends in the original key. Sometimes the modulation is long and sometimes it's short; it usually features ii, V, I in the new key pretty prominently (after all, you won't know you've modulated unless you hear the new key stated very clearly), but as long as it makes musical sense, particularly in the way the song gets to the new key and returns to the original key, it is doable. The feeling of modulation is varied, but in general, it is a kind of palette cleanser, giving the song a new harmonic lease on life.

3. There are special types of chords called modal interchange chords. These are chords that are borrowed from a different parallel key, usually a minor key. (This sounds more complicated than it is. The seven diatonic chords all come from a C major scale. I can also make diatonic sevenths from C minor scales. That's where most of these modal interchange chords come from. It's not necessary to figure out every possible type of modal interchange chord from all the scales out there. It's enough to focus on the common modal interchange chords that get used all the time.) The most common of these modal interchange chords are: the ii-7b5, which is like a more colorful ii-7 chord; the IV-7, which is similar, a kind of romantic sounding IV chord; the II7, a chord that puts off resolution—it's a way of holding on the second degree before the V7 kicks in and pushes us toward some resolution (think of the second chord of "Girl from Ipanema"), the IV7 chord, which is a bluesy IV chord; the bVII7, which is similar, another bluesy chord that usually takes the place of the IV; the #iv-7b5 chord is a kind of replacement for either I (or sometimes ii) and usually kicks off an extended series of chords that culminate in a I at the end. (Again, don't worry too much about memorizing all these chords right now. Being given all these types of chords without a context is a little like being told about a bunch of animals you've never seen or heard of—it won't mean much until you see them in their natural habitats. But when you encounter them later, they'll all have names and we'll understand a little bit about how they work.) (Okay, I know I just told you that they are hotels, but now they're animals, okay? Work with me, people, work with me.)

4. Passing chords. Sometimes chords are used to connect two chords. These connector chords can take me out of the key but they tend to lead strongly to the next chord. They are like secondary dominants in that they make any chord they are leading to more of a destination point. Passing chords are often a half step away from the chord

CHAPTER 2

> I am leading to. They can be any quality: dominant, minor7, major 7, etc. Sometimes passing chords are a whole step away from the chord they are passing to and these passing chords tend to be diatonic to the key—again this is simpler than it sounds—if you are on an Fmajor and you have a passing chord that is a whole step higher than the F, it's probably a Gminor7, the two chord in the key of F major.
>
> 5. Tritone substitutes. You can always replace either a V7 chord with the chord that is a tritone away, or a ii-7, V7 with a ii-7, V7 that is a tritone away. The reasons for this are more complicated than we really need to get into right now. Again, once you hear this substitution in action, it gets a lot more clear.

Okay, that's a fair amount of harmony, but that's everything we need to cover to start working on standards. Let's look at a real standard tune to see these components in action: "Bye Bye Blackbird."

"Bye Bye Blackbird" is a great tune for us to work on. We'll do it in Bb, since that is the key that many female singers do it in. (A quick aside here, I am not assuming that the target audience of this book, jazz singers, are all female but I am fairly certain that the world of jazz singers is more female than male. This, of course, is a wonderful thing for nerdy male pianists, since it gives them hope of a social life, but beyond that, my only interest in the gender of a singer is in relation to the keys that she will sing standards in. Most standards are written in keys that favor male voices, or (true) sopranos. Female jazz singers, whether capable of singing in the soprano range or not, tend to exploit their lower ranges more, singing as altos. If you are a woman and unsure of what key you sing a song in, a good place to start looking is probably a 4th (give or take a couple of half steps) away from the standard key, which for "Bye Bye Blackbird" is F. And, if possible, you might want to try to find keys like Bb, G, C, F, Eb and Ab, (as opposed to B, Gb and A) that players are used to playing in when you pick your keys. Personally, I like the challenge of playing tunes in unusual keys, but your bandmates, especially if they are young and not so experienced, may not. Besides, do you really want them practicing at playing in hard keys for the first time on your gig?)

"Bye Bye Blackbird" is a perfect example of the kind of problem the frustrated singer at the beginning of this chapter is likely to encounter. At first glance it seems to be as simple a tune as you can imagine. The melody is simplicity itself, mostly moving down a major scale with only a couple of accidentals (B naturals) toward the end of the tune. Clearly, this tune spends a lot of time in Bb, so how complicated could the chord changes really be?

Actually, "Bye Bye Blackbird" turns out to be a fairly complicated tune when it comes to the options available for its chord progression. The simple melody disguises the fact that a lot of different chord changes are possible. (Often a simple tune like "Bye Bye Blackbird" has a lot more (common) harmonic options than a more complicated tune like "Chelsea

CHAPTER 2

Bridge" or "Sophisticated Lady," where the melody more clearly designates one and only one common harmonic choice for most of the tune.) Still, if we look at a few different versions of these chords, we can get some sense of what's going on with the tune. We can understand these chord changes in terms of the harmonic story they are telling, and see how these different sets of changes tell the same story, each in a slightly different way.

Here is one set of changes for the first four bars.

1.

BbMaj7 / / / / | / / / / | / / / / | / / / / |

(next chord is BbMaj7)

For the first four bars we are hanging out in Bb, the I chord of the key. This is essentially standing still, waiting at the bus stop as we discussed above, so we can bet that a lot of the variations that we are likely to find on this tune will be about whether to use turnarounds in the first four bars or not. Sure enough, here are three other possibilities for the first four bars, all offering different turnaround possibilities:

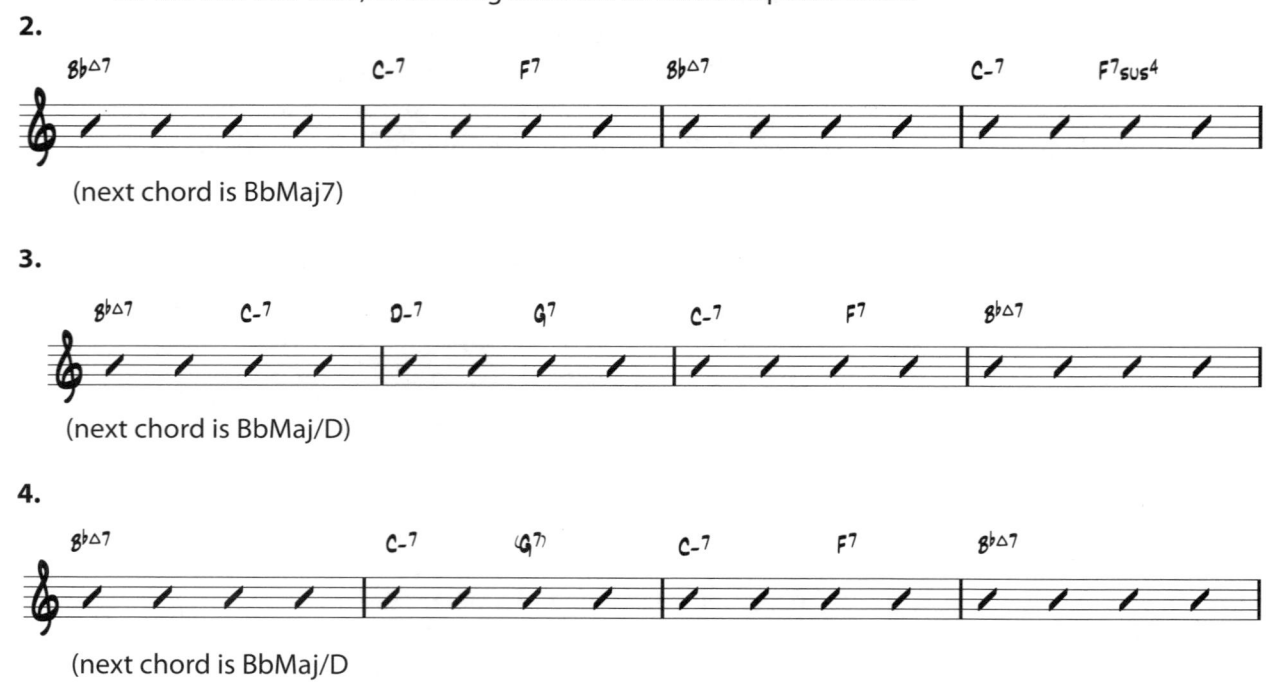

2.

BbMaj7 | C-7 F7 | BbMaj7 | C-7 F7sus4 |

(next chord is BbMaj7)

3.

BbMaj7 C-7 | D-7 G7 | C-7 F7 | BbMaj7 |

(next chord is BbMaj/D)

4.

BbMaj7 | C-7 (G7) | C-7 F7 | BbMaj7 |

(next chord is BbMaj/D

In progression two, we have a straightforward turnaround. This progression works fine, although there is a slight problem with the last chord—the F7sus4 doesn't really push forward to the next chord. An F7 would be a stronger chord, but the melody is Bb here so it would clash with the 3rd of the F7 chord and so I can't play it. (The "low" in "singing low" is the problematic word here.)

CHAPTER 2

(Actually, the phrase "I can't play it" isn't entirely accurate. Here is where some of the nuance and artistry in accompanying a singer comes in. I have to be careful about trying to play it because there is a potential clash with the melody, IF the singer is singing the melody exactly there. Maybe I CAN play it if the singer lays back on the melody or sings a slight variation. These are the things that good accompanists for singers decide in the moment, as the vocalist sings the melody of the tune. This is one of the reasons that singer/pianists are so great to listen to for pianists wanting to improve their accompanying of singers; singer/pianists always make the right choices, since they don't have to guess what the singer will do—they always know. That is why it's so important for you to learn about harmony when you are working on charts of your own. These are the decisions that you, as the singer, want to be able to make in choosing appropriate harmony for your rendition of the song.)

The third progression also works pretty well. The C-7 in the second half of the first measure is a (diatonic) passing chord leading to a related ii-7 chord in the second bar. The secondary dominant G7 leads the way to a ii-7, V7, IMaj7 for the last two bars. This progression has a slight problem with the D-7: there is an Eb in the melody at that point so there is a little potential for clashing here. Not to beat a dead horse here, but please keep in mind that I can't just assume that the Eb will clash with the melody. It can either clash and then resolve, or it may be that the way you actually sing the melody, the phrasing you use, will minimize this clash. ("Cares" is the problematic word here, to refer to the lyric that goes with the Eb in the melody.)

The fourth progression, the only one that I didn't find in a fake book, combines the two approaches from above to take care of the various problems with progressions two and three. The C-7 (a passing chord in bar 2) eliminates the possibility of the clash with the Eb, has an optional V7 of ii-7 and then follows the ii-V-I of the third version to follow the melody and avoid the problematic Bb on F7 of the second progression.

Even though these progressions are all a response to the first progression (what do we do while we are killing time for four bars in Bb major?) they all feel very different from each other. The second progression feels more like the pacing at the bus stop we talked about earlier. We are in a holding pattern waiting for the next phrase. The third progression feels a little more sensitized to the melody and may be a little bit closer to the original broadway version, but I'm not sure I like coming to rest in bar 4 like that. The third progression has the main resolution point in the 4th bar, whereas in the second progression, the 4th bar is setting up a resolution point in the next (5th) bar. The fourth progression feels like the third progression, with a variation in bar 2 to minimize the clash with the melody.

Sing the melody to the first four bars of the tune a capella. Where do you feel the harmony needs to rest? If you said, in the 4th bar, then maybe you will prefer the feeling of singing over the second progression more. Now play the first progression (BbMaj7 for four bars) and sing the melody over it. (Use the singer voicing from the previous

CHAPTER 2

chapter, or any voicing you wish. Also play the roots alone in your left hand and sing over them). Play the second, third and fourth progressions, singing the melody over each of them. Which do you think sounds best?

I'll repeat myself again (I have this tendency—perhaps you've noticed?) to tell you that understanding every tiny nuance of the harmony isn't really what I am after here for you. If you find some of this a little challenging to follow, believe me, you are not alone. Actually, the ability to write lead sheets of standards is a very difficult task. It's hard because it involves balancing options in subtle ways, and it's hard because there is an underlying harmony for each tune that can be expressed in many different sets of chord progressions. At the end of this chapter we'll recap some of the rules that you can bring to bear on these questions. But even if you don't follow every twist and turn in the road we are on, wrestling with these issues, playing changes on the piano, singing over them, and trying to make decisions about what you like and what you want to sing over is exactly the process you need to go through to learn about harmony and to learn what you like. If you haven't worked on this before now, no problem, you're doing it now. And you only get better at it with more experience.

Before we leave these four bars and go on to the next, let me point out that, as another option, you may choose to play either progression 3 or 4 for the first and last chorus of the tune (the melody choruses) and either progression 1 or 2 for the soloing choruses of the tune. This is because progression 3 and 4 are richer in the harmonic details that follow the melody, and progression 1 and 2 are more streamlined and easier to solo over.

Whew! That's a lot of analysis for about six seconds of music! Let's look at the next four bars:

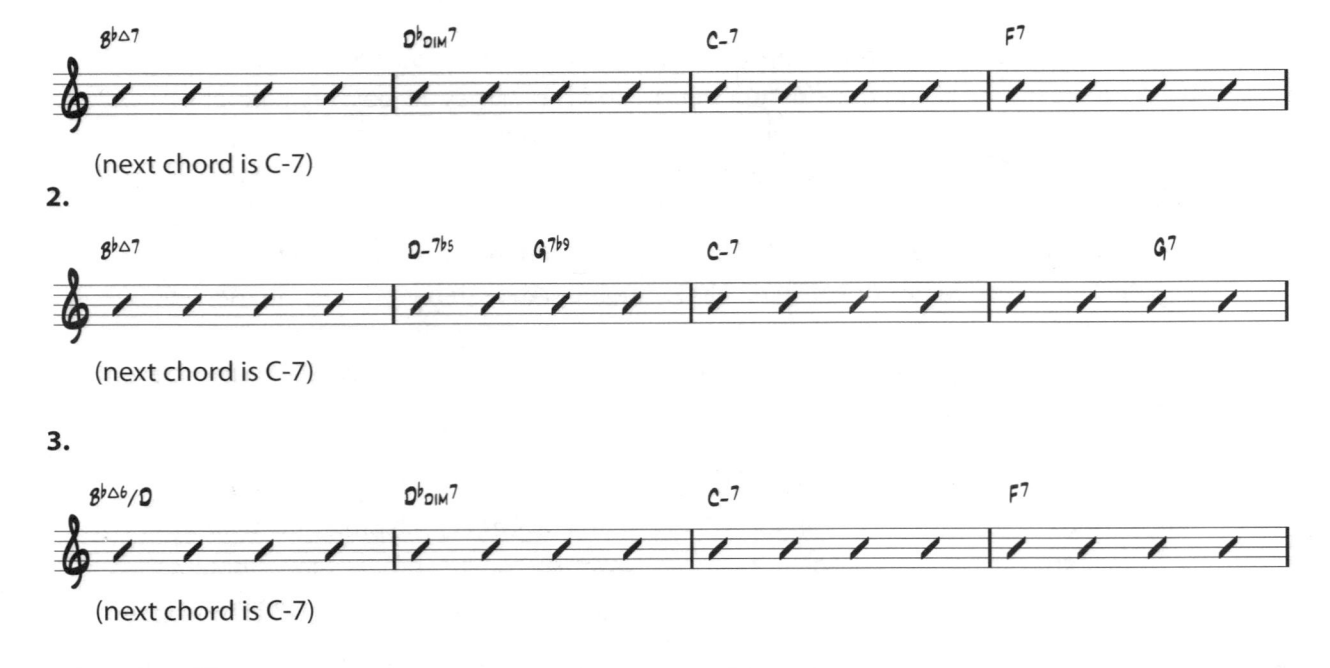

1.

| B♭△7 | D♭DIM7 | C-7 | F7 |

(next chord is C-7)

2.

| B♭△7 | D-7♭5 G7♭9 | C-7 | G7 |

(next chord is C-7)

3.

| B♭△6/D | D♭DIM7 | C-7 | F7 |

(next chord is C-7)

CHAPTER 2

Here we have a little more unanimity in approaches. Every one of these progressions has a tonic chord in the 5th bar (the first bar of the above four bar phrase), some kind of leading chord to ii-7 in the 6th bar and C-7 in the 7th bar. The first progression is probably the simplest, following the four bars of BbMaj7 with what is essentially a long turnaround. The second progression, with a secondary dominant and its related ii-7b5 chord leading to the C-7, (usually ii-7, V7 leads to a major chord and ii-7b5, V7, b9 leads to a minor chord) emphasizes the C-7 as the destination point, even more so by leaving out the dominant chord (F7) and replacing it with another secondary dominant to set up the fact that we are heading to the C-7 in bar 9. (The melody in the second bar is a little problematic with the note C in the melody on the G7b9 chord.)

The third version is the same as the first version, the only difference being the color change in the type of tonic chord used in bar 5. This progression connects to version 3 of the first four bars, which resolved to Bb in bar 4, so some sort of change between the Bb in bar 4 and the chord in bar 5 makes the harmonic flow feel more natural.

Play all of these versions singing the melody over them. (Again, try to play the chords in a variety of ways: roots only in the left hand two octaves or so below middle C, the singer voicing, any other voicings that we talked about in the piano chapter, or some other voicing that you may have worked out yourself, or learned somewhere.) Which progression feels the best to you? Which would you most enjoy singing the melody over? Which do you think would be easiest to scat over?

Let's look at the next 8 bars.

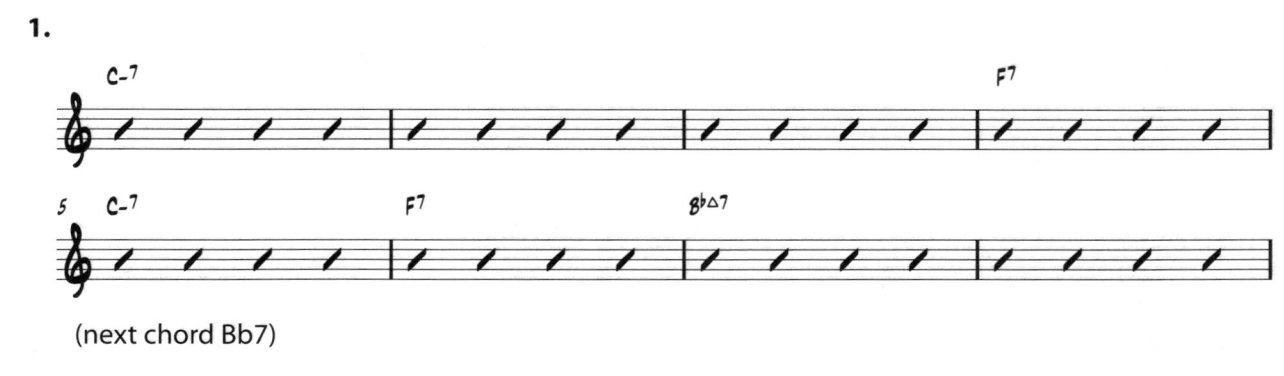

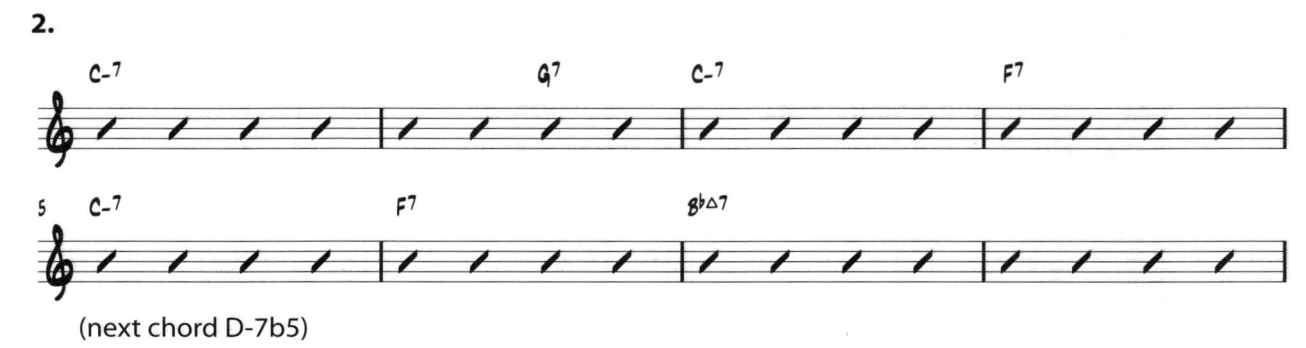

1.

(next chord Bb7)

2.

(next chord D-7b5)

43

CHAPTER 2

3.

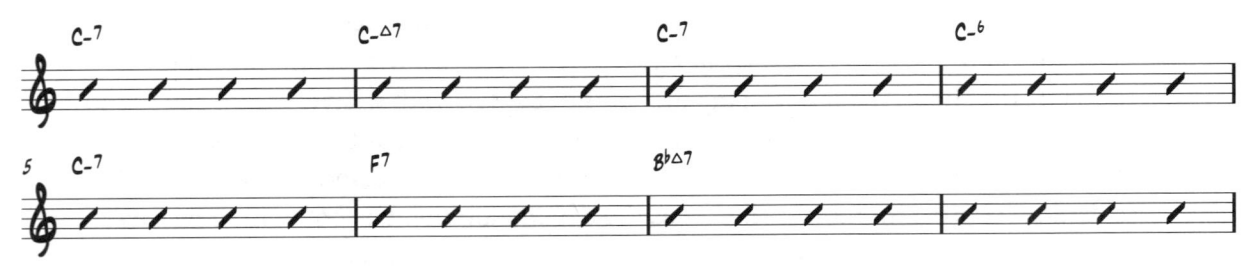

| C-7 | C-△7 | C-7 | C-6 |

| C-7 | F7 | B♭△7 | |

(next chord B♭7)

4.

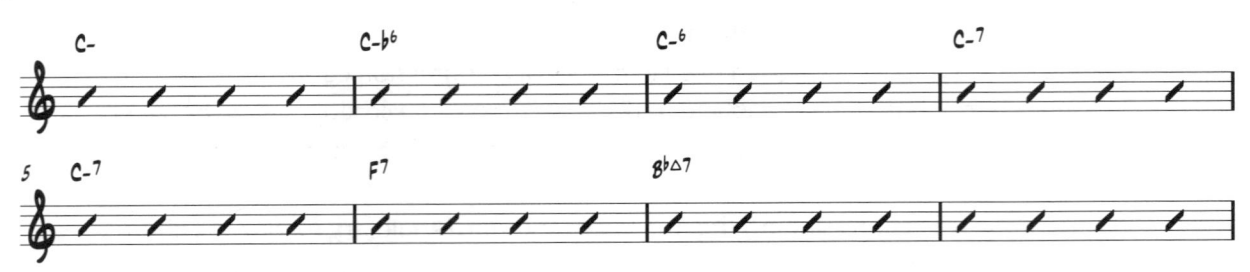

| C- | C-♭6 | C-6 | C-7 |

| C-7 | F7 | B♭△7 | |

(next chord B♭7)

For the second four bars of the above eight bars, there is universal agreement. The lyric, "Bye, Bye Blackbird" happens over ii, V I. There is a slight variation in the 4th version—the BbMaj7 changes to BbMaj6. The reason for this is that the melody goes from a C to a Bb, the root of the chord. Historically, arrangers have tried to avoid the dissonant interval that results from the root being played over a major seventh chord—here, the Bb (root) above the A natural (7th)—by using a major sixth chord instead of the major seventh in these situations.

[Musical example: B♭△7 chord with "BLACK - BIRD" melody, labeled "FLAT 9 INTERVAL CLASHES WITH MELODY"; and B♭△7 (as B♭6) with "BLACK - BIRD" labeled "NO CLASH WITH MELODY"]

Play a BbMaj7 and sing the root, Bb (the Bb below middle C.) Can you feel the clash of the minor second? This is what using the Bb6 allows you to avoid. **Now play a Bb major 6th,** replacing the 7th with a major 6th (voicing it Bb (1) and G (6) in the left hand, D (3) and F (5) in the right hand). Now sing the same Bb. Is this more comfortable? Progression 4 is the progression most sensitive to the melody (it connects to the previous four bars of progression 3), so it's not surprising that it contains this subtle distinction.

Let's consider the first four bars of the above progressions. Again, they all do more or less the same thing. The harmony holds on a C-7. Essentially what is going on here is this: we have a long ii-7 chord eventually leading to a V7, then ii-7, V7, I. As I said above, standard chord progressions sometimes we have ii-7, V7 without I, or a ii-7 for a while and then a V7, then back to ii-7, V7, and so on. This is a little like the turnaround situation, where we are pacing at the bus stop, but this time instead of pacing at the I chord bus line stop, we are pacing at the ii-7, V7 line. Of course, as usual, how we pace varies with each progression.

The first, again the simplest, just waits on the ii-7 chord before (reluctantly) going to the V7 chord in the fourth bar of the phrase. The second progression does almost the same thing, just adding a secondary dominant to the second half of the second bar. (This has the effect of saying, yes, I am still waiting on the ii-7 chord. Here it is again at the beginning of the third bar). The second two progressions do something interesting. They are also waiting at the ii-7 chord, but they want to give us something to do while we are waiting so they employ an inner line. Waiting on the ii-7 chord really means the bass note of the chord isn't going to change—it's C for the next three bars at least. But some other note in the chord CAN change while the bass is stuck waiting on the ii-7 chord. In this case, in progression 3, the 7—the note that you are playing with the thumb in your left hand—can change. The first chord of this progression is a C- chord. If you play the root in your left hand and double it up an octave, you will see this effect most clearly. (I know I told you not to double the root up an octave. I still mean it, oh, about 99.7 percent of the time. For now, though, to illustrate a point it's okay to do it. Don't you feel naughty?) For the next bar, the thumb of your left hand moves to the Maj7 (B natural). For bar 3 your thumb moves to the Bb and finally in the fourth bar to an A. This line creates interest and movement while the bass is stuck on one note.

The fourth progression does exactly the same thing, only it uses a different line for the thumb. To find this line, start by playing the 5th with the thumb of your left hand in the first bar (G). Now your thumb moves to Ab, then A and finally Bb in the fourth bar.

CHAPTER 2

These last two options, using a line in the tenor voice while the bass is stuck on one note, are extremely common. In the terminology of Berklee school of music these are called "line cliches." The first one is the one we associate most famously with "My Funny Valentine," and the second is probably most identified with the theme of the early James Bond movies.

Once again, play all of the above options, first just the roots and then voicings. Sing the melody over each of them. What do you think?

Here are the next four bars of the tune.

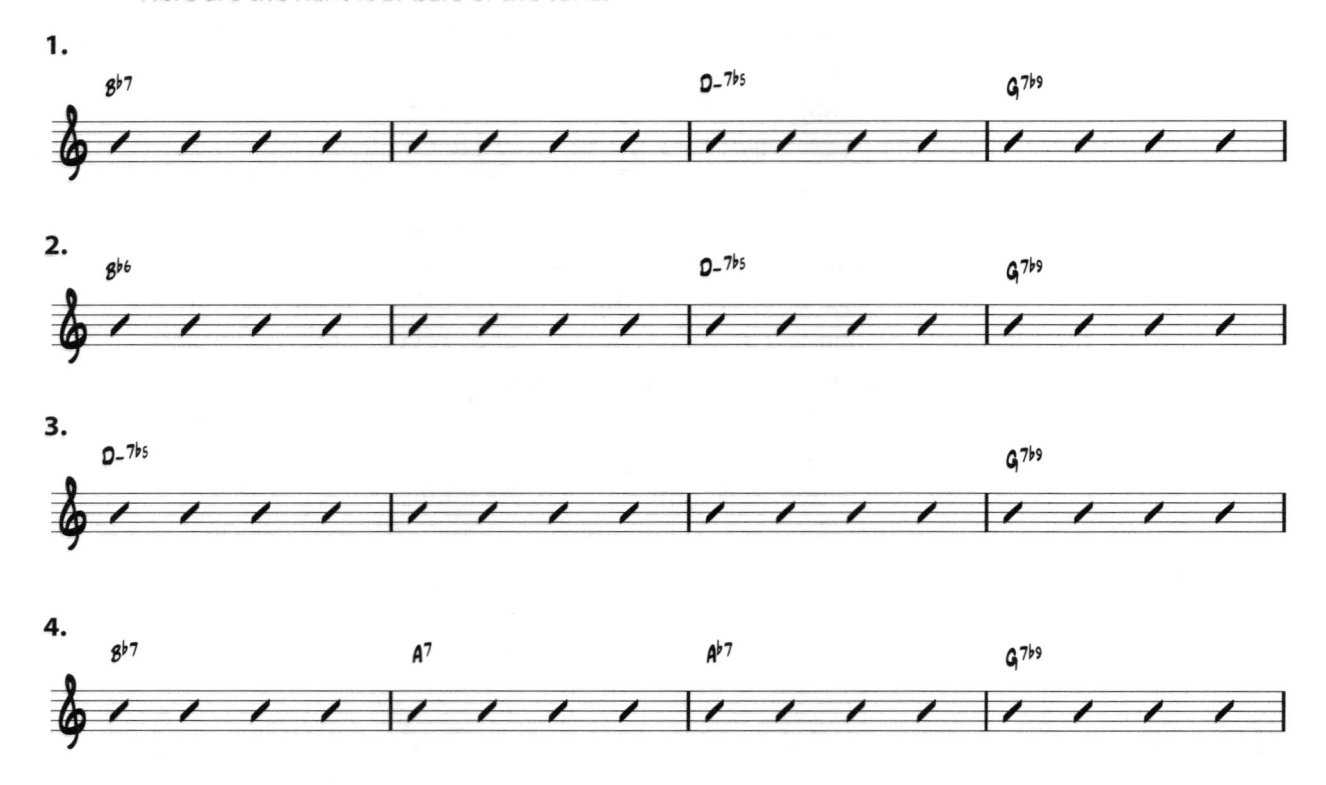

1. | Bb7 | | D-7b5 | G7b9 |

2. | Bb6 | | D-7b5 | G7b9 |

3. | D-7b5 | | | G7b9 |

4. | Bb7 | A7 | Ab7 | G7b9 |

Again, there is widespread agreement between these versions. The main point of these four bars is getting to the G7 (not to give away the ending or anything, but that's because the G7 will lead to C-7—but maybe you already guessed that.) The first three versions all agree about this, but they differ in terms of what sort of color we want to hear while we are waiting for that G7 to show up. The first progression (probably the most common) has us waiting on a dominant seventh, a bluesy sound. The second progression offers the more neutral sounding Bb6. The third progression goes with the D minor seventh flat 5. This is a colorful chord (as stated above, it's the ii-7b5 that goes with the G7 in a minor ii-7b5, V7, i progression, so it's a modal interchange chord) that makes waiting on this one sound potentially a little more exotic harmonically. The final progression has big problems with the melody in the second bar, but connects the Bb7 in the first bar pretty elegantly, moving down in half steps. (Take note, the Ab7 is a tritone away from the D7. This is a sort of tritone substitute that we talked about earlier.) This last progression is more likely to be found in the solo choruses of the tune than in melody choruses.

Once again, sing over these progressions as we have done with all of the other four bar sections of this tune. What do you think?

The next four bars, the last four bars of the bridge (well, it's not exactly a bridge but it more or less feels like one):

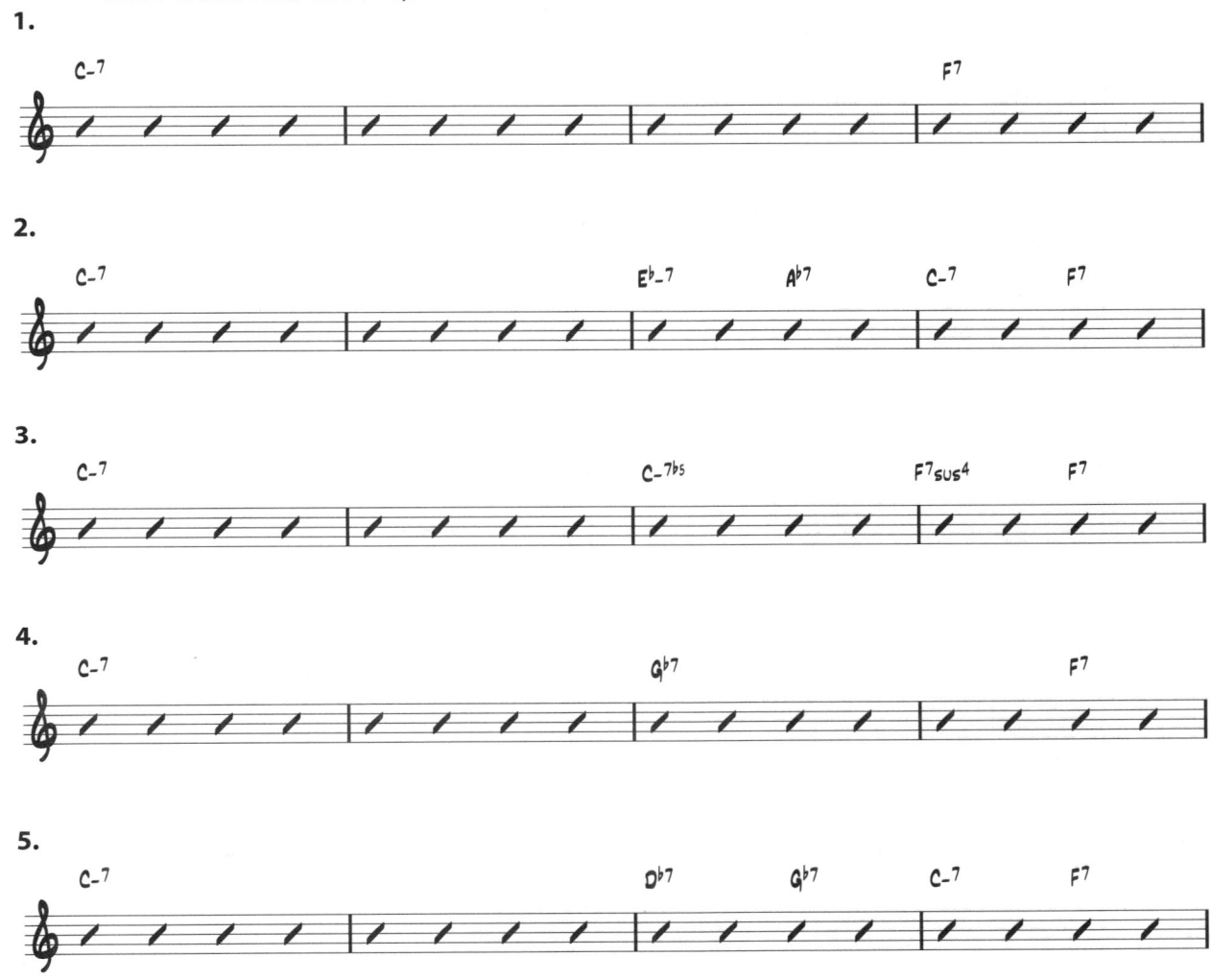

1. | C-7 | | | F7 |

2. | C-7 | | Eb-7 Ab7 | C-7 F7 |

3. | C-7 | | C-7b5 | F7sus4 F7 |

4. | C-7 | | Gb7 | F7 |

5. | C-7 | | Db7 Gb7 | C-7 F7 |

Again, you will perhaps be relieved to find widespread agreement here as well. Every version has C-7 for the first two bars. The second two bars serve the purpose of getting us back to the Bb that's coming next. Again, the first version is the simplest. We wait on the C-7 until we get to the F7 in the fourth bar (a ii-7 V7 progression, or half cadence we talked about earlier.) The second version is perhaps the most common. It's actually a variation of a modal interchange chord—the IV-7 (Eb-7). In this version, the V7 chord that goes along with it (also a modal interchange chord, the bVII7 is added). It has the effect of giving us a momentary surprise in the third bar (the melody has the root, Bb,

CHAPTER 2

so this unusual harmony is a little startling instead of the C minor seventh chord we were expecting. The third progression does something similar, but far less dramatic, by using the modal interchange chord C minor seventh flat 5 to create a color variation after the two bars of C-7b5. The F7sus4 creates problems with the melody, but that's easily fixed by omitting it and going straight to the F7. The fourth progression offers a tritone/passing chord variation of progression 3. The fifth progression embellishes the fourth with the additional related ii chord of the tritone substitute, creating a potential problem with the melody note of Bb.

Once again, try all of these yourself. Sing over them all. What do you think?

Finally, the last eight bars of the song!

1.

| Bb△7 | | D-7b5 | G7 |
| C-7 | F7 | Bb△7 | |

2.

| Bb△7 | C-7   F7 | Bb△7 | D-7b5   G7 |
| C-7 | F7sus4   F7 | Bb△7 | |

3.

| Bb△7 | | Ab7 | G7 |
| C-7 | C-7   F7 | Bb△7 | |

4.

| Bb△7 | A7 | Ab7 | G7 |
| C-7 | F7 | Bb△7 | |

The first four bars of this phrase also are about preparing us for the G7 that leads to C-7, F7 and BbMaj7, the ii, V, I phrase that ends the song. The simplest way to do this is probably the first: we hold on a BbMaj7 and then go to ii-7b5 chord of the V7 of ii-7, before the final ii, V, I. There is a problem, though, with the melody in the sixth bar, the "bird" of "Blackbird, Bye Bye." The melody is holding a Bb and this clashes with the F7. (Play an F7 and sing Bb and you'll see what I mean.) The second progression gives us a little more of the sense of pacing at the bus stop (this is the same progression that connects with progression 2 in the first four bars of the song, and it treats this part of the tune in a similar, turnaround-oriented way.) It also fixes the problem in bar 6, by preceding the F7 with an F7sus4 (voice this chord 1 and 7 in LH, 4 and 5 in RH, and then go to the 1,7,3,5 (singer) voicing for the F7 to see what I mean). The third progression gives us a tritone substitute/passing chord in the third bar of the song, and in its usual sensitivity to the melody, delays the F7 until the Bb in the melody has given way to an A. The fourth progression offers us, again, a series of chords in half steps connecting Bb with G7, although the A7 creates problems with the melody, so is probably best left for solo choruses if it is to be used at all.

Try all of these variations, singing and playing. Once again, what works best for you?

What have we learned from this lengthy examination of the possibilities for chord progressions on this song? I've said it at least five times, but I'll say it again: following every nuance of the harmonic moves that I was discussing isn't crucial for us right now. The important thing is to understand that in every phrase, the harmony is **doing something:** setting up an important chord in the next bar, waiting on a I major 7 chord, waiting on the ii chord of a ii-7 V7, I progression, resolving to ii-7, V7, I. Often, there is more than one way to accomplish each harmonic objective. Related ii-7 chords can be added to dominants, ii-7 chords can be taken away from dominants, passing or modal interchange chords can be added, various turnarounds can be added or subtracted. On a simple tune like "Bye Bye Blackbird," there are a lot of possible chord choices. (One can always re-harmonize a tune, meaning come up with a new harmony for it, so in a sense you always have lots of harmonic choices. But the harmonic choices above aren't re-harmonizations so much as realizations of the basic harmony of the tune, as we've been discussing. There tend to be a lot fewer choices for these basic sorts of harmonic realizations of more complicated tunes, as I mentioned earlier.)

Another thing to be gained from working on "Bye Bye Blackbird" in this kind of detail is to realize that YOU can gain control of your charts. **One thing you can do is compare different chord changes,** either from different fake books, or by listening and transcribing arrangements you like. **Try singing the melody over them.** Which changes give you more freedom? Which changes take away freedom? **Try singing over the bass notes alone.** Which bass lines create interesting countermelodies when you sing the melody over them?

CHAPTER 2

What's important is to develop a curious questioning mind when it comes to the harmony of tunes. Remember the story I told at the beginning of this chapter about the frustrated singer with the illegible charts? In retrospect what I should have said in response to her was, "Would you like me to show you some of the chords the pianists you hire have been fighting over? Then you can make your own choices." Whether or not my frustrated singer would have liked to get involved in harmony on that level, I encourage YOU to get involved.

Let's recap a few things to look for in your chord charts. Below is a list of common variations that you find in charts of standards, most of which we have discussed in this chapter. Be on the lookout for these things, and try to develop a sense of what harmonic devices are of particular interest to you. As I said before, being able to understand the harmony of standards you sing is a complex and difficult task. One of the hardest things I am asked to do is to write out the changes to a standard, because often there is a lot of variation in how I play it, depending on who I am playing with, and even chorus-to-chorus variations in response to what other musicians (the soloist, the bass player) are playing.

Still, ultimately, being able to come up with variations of chord changes or being able to settle on chord changes that you like is all about experience. The more you dig into this topic, comparing versions of chord changes, listening to great recordings of these tunes (from small group instrumental jazz recordings to Nelson Riddle, Mary Paich and other arrangements for Frank Sinatra, Ella Fitzgerald, Sammy Davis, Jr., etc.), the more you will have the listening experience to make good choices.

LIST OF COMMON HARMONIC VARIATIONS ON STANDARDS

1. Turnaround variations (adding turnarounds to extended I chord situations, subtracting turnarounds to make extended I chord situations.)
2. Adding ii-7 chords to V7 chords. Subtracting V7s or ii-7s from ii-7, V7 progressions to make extended I chord progressions.
3. Replacing one tonic chord (e.g., I major 7) with another (iii-7 or vi-7)
4. Replacing the ii-7 chord with the IV chord (and vice versa)
5. Replacing the V7 chord with the vii-7b5 chord (rare)
6. Adding secondary dominant chords before any diatonic seventh chord
7. Adding related ii-7 chords to secondary dominants, subtracting related ii-7 chords from secondary dominants.
8. Passing chords 1: preceding a chord with a chord of any quality (major 7, dom7, -7, etc.) a half step away from the target chord
9. Passing chords 2: preceding any chord with a diatonic chord one scale degree below or above it.
10. Using modal interchange chords: ii-7b5, IV7, IV-7, bVII7, #iv-7b5, II7.
11. Replacing ii-7 to V7 with V7sus4 to V7.
12. Tritone substitutes: substituting a dominant seventh with the dominant seventh a tritone away; substituting a ii-7, V7 with the ii-7, V7 a tritone away.

13. Substituting a chord with a different quality chord built on the same root, e.g. dom7 for major 7, dom7 for minor 7, dom7sus4 for dom7, minor major 7 for major 7. As long as this change doesn't clash with the melody, it's possible.
14. Adding lines in the tenor voice when you are on an extended I chord situation such as 1, major 7, min7, 6, or 5, b6, 6, b7.
15. Replacing diminished passing chords a half step below a chord (e.g., B diminished seventh to C-6) can be replaced by a V7 chord a 4th below the target chord (G7 to C-6) and vice versa. (We didn't talk about this one above, but I thought I'd throw that one in as an added bonus!)

Before we leave the subject of how to come up with chord changes on standards, let me just say a few things about intros, since often singers are confronted with the problem of creating introductions for their charts.

Like many of the things I learned about accompanying a singer, I learned a lot about intros from playing with Dakota Staton. I remember playing an intro to "My Funny Valentine" that had a recognizable motive in it from the tune, and she stopped me. "Don't play that!" she screamed. "You'll give it away!" She wanted me to play something that set the right mood, set up the key, but she wanted the moment she sang "My Funny Valentine" to be greeted with enthusiastic applause. (This was a hit for her in the late 50s or early 60s.) Of course, if I gave the tune away, people might clap during my intro, which was quite a different thing altogether.

So what should an intro be? Again, the best way to get a sense of this is to listen to a lot of recordings. Still, we can set down a few guidelines.

The first thing an intro should do is set up the key that the tune is in. (Q: Why did the singer always wait for hours outside her apartment door? A: She could never find her key.) Relatively few singers have perfect pitch, and if you do, you can take a lot more liberties with intros. (This was one of the pleasures of working with Jane Monheit.)

Turnarounds effectively set up the key in most situations, and this is one of the default options for intros. But of course, Dakota wouldn't have been satisfied with playing a turnaround repeatedly in front of the tune. "It's like a piano concerto," she'd say. "Play something and then hold a chord so I can come in." (Actually, she was probably a lot more cryptic than that. And a good deal meaner. She had a well-deserved reputation for tearing apart accompanists.) What I decided she meant about intros was the following: make some kind of statement, a motive, a line, an arpeggiation or something. Develop it in a way that feels consistent with the mood of the tune coming up. If it's a ballad, probably rubato is fine, even if the tune is in time. If it's a medium tune, then the groove should also set up the tune, and it becomes less of a "piano concerto." Still, the important thing is to present one idea and develop it, not just to blow over a chord progression or vamp over a turnaround.

CHAPTER 2

As far as that final chord of the intro is concerned, that depends on two factors: 1) Is there a pickup before the downbeat of the A section? and 2) What is the first chord? The intro should set up the first note the singer has to sing. That doesn't necessarily mean that the intro has to have the first note on top of the chord, but sometimes, that DOES help. If there is a pickup, it's particularly important that the intro sets that up, in addition to the key the song is in. For example, on "Autumn Leaves," an intro that sets up G minor in a medium tempo and then has a short downbeat on 1 of the eighth bar of the intro on a G7 altered with the note "G" on top of the voicing, will clearly set up the pickups to "Autumn Leaves" in Bb. All the elements are there: the key is stated; the V7 of the first chord (C-7, the ii-7) is played to suggest the next chord, the G; the first note the singer has to sing is clear in the chord voicing; and the rhythmic break leaves a space in the measure for the pickups. This intro is loosely based on Wynton Kelly's intro on this tune.

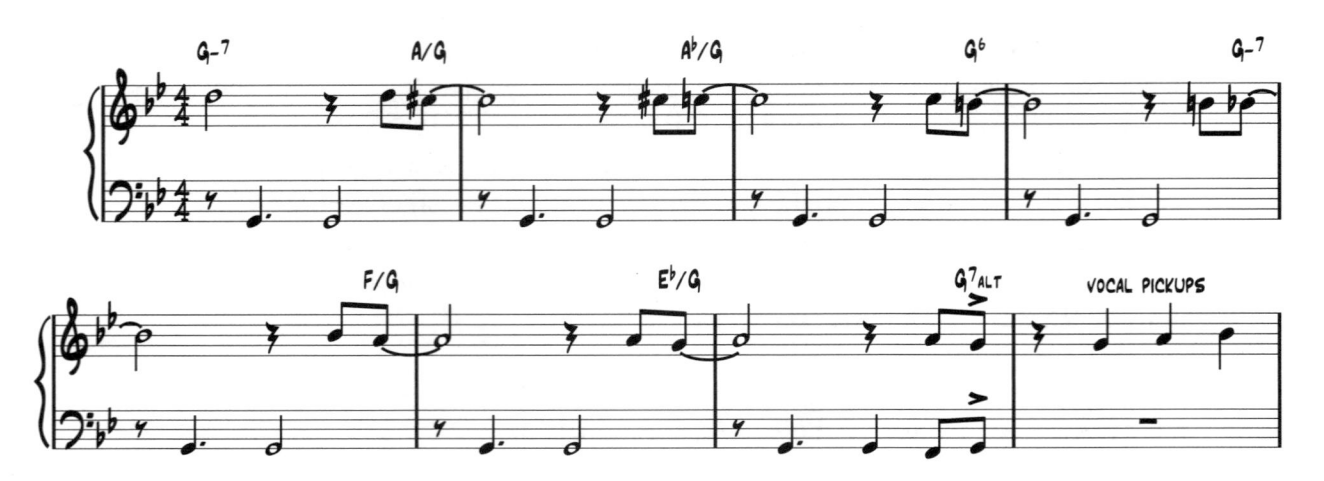

An intro to "My Funny Valentine" would be very different. Some strong melodic motive over CMaj7, something similar over Ab major 7, then F major 7, Eb major 7, Db major 7, G7susb9, to G7 altered with a slight ritard and then a strong downbeat on C-6 with the 5th of the chord on top of the voicing would set up this song well in C-. Again, the elements are there—something melodic, harmony that makes a mood, a slight ritard to signal that the intro is ending and a clear downbeat on one, because the singer is going to come in after the downbeat—there are no pickups this time. The C-6 chord clearly sets up the root of the chord (the first note) even though the 5th is on top of the voicing.

Those are some of the things to keep in mind with your intros. Try and be creative and don't overuse standard intros that have lost the ability to convey any mood. Also, for inexperienced singers, don't be too bossy about your intros, especially if they aren't terribly inspired to begin with. When I see a singer's chart that says: "play the last eight bars for an intro" or "I major 7, vi-7, ii-7, V7, for four bars," I am already suspicious. Why write down something that is so uninspired that it's only an option as a last resort?

The answer is that in many situations the singer and the pianist are both equally inexperienced. Or the singer just wants to know what he or she will get—something safe, if a little uninteresting. The "heart and soul" type turnarounds are not an inspired choice, but they do the job. It's making an intro "fast and dirty," as the great arranger Michael Mossman likes to put it. But of course we can all aim for something better, something that really intrigues the listener and makes you want to listen to the rest of the song.

And with that intro (to intros) let's leave this. Just like a good intro ought to do, we are now primed and ready to sink our teeth into the melody.

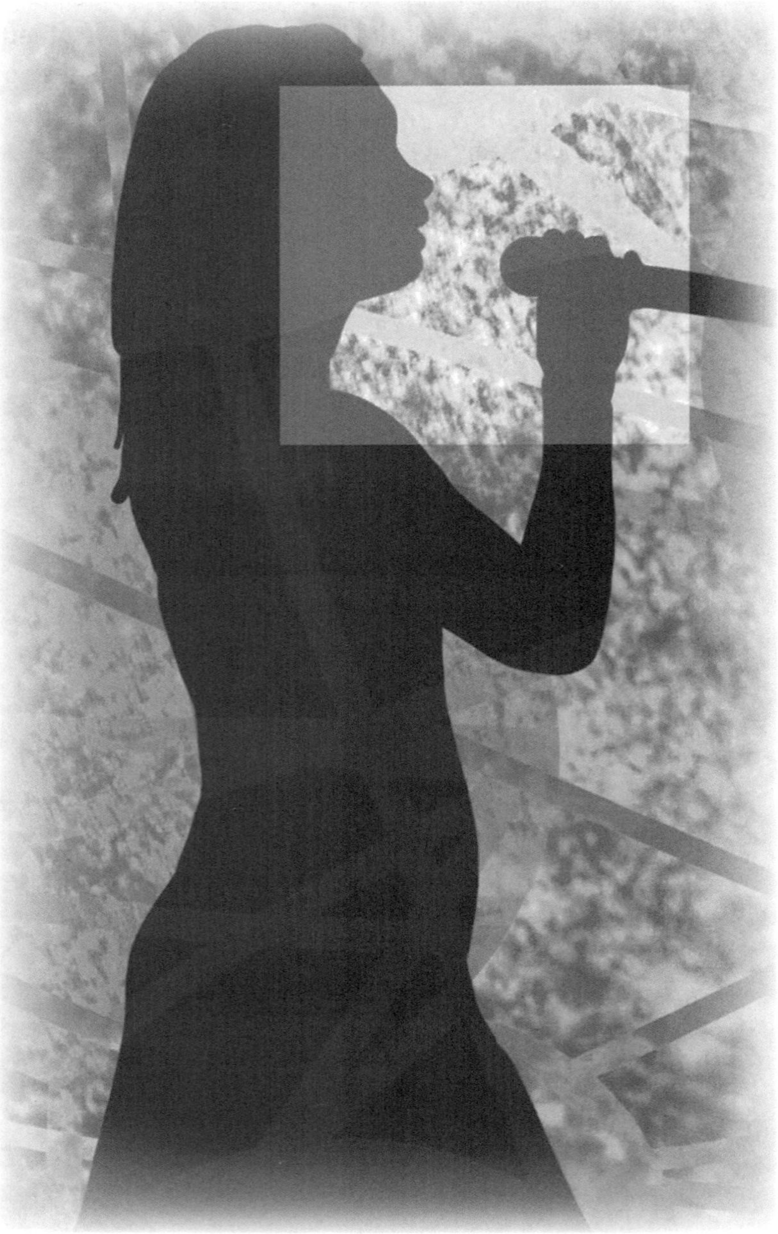

CHAPTER 3

The Melody of Songs

Congratulate yourself. You have gotten through a lot of piano and theory study to get here, the singing part of the program. (Either that or you skipped the first two chapters, but in either case, I congratulate you on either your industriousness or your cunning.)

I said in the intro to this book that an awareness of harmony can change how you sing the melodies of standards and now let's look at how that might be possible.

I can always tell when a drummer that I am working with can play the piano. There is a sensitivity to harmony in what he plays, in where he cadences and how strongly. It has to do with what we were talking about in the last chapter, the way chords create tension and drama, and you can tell from the way the drummer plays how sensitive he is to that kind of drama. Of course, many great drummers (Tony Williams, Jack DeJohnette, Bill Stewart, Jorge Rossy, to name a few) can play piano very well, but whether or not they play the instrument on a high level, I can tell when I am playing with a drummer how much he hears what is happening harmonically.

With singers, it's equally important to be tuned in to the harmonic aspect of things. The first step toward developing a greater awareness of the harmony of songs is to become more aware of the point at which each new chord change occurs, knowing where the downbeat of each new harmony is. This is particularly evident when you are singing a rubato ballad. In this situation, it is essential that you know where your melody notes fit with the chord progression. Does the phrase begin before the next chord change, or after that downbeat? What note (or what word if you are thinking of the lyric of the song) cues the chord change?

So in "All the Things You Are," we get:

> YOU
> ARE the
> PROmised kiss of
> SPRINGtime that
> MAKES the lonely
> WINter (chord) seem
> LONG

and in "Lush Life":

> I USED to visit
> ALL the very
> GAY places
> (REST) those come what
> MAY places

55

CHAPTER 3

(REST) where one re-
LAXES
ON the
AXIS
OF the
WHEEL of life
(REST)

Thinking of where the downbeats are encourages you to think about tunes in a different way from how you may be thinking of them. Melodies unfold in a horizontal way. What I mean by this is that you tend to think of the song as moving from one interval to the next over time. For example, the first phrase of "Lush Life" starts on the 5th of the key and then goes up a fourth to the root and then up the scale. The next phrase continues this movement. Single line instruments like the voice are usually more aware of the continuous movement of this line in a key. However, I can also think about this melody in a vertical way, meaning, what is the relationship between the notes of the melody and the chords or bass notes—the harmony that is changing all the time.

Thinking like a piano player, this is what "Lush Life" feels like:

(REST).... I
USED to visit
ALL the very
GAY places
(REST) those come what
MAY places
(REST) where one re-
LAXES
ON the
AXis
OF the
WHEEL of life,
(REST) etc.

Each phrase of the melody occurs over a different harmonic color. Of course, there is no such thing as hearing ENTIRELY vertically or ENTIRELY horizontally. But the fact that these two different ways of hearing exist accounts for a lot of the problems that come up with scatting, and with difficulties that pianists or instrumentalists in general have with vocalists. This is because practicing soloing over chord changes has a lot to do with what is happening VERTICALLY, over each chord as it moves forward in time. Being able to turn a series of different harmonic colors, like the chord progression for "Lush Life," into something that is an appealing HORIZONTAL melody is the difficulty the composer faces, and shows the artistry of Billy Strayhorn's composing—and is also demonstrated by jazz musicians who are capable of improvising lyrically (melodically) over this complex progression.

Being sensitive to the fact that each phrase has a unique harmonic color will make you easier to accompany when you are singing rubato. It's difficult to follow a singer who phrases "Lush Life" like this: I used to visitall the...verygayplacesthose....come whatmayplaces where....onerelaxes on....theaxis of the.....wheel of life-to-get a feel-of......... life. Granted, the above phrasing makes no sense in terms of the meaning of the words as well as the harmony. But in a somewhat milder form, I hear the way a lack of harmonic awareness puts vocalists and accompanists at odds when inexperienced singers and inexperienced accompanists work together. When a singer and pianist aren't together, the reason is usually either 1) the singer doesn't know which words of the song are the downbeat of a new harmony; 2) the pianist doesn't know which words of the song are the downbeat of a new harmony; 3) the singer or pianist thinks that if the harmony changes while the singer isn't singing, that space should be shorter (usually the singer thinks this) or longer (the pianist usually thinks this); 4) the pianist is playing too much; or 5) the singer is taking the tempo of the pianist even though he or she wants the piece at a different tempo.

So in addition to knowing where the chord changes change, it would be good to know what type of chord change you want. For example,

(Intro that sets up the key and then moves to a held dominant chord) (REST)**... I USED** (singer gives downbeat with the word "used"—short single chord simultaneous with the word used) **to visit**
ALL (singer gives downbeat with the word all—short single chord simultaneous with the word all) **the very**
GAY (singer gives downbeat with the word gay—single chord simultaneous with the word all, not as short as the others) **places**
(REST) (pianist gives downbeat after places—perhaps two attacks, a note to lead to the chord and then the held chord, without a lot of filling but more sustained than the others) **those come what**
MAY (singer gives downbeat with the word may—single chord simultaneous with the word may) **places**
(REST) (pianist gives downbeat after places—a note and then the chord without a lot of filling, same as above) **where one re-**
LAXes (singer gives downbeat with the word lax—single chord simultaneous with the word lax; these next 3 are all short)
ON (short chord simultaneous with on) **the**
AXis (short chord simultaneous with ax)
OF the (short chord simultaneous with of)
WHEEL (chord simultaneous with wheel, pianist will probably stretch this phrase a little more and try to connect it to the rest that starts the next phrase) **of life** and etc. At the end of the section, before it repeats, the pianist is likely to play a ii-7, V7 in the space before the melody, and cadences take longer than a single chord timed to coincide with a particular lyric.

CHAPTER 3

Of course, this is just one of many possible interpretations of how the singer and pianist could hook up on this tune. It could also work with the singer taking the downbeats (on phrases that start with "all" and "gay" for example) and the pianist coming in with a chord on the next word, or two words later. This would give it a slightly more relaxed feeling and would allow a little more leeway, since the singer and pianist wouldn't be both trying to hit the downbeat together, although eventually they probably would want to hit something together. Of course, how simple you want the piano accompaniment to be is a matter of personal taste, but you can't communicate with your accompanist if you don't know where the chord changes occur.

Of course, knowing where the chords change and being sensitive to the harmonic colors of each phrase effects more than just your rubato singing. It will also effect your phrasing. A lot of singers like to phrase the melody in a laid back way, singing a bit behind the beat. This is a great quality, when it is controlled. It makes the music feel relaxed and swinging, and many great singers—from Frank Sinatra and Ray Charles to Betty Carter, Norah Jones and Willie Nelson—exploit this to great effect. However, some singers lay back so far that they are singing a phrase that goes with the preceding chord change. They fall a chord change behind. This can be extremely uncomfortable to play with and makes little harmonic sense (at least, to me).

So check yourself on this. **Sing through your tunes playing the changes on the piano, or just the bass notes. Make sure you know where the phrases begin and end, and when the chords change.** Being able to play the chords for yourself as you sing the melody will increase your awareness of the changes, and make you much easier to comp for. **Sing the melodies away from the piano, as well, and tap your foot on the beat where you think the next chord change happens.** Notice if you tap only on the first beat of the bar, or if you are sensitive to when chords change two times in a measure on beats 1 and 3, or even if there are places in some of your charts where the chords change more than two times per measure. Try this on any standards that aren't in 4/4 meter—such as 3/4, 6/8 or any other meter you sing in.

I don't want to talk too much about phrasing the melody. That's a subject much better left to professional singers and coaches, and I think it is amply covered in other places. But I do want to talk about the next step in approaching the melody from a harmonic perspective, and that is to understand what notes you are singing over each chord.

Let's look at the bridge of "All the Things You Are." This is an interesting case of a melody that has a lot of harmonic details in it.

TRACK 1

The lyric has "You are the" (as pickups to the first bar of the bridge) and then we get "angel glow, that lights a star" with "angel" on the first two beats of the bar. "An" is the

4th or 11th of the A-7 chord; "gel" is the 3rd. Then the chord changes and "that" is an Eb on a D7 chord, followed by E natural, C and B (which is the 3rd of the GMaj7 in the next bar.) The notes on the D7 chord change are especially interesting—Eb can be thought of as a b9 leading to a natural 9, and C is the 7th, a chord tone. But, if you remember from our discussion of piano voicings in the first chapter, b9 and natural 9 don't often occur in the same chord, so in this case, I think we could view the Eb as a chromatic approach note leading to the 9. (We'll hear a lot about chromatic approach notes later on.) My main point in looking at these notes so closely is that the melody is extremely subtle in its use of chromatic approach notes and interesting note choices on the chords. It's very common to hear a singer sing this bridge like this:

In the above example, the unusual note choice on the D7 chord change—the chromatic approach note—is gone, the 9th and the interesting intervals (the C (7th) down to the Eb is a major 6th descending, the E natural up to the C is a minor 6th ascending) are gone in favor of a repeated chord tone.

Now, I am all in favor of freeing up the melody. That is the main reason why I want you to be able to study harmony—so that you'll have more freedom in creating melodies over chord changes, and altering existing melodies. This is what jazz musicians do, and this is the art that you are pursuing. But in the above case, interesting note choice has been sacrificed, and the melody becomes bland. This is one of the cardinal sins that inexperienced jazz singers commit. If you are going to change the written melody, do it with a sense of what is interesting, unique or important in the melodic details of the original melody. Try and add to what's there, and don't oversimplify unusual melodies because you weren't aware of harmonic details.

Having said that, the above simplified melody might be a good choice if the rhythm was altered in a particularly interesting way. But again, the main point remains. If you are singing the simplified melody because of a lack of awareness of the complexity of the original, then you'd be better off studying the melody more deeply.

What happens over the next dominant seventh in the bridge is also interesting: in this case we have a chromatic approach note to the root of the B7. (There is a variation of this particular melody that I learned a long time ago that has these two notes up a half step, so instead of the chromatic approach note to the root, we get the root to the b9. Sometimes you see it in fake books like that, but it is certainly the less common version.) Again, this melody is often made diatonic in a way similar to the example above.

TRACK 2

CHAPTER 3

So, how do you know if there are important harmonic details in the melody that you might wish to retain? The answer is to analyze the melody harmonically. A harmonic analysis of the melody does pretty much what I did in the above example; you figure out what scale degree every note of the melody is in relation to the chord it comes over. (This sounds a lot more difficult than it actually is. In practice, most melodies are pretty simple.) To get a little practice at this, let's look at "We'll Be Together Again," again. The first note of the melody is the 6th (or 13) of the G7 chord, then we get the root on the C major 7, and the rest of the first four bars as you can see below. (By convention, when analyzing a melody we use numbers smaller than 8. The rule is this: when you are thinking about melody lines, you are thinking of scale degrees and so use the numbers 1 to 7. When you are thinking about chords, you are thinking of chord tones and tensions and so use the numbers 1, 3, 5 and 7 for chord tones and 9, 11 and 13 for tensions. We'll get into this more when we discuss chord scales in the coming chapters. If it's easier for you to use 9, 11 and 13, though, it's fine, since these are just different names for the same notes.)

There are two reasons why this information is important and useful. The first is that hearing what notes you are singing over the chords helps your intonation. Traditionally, in big band writing the third or fourth trumpet is the improvising jazz player in the section. Arrangers will often try to give the altered tension, or note that clashes or rubs against another note in the chord, to this player, because he is sensitized to harmony, will hear how the note is functioning on the chord and will play it more in tune than a lead player (who is traditionally more of a stud, who can play high notes well, but usually is less advanced as an improviser over changes). In the same way, if you only think about the horizontal nature of the melody (in this case, singing down a 3rd, then up a minor 7th and down a minor 3rd, etc.) you are ignoring the fact that a C sung over a C major chord to a Bb on an Ab7 chord feels different from those same notes sung over a different harmony, a held C7 chord, say. We are effected by both the horizontal direction of the melody AND the vertical nature of what a given note's relationship is to the chord it is sounded over, whether we realize it or not.

Of course, the other reason why analyzing the melody is important is that knowing what notes the melody uses on each chord gives you insight into what chord scale the melody is based on and what other notes you might use to vary the melody. We'll tackle that next, when we look at singing second choruses, but for now, try this for yourself: **Take one of your tunes. Figure out what every note of the melody is, in relation to each chord.** You don't have to get into a deep analysis of chord scales here, as I said, most melodies are not that complex (in the sense that most standards are not outlining complex chord scales that change as they move chord to chord). You can think of this the same way we dealt with chords when you were working at the piano: for each chord there are the chord tones and tensions. The tensions are usually found a whole step above the chord tones, except on dominant chords, where you have all of the altered tensions as well. (The only difference between the available notes when you were making piano voicings and the available notes when you are doing a melodic analysis is that you will sometimes also find 4 (11) on major sevenths and dominant sevenths. On these chords, the 4th is a melodic passing note that usually resolves to the 3rd.)

What do you notice about your analysis? Perhaps you notice that a simple melody that just goes up and down the major scale has a lot of different numbers above it when you analyze the notes in terms of each chord. This may seem a little counterintuitive. Simple melodies are so clearly moving up and down the notes of a major scale that they are much easier to hear horizontally, moving along in a given key. Hearing the notes vertically can be a little challenging.

After you've written the numbers above each note of the melody, try singing the pitches using the numbers instead of the lyrics of the song. Try doing this over just the roots of the chords. When you do this, keep in mind that you are singing the number that defines the interval between the note you are singing and the root. For example, if you sing 4 to 3 (as you would for the first bar of the bridge of "All the Things You Are"), notice that you are singing a note that is a 4th above the root you are playing, and then a note that is a minor 3rd above the root you are playing, with a couple of octaves between these notes. (For me, writing 3 is good enough. You don't have to write b3 because if you see a 3 above a minor chord you know that the 3rd is flatted.)

So as you sing these numbers over the roots, you are doing a kind of interval ear training. **You could also try this on a standard you don't know. Analyze the notes of the melody in relation to the chords. Then, playing the roots only, force yourself to sing the interval specified by the number you are singing** (meaning that if you see 4 to 3, find the interval of a 4th in relation to the root and then the interval of a minor 3rd.) Is it possible to learn a melody this way, ignoring the horizontal intervals and concentrating only on the vertical ones? This will help your ability to hear the relationship between melody notes and the roots of the chord.

Now try singing the melody using the analyzed numbers over the full chords, using whatever voicings you like. Can you still hear the vertical relationship of these notes?

Do this many times with many of your tunes. After you have analyzed and practiced a melody in this way, do you notice any difference in what it feels like to sing the melody? Are you more secure? How about if you try to vary the melody a bit, in an intuitive manner. Do you have more ideas of how to change the notes but stay inside the vertical harmony of the song? If you don't notice a difference that's fine, but if you do, try to take note of it. Try this analysis process with songs that you've sung for a long time and songs that are new for you. Again, just try to notice if you can see any changes in what it feels like to sing songs this way.

SECOND CHORUSES

Now let's get to second choruses. Often, in any tune that is faster than a ballad, jazz singers will sing a second chorus that is not a scat solo. This is important, and it is one of the big differences between jazz and pop singing. Pop singing is usually concerned with delivering the words of the song and telling the story that the song is about. Jazz singers (as well as blues, gospel and some country and rock singing) are concerned with the words of the song, but not in the same literal story-telling way that pop musicians are. For example, many standards have only one set of lyrics for the form of the tune. A pop version of the song, as we mentioned in the last chapter, will seldom repeat the lyrics more than twice (once at the beginning of the tune and once on the way out), since the more times you tell the story the more anticlimactic its message becomes. A common jazz performance of a (non-ballad) standard will start with a chorus of the melody sung pretty faithfully, without too much deviation from the standard melody. The rhythm section may be in 2/4, meaning that the bass is playing a lot of half notes, not walking quarter notes. At the end of the first chorus, the rhythm section will (often) set up to go to swing and the energy level increases. Now, the singer sings another chorus of the lyrics of the song, in this new more energized setting. There isn't much point in doing this, of course, if you are going to sing the song exactly the same way again. You have to make changes in your interpretation of the melody, loosening up the rhythm and creating melodic variations. Indeed, this kind of improvising (along with the interpretation of the first melody chorus, which, as I said, tends to be a bit more faithful to the written melody of the song) is most of the improvising many jazz singers do.

It's important for you to sing second choruses, because it helps the band. More specifically, it gives the band more development options for the song. I mentioned earlier that one of the pleasures of playing with Jane Monheit is that she has perfect pitch and so playing intros for her was easy—you never had to worry if the key wasn't stated clearly, because she'd always find her note. One of the things that made playing with her challenging (at least at the time I played with her—that was quite a while ago and things may have changed) was that she often didn't sing second choruses on medium swing tunes. Either the band stays in 2/4 for the whole melody chorus and goes to 4/4 at the start of the instrumental solo, or the band is in 2/4 for only the first two A sections of the melody chorus and then goes to 4/4 at the bridge. Of course, there is no right or wrong way to develop a swing tune but the above options are a little bit limiting in the following ways: if the band goes to 4/4 at the start of the solo, it creates a feeling that the real energy of the song occurs when the singer isn't singing. There's a buildup (drum roll, please) and then boom! we are into walking, but the singer's role is over until the head out. (In a similar way, experienced singers often suggest to the band not to go back to 2/4 at the beginning of the head out because the resulting energy drop makes the last vocal statement of the melody seem anticlimactic, so the first two A's of the head out are often in 4/4 and either the bass goes back to 2/4 at the bridge, or at the end of the bridge for the last A, or not at all). The problem with the other option, going to 4/4 at the bridge in the first chorus, is that it condenses everything so much. We get 2/4 for 16 bars, then boom! walking in 4/4. There isn't another energy level to go to, and we've shot our wad and stay in 4/4 for the rest of the tune. Similarly, the problem with starting in 4/4 is that you don't have the possibility of the increase in energy level.

When I say that these things are "problems," you shouldn't assume that they can't be used as effective ways of developing a tune. You can have a beautiful version of a standard where the singer sings one chorus and the bass player walks from the beginning of the tune, from the bridge of the first chorus, or at the start of the solo chorus. My point is that, if you don't sing the second chorus (and are going to not sing any second choruses ALL NIGHT), then you have limited the possibilities, because one very traditional version of the development of a swing standard is this: intro, vocal melody in 2/4 (1 chorus), looser vocal improvising around the melody over 4/4 (one chorus), solos (? choruses), vocal melody out (one chorus), ending. It's a traditional way of playing a standard, because the pacing is very natural.

Another problem with not singing second choruses is solo length. On a medium or slow swing tune, singing two choruses (the melody in and out) takes between two and three minutes, depending on the tempo. The solo shouldn't be longer than the vocal choruses (at least not often, because this is, after all, the vocalist's gig) so the solo section might be one chorus of sax and one chorus of piano. If the sax player took more than one chorus, the pianist could probably still take one, but more would certainly be pushing it. In either case, not taking a second chorus (ever) severely limited the possible length of the solos, as well as the ability to build energy (the "story" that the rhythm section is telling, if you get what I mean) and make a feeling of direction over the course of the tune.

So being able to sing a second chorus helps the band and gives you the opportunity to solo, build energy, and still have the lyrics at your disposal. (Seasoned singers often use the freedom of the second chorus to slyly comment on the lyric; thus a very sentimental lyric in the first chorus might become slightly sarcastic or twisted in some way in the second chorus.) In addition to all of these musical reasons, singing second choruses allows you to ease into soloing without committing to the be-bop-a doo-wop of scatting.

So try singing a second chorus on one of the tunes that you have analyzed. See how you can loosen up the melody in an intuitive way. Spend a little time on this, singing many choruses of the lyrics over the bass notes or full two-handed comping. Now, look at your analysis. For example, to return to the bridge of "All the things You Are," the first bar, 4 to 3 on the minor chord is just one of the possible note choices that work over this chord. Other easy to hear options include: 4,5,3; 4,5,2,3; 4,5,6; 3,4,2.

CHAPTER 3

TRACK 3

[Musical notation: A-7 chord, four numbered examples]

(One quick note here: once we start working on scales and patterns, feel free to transpose the given selections up and down octaves wherever you wish. Many of the examples in this book are written in the middle to upper part of the treble clef, but that doesn't mean you need to sing them there. Take them down an octave if that feels more comfortable.)

You can easily invent these all day, which is exactly what I suggest you try and do! As with the melody, you need to try these patterns both with and without the lyrics. Singing melodies without the lyrics is very liberating, but once you bring back the words of the song, you may feel a little bit stuck in the melody of the tune and have a harder time loosening up the note choice. **You should work back and forth on this, singing the melody with the lyric and without,** finding melodic variations with the words and without the words, and then seeing how you can fit the lyrics to the variations you find.

Staying with the bridge of "All the Things You Are," in the next bar, the melody gives us b9 as a chromatic approach note to 9 and then 7 over the D7 change. Try replacing some of these notes with other interesting notes on this chord, such as the examples below.

TRACK 4

[Musical notation: D7, G△7, D7, G△7 chords, two numbered examples]

Write down some of your favorite patterns that you discover in this way, gradually building a vocabulary of ideas for the eight bars of the bridge. Practice singing different patterns. Perhaps it might be helpful to compose a chorus of these variations of the melody, or if you like this process, you could compose several choruses.

I should probably point out something here. When I am working with a singer on some of these approaches, he or she always asks the same question: "Do I always have to know the scale degree number of every note that I am singing? Do all singers that can scat know every note as they sing it?" The answer to this is, of course, no, you don't have to know every note before you sing it. Singing shouldn't be merely an intellectual exercise of finding the right notes on chords. BUT, when you are practicing it's okay to be a little bit intellectual about working on these things. Finding unusual notes, composing melodic variations that you can't improvise intuitively right now, doing analysis and ear training to hear harmony better—these are all things that you CAN do when you are practicing. In performance, close your eyes, forget everything and sing whatever you hear or feel.

CHAPTER 3

I have a vision for you, and for some of you this is radically different from what your musical life has been like up until now. I imagine that you can spend hours productively, studying, singing, playing the piano, analyzing harmony, writing changes, and ultimately, arranging and composing interesting music. This isn't something that is reserved for genius singers, or something that only pianists and arrangers have the license to do. It's a kind of practice that you can do, and you can see steady progress and musical growth through doing it. This sort of practice can change the way you hear music and sing it. It will make you more fun to work with and it will enrich your musical life.

Here's one last thing I'd like you to consider before we move on to the true scatting portions of this book. If you listen to Louis Armstrong you may have noticed that often when he sings the melody on swing tunes, he scats short solo lines in the spaces of the melody around the lyric. Essentially, this is like when a singer sings a solo with a sax player playing what is called obbligato, solo lines around the singer's melody. (If you can't imagine what this sounds like clearly, listen to some of the Billie Holliday recordings with Lester Young playing some sublime yet simple obbligato sax behind her). These lines comment on the melody and respond to it, and this is another way to begin soloing. **Often for scatting novices, it's easier to answer the melody with improvised melodies, than to sing a completely improvised solo. So, try this as well, again, over bass notes and over two-handed voicings.**

TRACK 5 To return to our staple, "We'll Be Together Again," here is an idea to start you off.

Keep in mind, that all of these things will be affected by the upcoming work we will be doing on scatting. Still, it's very helpful to try these things in an intuitive way before buckling down and working on the theory that underpins them. We will be revisiting all of this in later chapters so, for now, see what you can come up with, and when you are ready, move on.

MELODIC STUDY WRAPUP

1. Pick several of the tunes you normally sing. Sing the melody of some of your tunes at the piano, first over bass notes and then over two-handed voicings, noticing where each chord changes and what note and lyric of the melody this happens on. Away from the piano (not looking at the chart) sing the melody and tap your foot at the point of every chord change.
2. Analyze the melody by writing the scale degree above each pitch. The scale degrees should be in relation to each chord the notes of the melody are sounded over.

CHAPTER 3

3. Sing the melody over the roots alone and then over two-handed chords using the scale degree numbers instead of the lyric. Try to hear the vertical (intervalic) relationship of each pitch to the root and then the whole chord.
4. After working this way for a while, sing the melody with the lyric. Does it feel different than before you worked on your analysis? Repeat this process with many tunes.
5. Analyze a song you don't know. Play the roots and sing the melody by singing the vertical interval above the root, not by learning the melody in a horizontal way.
6. Practice loosening up the melody on second choruses of some of the tunes you have analyzed. Sing many choruses of each tune, trying to change the melody in subtle ways.
7. Return to your analysis; look at the notes that the melody uses on the first harmony.
8. Working slowly on one chord change, create variations by changing the order of pitches, adding chord tones or adjacent notes from the scale. On dominant seventh chords try adding altered tensions. Alternate composing with improvising. Keep a record of some of the variations you like. Try doing this without the lyric; sing the numbers of the scale degrees.
9. Continue working through each chord of the tune (or of an A section; you don't need to finish this necessarily—whatever you do will help you become more comfortable with creating ornamentations and variations in the melody that will be appropriate for second choruses). Keep a record of some of your variations. Now try singing some of these with the lyrics.
10. Combine some of these variations in a composed second chorus

Keep in mind that these lists of things to do are only suggestions. Your practicing may take a different turn, and not all of the things I suggest will be helpful and fun. Monitor your interest level and notice what work most appeals to you. If it's not fun for you, try something else.

CHAPTER 4

Practicing Scatting 1:
The Chord Tones and Tensions of Progressions

So now we are halfway through the book and almost to the exercises that motivated me to write this book in the first place.

Almost, but not quite. I just want to say one word about scat syllables. To be honest, a thorough discussion of scat syllables is beyond the scope of this book. Once again, I am allowed to play the I-am-not-a-singer card and tell you that I don't perform as a scat artist so I don't really know what syllables are comfortable to sing (at least in public). For me, I am very much in the "be da boo da ba da be ya ba da be" camp, with "bop" or "dop" for the short sounds. The most important thing about scat syllables is that they sound natural (and not stupid) to you, and that the articulations should feel right in the same way that an instrumentalist's articulation needs to feel right. Some novice scatters have probably never thought about why scat singers use the syllables they use. Essentially, scat syllables are meant to imitate an instrumental soloist's articulations. The articulations should convey the swinging rhythmic quality of the line. ("Da" is an accented syllable, tongued like a sax player and "ya" is softer, an articulation that is slurred to the next note. "Be" is a harder accent than "ba," and as I said, "bop" or "dop" is short. You need a few different vowel and consonant sounds because singing ba ba ba ba is harder than singing ba-de-ah-ba. Changing the vowels makes it swing more too. (Having said that I won't say much about scat syllables I have a surprising amount to say.) Any syllable within reason will pretty much work as long as you believe in it. To prove that point, check out Louis' slightly unlikely choice of "za" or, for that matter, his gravelly delivery that singers imitate at their peril. (He is my favorite jazz singer and I continue to be amazed at his incredible sense of swing.) If you listen to Chet Baker, Jon Hendricks, Bobby McFerrin, Ella Fitzgerald and other great scatters you will get ideas, but keep in mind that the scat syllable tradition is an attempt to imitate horns and so you need to also keep listening to jazz instrumentalists to refine your sense of what all this is about. On a gig with the extremely talented and crazy Miles Griffith, I once complained that no singers ever used the consonant "q" when they scat and he launched into a set of "qua-quiddity qua-ka das" until audience members begged him to stop.

Okay, now I really am done with talking about scat syllables. Let's move on to something that I feel more qualified to help you with.

You probably have noticed that I continue to suggest to you that you should work on harmony using both two-handed voicings at the piano and roots alone. This is because the roots of the chord changes are potent tools in hearing the harmony. If I am trying to remember a standard that I haven't played in a while, or if I am on a gig and playing a standard that I am not so familiar with, I will sing the bass notes to myself as the tune goes by, reminding myself of the harmony. The bassline is a kind of second melody that accompanies the main melody of the song, and hearing that bassline as I improvise over the tune allows me to keep my place while I am busy soloing over the changes.

CHAPTER 4

You can do the following exercises on any tunes of yours, but for now, I am going to use the A sections of "Autumn Leaves." "Autumn Leaves" is a perfect practice tune because it consists of ii- V I (IV) major and ii- 7b5 V7b9 I minor (+ in the major key: V7 of ii-7 at the end of the form to get you back to the top of the song).

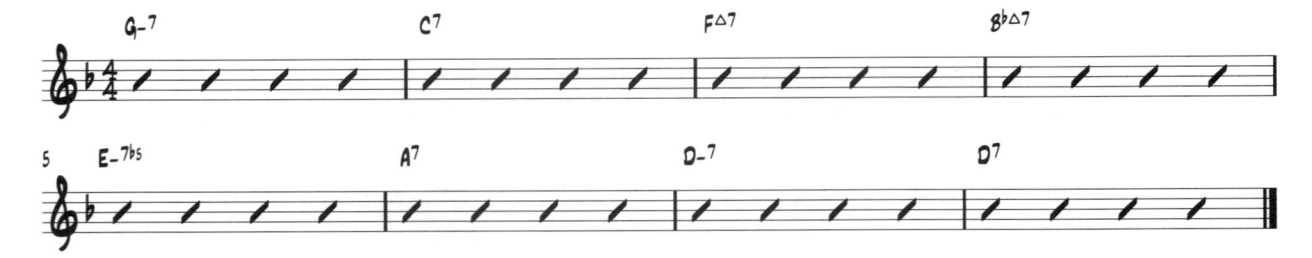

[Musical notation: 8 bars with chords G-7 | C7 | F△7 | Bb△7 | E-7b5 | A7 | D-7 | D7]

Start by learning the bassline as a second melody. Sing the roots and play the melody at the piano. Then play the roots and sing the melody. Actually, with this tune it's possible to sing the melody AND sing the roots, something like this:

TRACK 6

[Musical notation showing alternating MELODY and ROOTS under chords G-7, C7, F△7, Bb△7]

After you really have the sound of these roots in your ear, try singing the 3rds of each chord as you play the roots. Make sure you distinguish clearly between major and minor 3rds, checking yourself on the piano to make sure you are correct.

TRACK 7

[Musical notation with PLAY/SING markings under chords G-7, C7, F△7, Bb△7]

(Play the roots an octave below where they are written in the above example.)

Next, try singing the root and the 3rd (consecutively, unless you have the ability to sing two notes at once, like a student I had recently) **while you play the chords. Try singing the root and the 3rd,**

TRACK 8

[Musical notation with SING marking under chords G-7, C7, F△7, Bb△7]

and also try playing the 3rds alone and singing the roots.

TRACK 9

[Musical notation with PLAY/SING markings under chords G-7, C7, F△7, Bb△7]

When you feel that you have a strong idea about the sound of the 3rds and their relationship to the roots of the chords, move on to the 5ths, going through all these combinations:

1. play roots, sing 5ths for each chord in the progression
2. play full chords, sing 5ths for each chord in the progression
3. play 5ths, sing roots for each chord in the progression
4. play roots, and afterward two-handed voicings of the chords, sing 5,1 for each chord in the progression
5. play roots, and afterward two-handed voicings of the chords, sing 1,5 for each chord in the progression
6. play roots, and afterward two-handed voicings of the chords, sing 3,5 for each chord in the progression
7. play roots, and afterward two-handed voicings of the chords, sing 5,3 for each chord in the progression
8. play roots, and afterward two-handed voicings of the chords, sing 5,1,3 for each chord in the progression
9. play roots, and afterward two-handed voicings of the chords, sing 1,5,3 for each chord in the progression
10. play roots, and afterward two-handed voicings of the chords, sing 3,5,1 for each chord in the progression
11. play roots, and afterward two-handed voicings of the chords, sing 3,1,5 for each chord in the progression

You get the idea. As you work on hearing each new chord tone, practice singing it through all the chords, then add the preceding chord tones, varying the order of these notes.

Next come the 7ths, which you should work on in exactly the same way, 7ths alone and then with each chord tone, root, 3rd and 5th. Then with two chord tones, 7,5,3 and the different ways you can order these pitches; 7,3,1 and the different orders of **THESE pitches; then 7,5,3,1 and all the different arrangement of these pitches.** (There are 24 possible orders: 1,3,5,7; 1,3,7,5; 1,5,3,7; 1,5,7,3; 1,7,3,5; 1,7,5,3; 3,5,7,1; 3,5,1,7; 3,1,7,5; 3,1,5,7; 3,7,5,1; 3,7,1,5; 5,1,3,7; 5,1,7,3; 5,3,1,7; 5,3,7,1; 5,7,1,3; 5,7,3,1; 7,1,3,5; 7,1,5,3 7,3,1,5; 7,3,5,1; 7,5,3,1; 7,5,1,3.)

Now, it's not important to drill yourself on every one of these, but what is worthwhile is to drill enough of these arrangements of notes so that you can hear each note on the chords. Pick a few of these and work on them until you start to feel more confident that you can find the chord tones of the progression easily. As always, try to work on these at the piano, with roots of the chords alone and then with two-handed voicings. Also, try and work on these away from the piano (in the shower or in your car stuck

CHAPTER 4

in traffic are two good places to do this; at the library or in traffic court are two rather bad places to try this), hearing the harmony in your head and singing as much of the chords as you can.

Next come the 9ths. On the minor chords and the major sevenths, you have only one possible choice: you have to sing the natural 9th. On the dominant chords, you have several choices, but I am going to limit them to one choice. Sing the b9. Why is this? Mainly, because I want you to get practice hearing this altered sound. Beyond that, however, the dominant seventh chords in this progression are particularly suited to using altered notes. Whenever you have a V to I situation (as you do repeatedly in this song) altered tensions are a good choice. Dominant seventh chords appear in a lot of different situations, and sometimes they don't resolve as clearly as they do here. Whenever you see a dominant seventh that is moving up a fourth to the next chord, I want you to think of altered dominants. Using these altered notes helps push the harmony forward and make the resolution (when it comes) feel stronger.

So, now repeat the above practice with 9ths, first 9ths alone, then 9ths and roots, 9ths and 3rds, 9ths and 5ths and 9ths and 7ths. Then 9,1,3 (and 9,3,1; 1,9,3; 1,3,9; 3,9,1; 3,1,9) 9,1,5 (and different combinations) 9,1,7 (and different combinations), 9,3,5 (and different combinations), 9,3,7 (and different combinations), 9,5,7 (and different combinations). Then four-note groups. Finally you can practice some five-note combinations.

I am a little torn here. On the one hand, writing down many combinations performs a service for you: you can pick a few from the list and practice them. On the other hand, having huge lists of all the different orders of 1,2,3,4 and 5-note sequences is a little daunting for some. I have never practiced in a rigidly mathematical way (well, maybe when I was younger, but I got tendonitis and stopped.). Nowadays, I practice what is enjoyable (and reasonable) for me. However, if I am working on something that uses a somewhat mathematical approach (for example, breaking down an odd meter into different patterns, or working on some kind of rhythmic exercise between two hands, to cite two recent examples from my own practicing), I try to work on a representative sample of those combinations. When we are talking about the number of different combinations of five pitches, the numbers are truly huge and I don't expect you to dutifully work through each one of them. (Although being able to command hordes of singers to work so submissively is kind of exciting.) Keep your eyes on the prize, as the old saying goes, and in this case the goal is to be able to sing (slowly and in a practicing situation, not necessarily in performance for now) any chord tone or tension on any chord as you wish.

With that disclaimer disclaimed, let's push on. **Next are 11ths.** Again, there are no decisions to make regarding which 11ths to use: natural 11 on minor chords, #11 on major and dominant sevenths. **Practice all ways as above.**

Finally, 13ths. I am going to make the same rule I made for 9ths (for the same reason), on dominant chords, sing the b13th. On minor chords and major sevenths, sing the natural 13th. **Drill in all combinations, all ways, away from the piano, at the piano, in the shower, at the beach, etc.**

This is the first step toward hearing the harmony better and being able to scat on each chord change—getting to know each chord intimately—all of the tensions, all of the chord tones, everything. I do know some singers who have worked on this material and I see a definite improvement in their scatting because of it. **While you are at work on this, take time, occasionally, to play the chords and scat over them, not paying too much attention to what you are singing when you do this.** As you develop, you are always working on two levels: what you can do in a slow and controlled practicing situation and what you can do in a playing situation. Both are important. For some singers, the practicing situation will be new. If you haven't done this before, it may take a bit of time to get used to it. But this is good news. If you haven't done serious practicing of harmony before, it's no wonder your scatting isn't as strong as you'd like it to be. So hang in there and try it. As I said above, you will not be held to any new standards of chord knowledge when you are in a performance situation. Just keep practicing and allow the playing to move in a relaxed, unhurried manner. When you are playing, don't judge, and let anything happen. If you keep practicing, your practice will effect your playing in ways that may surprise you.

After you have spent some time with the above chords and are starting to feel confident of your ability to hear all of the notes on each chord change, try composing a new melody, or a solo chorus over these changes. Learn it thoroughly, and try composing another. Again, as above, when you are performing, don't make any special attempt to quote these previously composed choruses—just let them come into your solo if it seems to be happening organically.

One final note here. Should you do the above exercise for every one of your tunes, singing each chord tone and tension over the progressions? Sure, why not? Does it sound like an impossibly large task? Okay, then do a little piece of it. Pick one tune to do the above exercises on. Take a song that has easy and clear one chord-per-bar changes, leaving out a change or two if that simplifies the form. ("Cherokee," "I Thought About You," "Summertime" and "Beautiful Friendship" are good choices among the thousands of possibilities). In the end, you will not have to do this exercise over every tune to see a benefit in your scatting in general. Standard tunes work in similar ways, and things that you learn on one tune will transfer to another.

Let's recap the steps that you went through in this chapter.

1. Learn the roots to the A sections of "Autumn Leaves." Learn them like a second melody of the tune and be able to sing them at the piano and away from it.
2. Sing the melody and the roots.

CHAPTER 4

3. Sing the 3rds for each chord of the progression; play the roots, then the full chords. Play the 3rds, sing the roots, play the roots, then chords and sing 1,3 over each chord, then 3,1.
4. Repeat in the manner of step 3, all combinations of singing the 5ths and the other chord tones.
5. Repeat in the manner of step 3, all combinations of singing the 7ths and the other chord tones.
6. Repeat in the manner of step 3, all combinations of singing the 9ths and the chord tones. Use b9 for dominant sevenths, natural 9 for minor sevenths, minor seventh flat 5s, and major seventh chords.
7. Repeat in the manner of step 3, all combinations of singing the 11ths and the chord tones and 9ths. Use #11 for dominant sevenths and major sevenths. Natural 11 for all other chords.
8. Repeat in the manner of step 3, all combinations of singing the 13th and the other chord tones and tensions. Use b13 for dominant sevenths, natural 13th for all other chords.
9. Scat freely over the tune each time after you finish practicing. Compose a chorus of solo on these changes, and memorize it. If this is enjoyable, compose a second chorus and memorize that one as well.
10. Repeat the above steps with another (reasonably simple) standard of your choosing.

One aspect of practicing that we haven't mentioned is important. It takes time. Don't put too much pressure on yourself to see improvement in your overall scatting immediately, on "Autumn Leaves" or your other tunes. Just practice and see what happens. There are a lot of exercises we will try and some of these are likely to be more useful for you than others. In the end, you can choose which ways to practice are most enjoyable and effective for you. In the meantime, try all of the above suggestions and see if anything changes.

For those of you who are new to this sort of approach, try it for a few months before you judge how effective it is. Keep in mind that you are now practicing scatting in a way that is similar to how instrumentalists practice soloing. And if you've ever lived with a serious saxophonist working on soloing, you know that they can practice a long, long time.

CHAPTER 5

Practicing Scatting 2:
Chord Scales, Friend or Foe? (Friend!)

We've avoided them until now, but like incredibly humid days in August, or relatives you aren't fond of, eventually you have to deal with them.

Actually, they aren't all that bad, these chord scales. You already have a sense of what notes are available on each chord, so a bit more theory will only clear up any lingering questions you might have had about how these things work.

Knowing the chord tones for each chord you encounter, there are only three additional notes that you have to decide on to complete each chord scale (or scale that is implied by a given chord): the 2nd, the 4th and 6th note of each scale. (One more time for those of you that might have been napping earlier: when we are addressing these notes as scale degrees we tend to use 2,4 and 6 to designate them, as opposed to when we are thinking of them as the upper notes of a chord stacked in 3rds, the tensions: 9, 11 and 13.) Up until now, I've suggested that either you think of these notes as up a whole tone from the chord tones, or use your ears to make good choices. However, we can also learn a little bit of theory to refine these choices, and give our ears something to sink their teeth into (a truly frightening image, that).

Where do chord scales come from? The most common chord scales in jazz come from two scales, the major scale and the melodic minor scale. As we saw when we looked at the diatonic sevenths for the key of CMaj7 (see page 35), we find minor sevenths, major sevenths, dominant sevenths and minor seventh flat 5 chords on the scale degrees of the major scale when we stack 3rds starting on each of the notes of the scale. When we think of the major scale, we think of do, re, mi, fa, so, la, ti, or major scale degrees 1 through 7. But it's also possible to make a scale that starts on re: re, mi, fa, so, la, ti, do. This scale is called a "mode" of the major scale, it's a major scale moved over to start on a different pitch. There are seven different pitches in a major scale, so there are 7 modes of the major scale: Ionian, which starts on 1; Dorian, which starts on 2; Phrygian, which starts on 3; Lydian, which starts on 4; Mixolydian, which starts on 5; Aeolian, which starts on 6; and Locrian, which starts on 7.

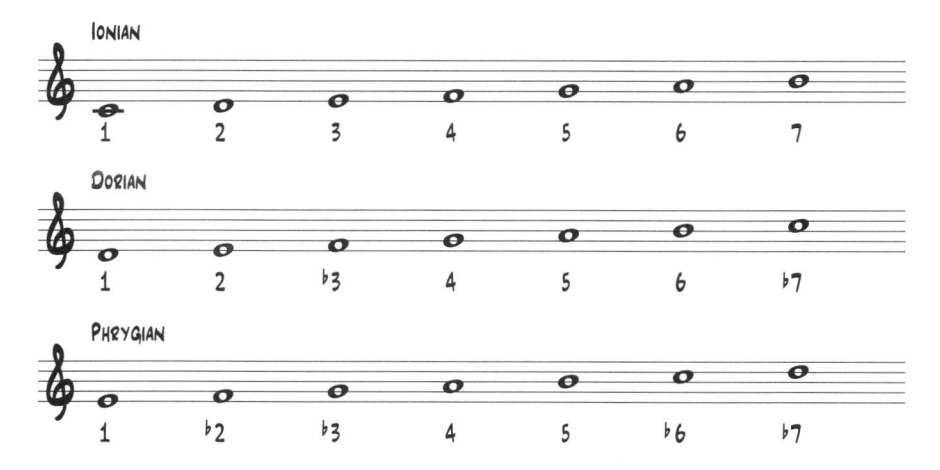

IONIAN
1 2 3 4 5 6 7

DORIAN
1 2 ♭3 4 5 6 ♭7

PHRYGIAN
1 ♭2 ♭3 4 5 ♭6 ♭7

73

CHAPTER 5

LYDIAN

1, 2, 3, #4, 5, 6, 7

MIXOLYDIAN

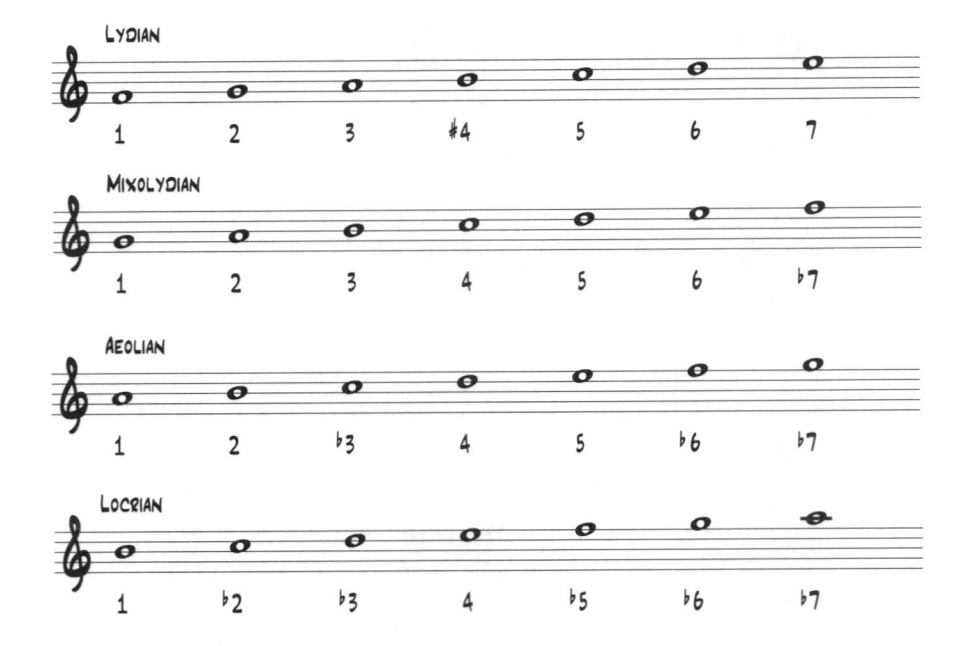

1, 2, 3, 4, 5, 6, b7

AEOLIAN

1, 2, b3, 4, 5, b6, b7

LOCRIAN

1, b2, b3, 4, b5, b6, b7

Even though these scales have all the same notes in them (they are all from the parent scale of C major, aka C Ionian) they all have different arrangements of half steps and whole steps when we look at them from each starting note, each different scale degree. What I mean by that is that when you look at D Dorian, it's important not to think of this as a variety of C major scale. It isn't. It's a kind of D scale. Specifically it's a D scale with these scale degrees: 1, 2, b3, 4, 5, 6, b7. (When using scale degree numbers, we are always thinking relative to a major scale. The D major scale (or D ionian) would be 1,2,3,4,5,6,7 and so a D dorian is a D major scale with the 3rd and 7th degrees flatted.) This scale works well with the minor seventh chord, because that is the chord that is built on the second degree of the major scale, and the minor seventh is a chord built on the second degree of the major scale.

The other modes also follow this pattern: they work with each of the chord types that are built on the degrees of the scale that they start on. So E Phrygian is a scale that works with an E-7; F Lydian works with F major7; G Mixolydian works with a G7 chord; A Aeolian fits an A-7 chord and B Locrian fits a B-7b5 chord.

To repeat, it's interesting and I guess somewhat important to know where these scales come from, but in the end it is much more important to view these scales from each root. A Dorian scale (for example) is a scale that starts on any pitch, and has these degrees: 1, 2, b3, 4, 5, 6, b7 as explained above. Incidentally, it will be a mode of a major scale (meaning that it has the same pitches as the major scale of its b7th degree) but if you forget that, or don't immediately know what major scale it shares its notes with, that doesn't really matter, as long as you know what pitches it has in relation to its root.

If we look at all of these scales, we notice something. There's more than one scale that works with minor sevenths! There is more than one scale that works with major sevenths! If that's the case, how do I know which scale to use when I see a major seventh, or a minor seventh?

Good question! (Although it is fairly easy to come up with good questions when you are writing both the questions and the answers.) What you need to know is that for the most common chords, there are at least two common scales that go with each of them. Generally speaking, there is a neutral or regular sounding scale and a slightly more colorful choice. Also, in the same way that I suggested in the last chapter that you use altered tensions on dominant sevenths that resolve up a 4th, there are other "common use" situations where one scale is favored over another choice.

You probably also noticed that there was only one scale for the dominant seventh chord in the modes of the major scale. The astute among you may have even noticed that this scale has no altered tensions in it. This can't be all the scales there are for dominant sevenths, and of course, it isn't. We also have modes of the melodic minor to consider. This is a C melodic minor scale:

Melodic Minor

1 2 ♭3 4 5 6 7

(Please note that in jazz theory, the melodic minor scale is the same ascending and descending, just like every other scale. In classical theory this is not the case.)

Not every mode of the melodic minor scale is important for us to consider. We really only need the mode built on the first degree of the scale (above), which works with C-Maj7 and C-6; the mode that's built on the 4th degree of the scale, which works well with dominant chords;

Lydian flat 7

1 2 3 ♯4 5 6 ♭7

the mode that's built from the 6th degree of the scale, which works well with minor seventh flat 5 chords;

Locrian Natural 9

1 2 ♭3 4 ♭5 ♭6 ♭7

and the mode that's built from the 7th degree of the scale, which works well with dominant sevenths with altered tensions.

CHAPTER 5

ALTERED

[musical notation: 1, b9, #9, 3, #11, b13, b7]

(The altered scale is often written with numbers larger than 7 to make the point: this is a scale that has the 1, 3 and b7 chord tones of a dominant chord plus all of the altered tensions: b9, #9, #11 and b13. It could also, of course, be written with b2, #2, #4, and b6 or #5.)

Just as with the modes of the major scale, the important thing is not to remember the parent melodic minor scale that the mode is from, but to know the scale degrees for each scale working from the root of each chord.

There are three more scales that we need to look at. The first of these is the diminished scale. This is an extremely unusual scale that has an extra note in it (an 8-note scale, this is sometimes called the "octotonic" scale). The pattern for how it is constructed is extremely easy to remember: start on any pitch. Go up a half step, then a whole step, then a half step, then a whole step, then a half step, then a whole step, then a half step, then a whole step. That's the scale. I can also write it using scale degrees if I wish: 1, b9, #9, 3, #11, 5, 13, b7. This scale works on dominant sevenths with altered 9ths and natural 13ths. This scale is called the "half/whole diminished." (This scale is also sometimes written with numbers larger than 8 because of its similarity to the altered scale. Of course, it could also be written as 1, b2, b3, 3, #4, 5, 6, b7. Use whatever numbers are easiest for you.)

HALF/WHOLE DIMINISHED SCALE

[musical notation: 1, b9, #9, 3, #11, 5, 13, b7]

There is another mode of this scale that also has an easy pattern for its construction. Start on any pitch. Go up a whole step, then a half step, then a whole step, then a half step, then a whole step, then a half step, then a whole step, then a half step. I can also write this scale using scale degrees: 1, 2, b3, 4, b5, b6, 6, 7. This scale is called the "whole/half diminished scale" and it works with diminished chords.

WHOLE/HALF DIMINISHED SCALE

[musical notation: 1, 2, b3, 4, b5, b6, 6, 7]

The last scale is a mode of the harmonic minor (the harmonic minor is 1, 2, b3, 4, 5, b6, 7) and works well with dominant sevenths, especially dominant sevenths that are leading to a minor chord.

5TH MODE OF HARMONIC MINOR (DOM 7 ♭9♭13 SCALE)

1   ♭2   3   4   5   ♭6   ♭7

And that's all the scales you need to know for now. There are a few other scales that are in common use for specialized situations, but the ones I've mentioned above account for 95 percent of what you encounter on standards.

How to practice this mess? First of all, don't be put off by the amount of scales you will be working with. Work on a few scales each day. Proceed by playing 1, 3 and 7 of the chord change in your left hand (1,3,5,7 for diminished and minor seventh flat 5 chords) and play the scale slowly with your right hand, ascending and descending, one octave. Then sing the scale as you play it. Finally, sing it over your left hand voicing without playing the scale with your right hand, checking the pitches occasionally to make sure the sounds are in your ear and your intonation is good. Now move on to the next key, going up a 4th (or down a 5th) from the last one.

I can hear the agonized screams from some of you, saying: "Do I really have to learn to sing every chord scale? Do you expect me to always know exactly what chord scale I am on when I am scatting? I thought you were going to try to make working on improvising more vocal-friendly and here we are doing scales just like a piano student!
I want my $26 back. This book is stupid!"

Okay, take a deep breath. Relax and have a drink of something soothing. I am not expecting you to memorize each of these scales by ear and be able to recall them perfectly when you see a chord change. I DO expect you to be able to have the theoretical knowledge to know what chord scale goes with what chord. This is a way to introduce chord scale sounds to you. That will generate further exercises where you can work on improvising with these scales. Eventually, these sounds will creep into your head, and when you least expect it, you will be singing something and, suddenly, out will pop a piece of the scale.

Of course, that will never happen if you don't spend some time investigating these scales and what they sound like. So here is an approach to begin with.

Let's look at each scale in terms of the chord that it belongs with. On each chord, I've grouped the most common scales, starting with the most neutral sounding scale and proceeding to a scale that is a little more exotic sounding and finally, to the scale or scales that are the darkest.

CHAPTER 5

MINOR 7THS	MAJOR 7THS	MINOR7 b5
Dorian, 1 2 b3 4 5 6 b7 (neutral, most common)	Ionian, 1 2 3 4 5 6 7 (neutral, common)	Locrian, 1 b2 b3 4 b5 b6 b7 (more neutral, common)
Aeolian, 1 2 b3 4 5 b6 b7 (a bit darker, not as common)	Lydian, 1 2 3 #4 5 6 7 (slightly spicier, common)	Locrian natural 9, 1 2 b3 4 b5 b6 b7 (slightly spicier, common)
Phrygian, 1 b2 b3 4 5 b6 b7 (darkest, least common)		

DIMINISHED 7TH	MINOR 6TH OR MINOR MAJOR 7TH	DOMINANT 7TH SUS 4
Whole/half diminished, 1 2 b3 4 b5 b6 6 7 (most common choice)	Melodic minor, 1 2 b3 4 5 6 7 (most common)	Mixolydian, 1 2 3 4 5 6 b7 (most common)
		Phrygian, when the chord has a b9 and b13 1 b2 b3 4 5 b6 b7 (common choice for this chord, but the chord is uncommon)

DOMINANT 7THS
Mixolydian, 1 2 3 4 5 6 b7 (most neutral)
Mixolydian #11, 1 2 3 #4 5 6 b7 (slightly less neutral)
Diminished half/whole 1 2 3 4 5 6 b7 (colorful, use when the seventh chord will resolve up a fourth)
5th mode of the harmonic minor or dominant seventh, b9, b13 scale, 1 b2 3 4 5 b6 b7 (dark, colorful, a colorful scale to use when the dominant seventh will resolve up a fourth to a minor chord)
Altered scale, 1 b2 b3 3 #4 b6 b7 (darkest, colorful, use when the dominant seventh will resolve up a fourth to a major or minor chord)

Some chords only have one common scale choice; others have two or three. The dominant seventh has the most common choices and we'll talk more about how to distinguish these scales in a few pages. **As stated above, work slowly, going scale to scale, playing and singing, focusing on a single chord and scale type and taking it through all 12 keys before moving on to the next scale type for the same chord until you have been through all the scales available for a given chord quality. Then move on to the next chord quality and repeat the process.** I suggest that you focus on the most common chord qualities first: major seventh, minor seventh, minor seventh flat 5, minor sixth, minor major seventh, diminished seventh and dominant seventh. **Try and do 30 minutes or so a day, and if possible, be consistent, picking up the next day where you left off the day before.** This is potentially the least interesting thing I will ask you to practice, and so I would work through it slowly, looking for interesting sounds that you will encounter along the way. Still, it's something that almost every jazz instrumentalist has spent at least some time with, and I encourage you to give it its due and not skip on to something more interesting.

Having said all that, I am not sure that you will find this to be uninteresting work. After all, these scales with their unique colors each imply different melodies and so will give you many ideas for creating melodies that are different from the ones that you have been able to improvise so far. For some singers who scat mostly on the major scale on each tune, this may indeed be liberating. Again, try to approach it without large expectations, working steadily and seeing what effect it has on your soloing over time.

CHAPTER 6

Practicing Scatting 3:
Applying Chord Scales to a Tune

We will now work at these same scales in the context of the A section of the "Autumn Leaves" progression that we worked on in Chapter 4. Learning scales is something that can happen both in the abstract theoretical way I discussed in the last chapter and also applied to a particular song. So, if you really dislike working on the scales divorced from tunes, maybe seeing them in context will make the work easier or more fun.

So what are the appropriate chord scales for this progression? The first chord is a ii-7 chord and whenever you see a minor seventh that is functioning as a ii-7 chord (that means whenever it is followed by a dominant seventh whose root is a 4th up) that chord takes a Dorian scale. Because of the fact that there are so many ii-7, V7 situations in jazz, almost every time you see a minor seventh you can assume that Dorian will work for it. I've already told you that dominant sevenths leading up a 4th should get altered tensions, so let's extend this to say that in such situations you should use the altered scale (unless the dominant seventh is leading to a minor chord, in which case you should use the dom7 b9 b13 scale). So altered it is for the C7. The FMaj7 gets Ionian because it is the I chord in the key and the I chord takes Ionian. The BbMaj7 gets Lydian, because it is a major seventh built on the 4th scale degree (and the 4th mode of the major scale is Lydian scale). The E minor seventh flat 5 chord gets Locrian, the more neutral of the two available minor seventh flat 5 scales, (also because this chord is built on the 7th degree of the F major scale) the A7, dominant seventh scale, leading to a minor chord can take either dom7 b9 b13 or altered and I am going to say altered in order to give you greater familiarity with this extremely colorful scale. The D minor sixth chord gets melodic minor, and the D seventh, leading back to the G minor seventh (the first chord of the progression) will take altered.

There you have it, easy as pie! Finding the appropriate chord scale for each chord is relatively simple, once you keep a few rules in mind.

1. For any diatonic seventh chords, you can use the mode of the major scale that has the same root as that particular seventh chord.
2. Nearly all minor sevenths get Dorian
3. Some chords have only one common scale associated with them, so whenever you see one of these chords you play the appropriate chord scale: diminished sevenths, dominant 7sus 4 chords (natural 9), minor major sevenths, minor sixths
4. For dominant sevenths follow these 3 rules: 1) if the dominant seventh resolves up a fourth to any chord that is not a minor chord, play either half/whole diminished scale or the altered scale; 2) if the dominant seventh resolves up a fourth to a minor chord, play either dominant seventh b9 b13 or the altered scale; 3) if the dominant seventh doesn't fit any of the above conditions, play Mixolydian or Mixolydian #11, whichever sounds better to you.

CHAPTER 6

Of course, after you are more familiar with these chord scale sounds, you will have much more latitude in choosing the sounds you like. Whenever your ears tell you to break one of these rules (or any other rule) that I set down for you, be my guest. Still, you need some guidelines to begin working. In general, the above suggestions will steer you toward the normal uses of these scales.

Knowing which scale to use will not make you a great jazz soloist. The next step is to practice making melodies from scales. This is a crucial skill in improvising. Fortunately, it's something you can practice pretty easily, and it's pleasant to do.

You can start in the same way I suggested you practice the scales at the beginning of the chapter. For the first chord of the progression, G-7, play 1, 3 and 7 in your left hand, and play the G Dorian scale in your right, singing the notes as you play them. Then try singing the scale without playing the notes. When you can do this easily, try singing just the first five notes of the scale. Now sing some patterns. To get you started here are a few off the top of my head: 1,3,4,3,1; 1,5,4,3,4,5; 5,3,1,b7,1; 1,5,6,5,3, 5, 8(1); and 5,10(3),9(2),8,(1).

TRACK 10

These are all patterns that come out of the scale. I am just trying to find motives that are interesting, getting to know the scale melodic bit by melodic bit. What makes a pattern sound like the kernel of a melody?—this is what I am trying to find out with this kind of improvising.

Make some of your own patterns in this fashion. Play the chord and sing some lines over the chord and see what you are singing. Can you stay within the scale when you sing lines over the change? Are you adding notes? Sometimes people add the #4 to the 1,3,4,5,7 of the Dorian scale to make a blues scale (we'll talk about this in the blues chapter). **Try to notice what you are singing and to see if, just working with one scale, you can make appealing melodies from pieces of that scale. Keep a record of some of the patterns that you like and return to them next time you practice. Try and improvise new patterns each day.**

Now let's move on to the next chord, the C7. As we discussed, you will play the altered scale over it. Again, play 1,3 and 7 in your left hand and sing the scale slowly as you play it in your right hand. Keep singing it until you can sing it without playing it. When you can do this easily, try singing just the first few notes of the scale. Vary the order of those notes. Try singing small pieces of this unusual scale. Try: 1,b2,3; b7,1,b3,3; 1,b7,b3,3,b2,1; b3,3,b10 (b3),b9,(b2),8 (1); b2,b3,3,1,#4,b6,b7.

CHAPTER 6

TRACK 11

Again, keep a record of some of the interesting patterns that you come up with and return to them whenever you practice. After you've spent some time practicing the scale and patterns over 1,3 and 7 in your left hand, play the C7 using a two-handed voicing. Use a voicing that conveys the altered sound of the chord, such as 1 and 7 in the left hand, b9, 3 and b13 in the right hand.

Now just sing melodies. What sort of melodies does this chord suggest to you? Are the notes of these melodies all falling within the altered scale, or are you adding other notes? If you are singing other notes, try to figure out some of what you are singing. Perhaps you are hearing other scales over this chord. If so, it would be good to know what they are.

In this way, you can work through all eight scales of the progression. Spend time on each chord, getting to know the scale and making patterns with it. Keep some notes of interesting patterns. Spend some time playing a two-handed voicing for each chord change and seeing if you can stay within the scale you have been practicing, or seeing if the chord might suggest other scales to you.

Keep working on these scales in this fashion for a while. How long is up to you, of course, but you need to let these things sink in over time. I have already given you a lot to do between the 1,3,5,7,9,11,13 oriented work and now this chord scale work, so you have to be careful not to rush through this. If the last two chapters in this book were weekly private lessons, we'd would probably be into our second month by now. Maybe less if you are working quickly, but for those of you that are new to practicing scatting in this manner, don't try to do too much too quickly.

The next step is to work on connecting these scales one to the other. To do this you will need to look back over the patterns you have been keeping notes of. **Try and find patterns, or make new ones, that are only a few notes, maybe no more than 4.** Try and find several three and four note patterns for each chord. If you are having trouble with this approach here are a few standard patterns that you might try: 1,2,3,5; 1,3,4,5; 1,3,5,7; 3,5,7,9; 5,7,1,2. Try some of the patterns from your 1,3,5,7,9,11,13 work on the chords.

TRACK 12

TRACK 13

Now try playing through the progression very slowly. If necessary, use 1, 3 and 7 in your left hand and play the first note of one of the patterns on the downbeat of the each measure. Then sing the pattern, changing patterns as you move chord to chord. If necessary, as a preliminary step, you can play the patterns in your right hand and play 1,3 and 7 in your left, or just the roots of the chords. Connect the patterns you've written down in a random sort of way, not really worrying too much about the effect of how they connect, just hearing them consecutively over the chord changes. Keep the tempo slow, so that you can do this without stopping and starting much. Try to go through all of the 4-note patterns that you have written down, connecting different patterns over the changes in different combinations, so that each time you play through the chorus you are playing different combinations of these patterns are connecting and you are making different choruses of combined patterns (scale fragments).

Do this repeatedly until you can sing the patterns without playing them, or with only playing a note here or there to keep you on track. How does this sound to you? Can you make music this way, by connecting scale fragments, or does it still feel kind of academic? Notice if you are creating sounds you like, and (even though this sounds a little obvious) try to make sounds that you like more, using the patterns that seem most interesting to you.

When you are working in this way, you are accentuating the kind of vertical hearing that we were talking about in Chapter 3. All that matters is connecting patterns on each chord. You aren't really thinking much about the melodies you are making over several bars.

Although we are stressing the vertical here, meaning trying to hear what happens over each chord, music doesn't work ENTIRELY in a vertical way, proceeding chord to chord, starting each idea at the downbeat of each new harmony. Ideas can last longer than one measure and what you improvise over the G-7 can effect what you sing on the C7, FMaj7, over the whole 8-bar progression.

Here is another way to think about what happens in a jazz solo. I play some kind of idea, say 2,3,5,6, on the G Dorian change, and then I let the C7 altered scale work on those same notes when I get to the next bar. So the altered scale changes these notes to b6,b2,b3,3, and the next scale, over the FMaj7, massages the notes again, to 3,5,7,9. On the BbMaj7, the notes get tweaked to 7,3,4 (#4, because the scale is Lydian),5. The same notes morph into 3,b5,b7,1 on the E-7b5; 7,b9,b3,3 on the A7; 3,6,7,9 on the D-Maj7 and finally 3,b13,7,b9 on the D7 (altered).

CHAPTER 6

This is part of what happens when you are improvising, although not quite in as extreme a form as the above example. While you are improvising, there is always a kind of give and take between the sense that each new chord is a new starting point for an idea and the sense that the new chord change is a color change in which to develop the idea from the previous bar. I play an idea, and then the chord changes and I have some new notes at my disposal, and so I can play some of the last chord's idea with these new notes. For example, let's take the Ab in the second bar of the above progression, the one that occurs on the C7 altered scale. I didn't have an Ab available in the first bar over the G Dorian, and I have one now on this new scale, so the Ab effects the idea. In the next bar I have an A natural on the F major 7 and so this note is again a new available sound for me to use.

This raises one point that I think is important to singing well over chord changes. Chord scales often have many notes in common as you move chord to chord. In our progression, the first chord and the second chord have only three notes in common. The next chord, the F major seventh, also has three shared notes with the previous chord. The Bb major seventh has all the notes of its scale in common with the F major seventh as does the E minor seventh flat 5. The A7 has 6 notes in common with the E minor seventh flat 5 chord, and 6 notes in common with the D minor major seventh. The D7b9 b13 chord has 4 notes in common with the D minor major seventh.

G, Bb, C, F can be played on most of the chords in this progression and sometimes people suggest to novice improvisers that the way to begin improvising is to ignore the chord changes and focus on the common notes of the chord progression. There are two problems with this approach. The first is, that it doesn't lead anywhere. If you don't try to hear the subtle harmonic differences that are caused by the changing available notes on the chords, then you aren't learning to sing over the chords. At best, you are learning to sing in a key. The second problem with this approach is that it doesn't sound very good. It doesn't sound like you are singing the changes, because you aren't focusing on the notes that CHANGE, the new available notes that you get when you get a new chord change in the chord progression.

It's a little like that terrible joke about the guy who owns a talking dog. The dog owner wants to get his dog on a TV show and he takes him into the talent agent's office and asks him what the top of a house is called. The dog barks, "ROOF." Then he asks the dog what sandpaper feels like and the dog barks, "RUFF." Then the guy asks the dog who was the greatest baseball player and the dog barks "RUTH." The talent agent throws the owner and the dog out on the street, at which point the dog turns to the guy and says, "You think maybe I should have said DiMaggio?" If the dog could really talk, why did he only pick words that sounded like barking, and if you really know how to play on chord changes, why are you only using the safe notes that don't change when moving chord to chord?

This brings up my biggest gripe with the way singers usually scat. Scat solos tend to be extremely reactive. What I mean by that is, the singer listens to the band and tries to find notes that are consonant with harmony. The chord changes. The singer listens to the new chord and tries to find pitches that are consonant with this new harmony. This is not how instrumentalists solo. Instrumentalists anticipate the coming harmony, plan for it, exploit chord scales of their choosing. I can be PRO-active instead of just RE-active. And this is what is missing from most scatting. Scatters who are entirely reactive can never choose a note from a chord that is about to be played, can never maintain tension by intentionally choosing a note at odds with the harmony that resolves a bar later. Scatters limited to reacting can never lead and so, even if they can find consonant notes relatively quickly, their solos tend to be very conservative in note choice and not very interesting.

Fortunately, what we are working on is scatting over harmony, not responding to what was just played. If you have the progression in your head and if you know what scales are suggested by the chords you are hearing, then you are singing both with the band in the present moment and with your sense of the form of the song that is playing simultaneously in your head. And you are not passively reacting to the harmony. You are making harmonic decisions based on what you've learned. (One quick caveat: reacting to what others play is often a good thing and I don't advise you to play only with the harmony in your head, ignoring what the piano player comps. It's a balance, but let's say that many scatters are too far at one end of the scale.)

So, to return to our progression, try using the pattern-morphing idea by altering the pattern that you use over the G-7 in the other bars of the progression. Try using several of your initial patterns, tweaking them as they move from chord to chord. See if this helps make your choruses more organic feeling and see if you can create some melodies that you like by combining this method with some of your favorite patterns. Keep in mind that morphing the idea on each chord doesn't mean repeating the idea exactly with different accidentals. Try to let the idea change shape and develop as it moves through the progression.

Finally, after spending more time with these patterns, morphed and unmorphed, write down some of your favorite ideas. See if you can create a chorus of solo that you like this way. Feel free to vary the ideas rhythmically, adding rests and notes of different time values. If composing works well for you, try writing several choruses. Memorize them and then forget them when you scat on this tune, unless parts of them sneak out organically without your planning it. Then repeat all the steps that we did on the A section of "Autumn Leaves" on one of your tunes that you worked on in Chapter 4. To aid you with this, let's recap what we did in this chapter.

CHAPTER 6

SCALE APPLICATION TO TUNES WRAP-UP

1. Find the "right" chord scales for the chords in the progression. To find the appropriate chord, follow these guidelines:
   a. For any diatonic seventh chords, you can use the mode of the major scale that has the same root as that particular seventh chord. (That sounds complicated, I just mean that the IV Major7 chord, for example, gets the fourth mode of the major scale, the lydian mode. The ii-7 chord gets the second mode of the major scale, the dorian mode, etc.)
   b. Nearly all minor sevenths get Dorian
   c. Some chords have only one common scale associated with them, so whenever you see one of these chords you play the appropriate chord scale: diminished sevenths, dominant 7sus 4 chords (natural 9), minor major sevenths, minor sixths
   d. For dominant sevenths, follow these 3 rules: 1) if the dominant seventh resolves up a 4th to any chord that is not a minor chord, play either half/whole diminished scale or the altered scale; 2) if the dominant seventh resolves up a 4th to a minor chord, play dominant seventh b9 b13; 3) if the dominant seventh doesn't fit any of the above conditions, play Mixolydian or Mixolydian #11, whichever sounds better to you.
2. Play 1, 3, and 7 in your left hand for the first chord change in the progression. Sing and play the scale. When you are able to, sing the scale without playing it, checking to make sure you really have internalized the pitches, checking occasionally for intonation.
3. Sing the first five notes of the scale or other fragments. Change the order of the pitches. Do this randomly or looking for patterns by ear. Keep singing pieces of the scale and melodies that you find; keep notes of patterns that you like on this chord and keep coming back to these patterns whenever you come back to working on the progression.
4. One by one, follow the same process for each chord of the progression.
5. After you have a number of patterns you like, reduce them to 3- or 4-note pieces. Practice going from one 3- or 4-note pattern on one chord to another pattern on the next chord change, building choruses of pattern combinations that are different each time. Start by playing 1, 3 and 7 in your left hand and playing the patterns as you sing them with your right hand. Eventually, sing the patterns without playing them, occasionally checking with the piano for intonation.
6. Try picking one pattern you like on the first chord change, and then try to keep elements of the pattern intact as it moves through the chord progression. Let each chord "tweak" the pattern so that it morphs and develops as it moves through the chord progression.
7. Compose some choruses based on this work. Learn them, memorize them and forget them when you sing, unless pieces of these melodies come to you unconsciously.
8. Repeat all of these steps with another tune of your own choosing. (Make it a fairly simple one with one change per bar.)

Practicing Scatting 4: A Tetrachord Approach to Chord Scales

CHAPTER 7

I've always liked the word, "tetrachord," although I didn't fully understand exactly what they were until several years back. (That's what joining academia will to do for you.) "Tetrachord" means a 4-note piece of a scale, so each scale that we have been studying can be understood as two tetrachords. For example, the major scale has one tetrachord with these intervals: whole step, whole step, half step, (in C: C, D, E, F) and a second tetrachord that starts a whole step above the last note of the first tetrachord that is the same—also whole step, whole step, half step (G, A, B, C). The Dorian scale also is comprised of two tetrachords a whole step apart with the same intervals, whole step, half step, whole step (C, D, Eb, F and G, A, Bb, C). It turns out there are only so many sorts of tetrachords, and together they are the building blocks of scales.

Here are the types of tetrachords that exist in the world of scales:

- whole, whole, half
- whole, half, whole
- half, whole, half
- half, whole whole
- whole, whole, whole

You can make every scale that we've been discussing from these five tetrachords (except the dom7b9 b13; for that scale you need one more, an odd one: half, minor 3rd, half).

"Okay, all very interesting in a rather nerdy theory kind of way but what does this have to do with anything?" you might be asking. There are a number of things that can be gained by understanding scales as tetrachords. One is, that you can see similarities between scales faster. For example, you may have noticed that the half, whole diminished scale starts the same way as the altered scale, or that the melodic minor scale has a bottom half that looks like a minor scale and a top half that looks like a major scale, or that most minor scales start off the same way. These things are useful to help you orient yourself when you are playing melodies derived from scales, even more so when you are connecting different scales.

Another thing that makes this approach useful, especially for vocalists, is the difficulty of range considerations when singing scales. Tetrachords are a great way to focus on the changing notes of different scales, but each tetrachord has the range of a fourth instead of the octave that a seven note scale has.

So let's see how we can adapt this approach to what we've been doing with the changes of "Autumn Leaves." **If we start on the bottom tetrachord of the first chord, I can continue using the lower tetrachords for all of the chords.**

CHAPTER 7

[Musical notation: G-7, C7, F△7, B♭△7, E-7♭5, A7, D-7, D7]

The only problem with this is that it doesn't help us much with range considerations. **How about if we use the upper tetrachords?**

[Musical notation: G-7, C7, F△7, B♭△7, E-7♭5, A7, D-△7, D7]

Okay, that's no better. How about this, whenever you want to, you can change from one variety of tetrachord, either the lower or the upper, to the other variety. Also, let's use the upper tetrachords in reversed order going downward from the root.

TRACK 15

[Musical notation: G-7, C7, F△7, B♭△7, E-7♭5, A7, D-△7, D7]

(Okay, that last tetrachord was an upper tetrachord and so should have descended, but I thought it sounded better like that. Feel free to change the direction of these tetrachords when it suits your musical purposes.)

The fact that you are changing direction whenever you want to, allows you to take many different paths through these chord changes.

TRACK 16

[Musical notation: G-7, C7, F△7, B♭△7, E-7♭5, A7, D-△7, D7]

88

CHAPTER 7

Try to find many different paths through the chord changes, eventually improvising where you change directions.

The next step is to try moving from tetrachord to tetrachord, but not proceeding straight up the scale. Try varying the order of the pitches. This is much easier to do after you have spent a fair amount of time with the earlier stages of the tetrachord process, so don't skip them! After you are comfortable with singing straight up and down the tetrachords, you can find more circuitous routes through the changes, and singing at a slightly slower tempo, you can use rhythms based on eighth notes instead of the quarter-note rhythms that we have been using.

When you are practicing, try keeping 1, 3 and 7 in your left hand and using your right hand to prompt yourself and to check intonation.

Once again, after you have spent a lot of time working on tetrachords, try composing a line that uses the notes of the tetrachords in different orders. I keep suggesting that you compose lines over this progression for a simple reason. Improvising is really comprised of two different skills. The first skill is knowing how to make melodies from the underlying harmony. That means being able to use and understand all of the various techniques we have been employing up until now: arpeggios, finding chord tones and tensions, scales, patterns derived from scales, creating a pattern and being able to morph it through a series of chords, tetrachords. The second skill is being able to implement these things in time. Often, people confuse these two skills. Being able to create lines that utilize a given technique is very important. It means you understand the concept and can hear it when you have enough time to move slowly and make mistakes and fix them. If you can compose it, eventually you can improvise it. But since improvising is actually the culmination of both of these skills, the knowing AND the doing, it's sometimes hard to hear how much you know from a given improvised performance. If I hear you sing and something is missing, I ask myself, do you under-

CHAPTER 7

stand how to make lines? Do you know what a line over a chord change sounds like? Is the problem in the understanding or the implementation? That's where composing helps. When you compose a line, think of it this way. You are writing down what your improvising will sound like at some point in the future. You get to hear a preview of what you are going to sound like a few years from now, when your ability to improvise lines in the moment catches up with your knowledge of how lines are constructed.

Of course, if composing doesn't work for you, you don't have to do it. All of these techniques are ideas of things you might try, and please remember what I said all those pages ago—monitor your progress and your level of interest and try to do only what is fun and effective for you. However, if the first time you try something, it is not so much fun or so very interesting, that doesn't mean that it won't engage you in the future. Put it aside for now and come back to it from time to time to see if it engages you more than it did the last time you tried it.

So let's add something more to our tetrachord concept. This is a variation on what are known as bebop scales. A bebop scale is not really a new scale—it's all of the same scales you have been studying with one note added to any of these scales. There is a Mixolydian bebop scale, a major, or Ionian, bebop scale, a Dorian bebop scale and an altered bebop scale—in short, a bebop scale for each of the scales you've learned. The reason we need bebop scales has to do with the strong and weak beats of a measure. Notes that come on the beat (1,2,3,4 in 4/4 time) are called "downbeats" and they tend to be stressed a bit more than notes that come off the beat, called "upbeats" (the "and" of 1, the "and" of 2, the "and" of 3, the "and" of 4). So a bar of 4/4 is divided into eight parts, and the downbeats are strong (or accented) and the upbeats are weak (or unaccented). If you play a 7-note scale in two octaves every note gets to be on a strong beat and a weak beat, which means, every note is accented about as much as every other note. All that changes if I add one half step to the 7-note scale. Now, the 1, 3, 5 and 6 or the 1, 3, 5 and 7 will always fall on the downbeats, and the other notes will fall on the weaker upbeats. This is useful because it makes the chord scale sound more like it is connected to the chord that it goes with.

The notes that are added to make scales into bebop scales follow a pattern. For any scale that has a major 7th in it, add the #5. For any scale that has a flat 7th in it, add the major 7th. So for an F Mixolydian bebop scale I add the E natural to the scale, and for a Bb major bebop scale I add the F#.

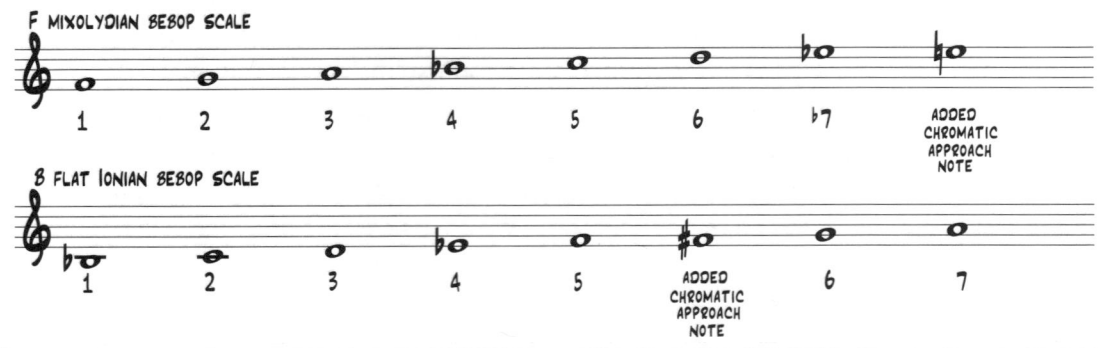

CHAPTER 7

Let's put all of this bebop scale information into the tetrachord context. First, adding a note to make a bebop scale only effects the upper tetrachord of the scale. The lower tetrachord remains exactly the same. Second, bebop scales are most effective when you use the simpler (more neutral) scale choices we talked about back in chapter 5.

For these reasons, let's change the chord scales we've been using and limit the tetrachords to only the upper tetrachords of each scale. For dominant sevenths, we will use the Mixolydian scale, which has an upper tetrachord of whole, half, whole. If we add a half step this tetrachord becomes whole, half, half, half. This is the same tetrachord for minor sevenths as well. For major sevenths, the upper tetrachord becomes half, half, whole, half. So here are the upper bebop tetrachords for our progression.

TRACK 19

Let's sing through the upper tetrachords with the additional bebop scale notes for this progression. Because we are not using any of the lower tetrachords, we will have to skip around a bit. Let's sing through the upper tetrachords with the additional bebop scale notes for this progression. Because we are not using any of the lower tetrachords, we will have to skip around a bit.

You should practice these lines as you did the other lines, with 1, 3 and 7 in your left hand and your right hand playing the notes of the tetrachord + chromatic passing note. We are just getting to chromatic approach notes and we will study these in much more depth in the next chapter, but these notes are difficult to sing in tune. Please watch your intonation closely, using your right hand on the piano to prompt you (if anything) more than you have with the last few exercises.

Chapter 7

Try the above tetrachords + chromatic passing notes both ascending and descending.

Finally, mix and match the various tetrachord approaches that we've tried this chapter. Try singing various combinations of tetrachords, tetrachords + bebop passing notes. If you wish, compose a line that incorporates these various techniques and learn it. Also, try all of these techniques on another song that you've been working on.

TETRACHORD RECAP

1. Find the tetrachords for the A section of "Autumn Leaves."
2. Connect all of the lower tetrachords (ascending) playing only, not singing.
3. Connect all of the upper tetrachords (descending) playing only, not singing.
4. Connect all of the lower tetrachords (descending) playing only, not singing.
5. Connect all of the upper tetrachords (descending) playing only, not singing.
6. Connect the tetrachords, starting on the lower tetrachord, changing direction (and changing to the upper tetrachord) whenever you wish. Switch back and forth as you want. First do this playing and singing, gradually limiting the amount you are prompting with your right hand until you are singing without piano assistance.
7. Repeat step 6 many times, finding different routes through the tetrachords of the tune.
8. Connect the tetrachords, again switching whenever you wish but varying the order of the pitches of the tetrachord so you aren't going straight up or down each scale fragment. First do this playing and singing, gradually limiting the amount you are prompting with your right hand until you are singing without piano assistance.
9. Compose a line using this technique. Learn to sing it. Memorize.
10. Add bebop passing chromatic pitches to the upper tetrachords. Use Mixolydian on dominants. Practice singing only upper tetrachords descending in this rhythm four eighth notes, one quarter note, one quarter rest.
11. Repeat step 10, upper tetrachords with chromatic passing note, descending.
12. Combine all tetrachord approaches: using upper and lower tetrachords, upper tetrachords with passing chromatic notes, varying the order of the pitches. Practice singing with the right hand of the piano and without.
13. Compose a chorus with all these techniques.
14. Repeat these techniques on another tune of your choosing.

CHAPTER 7

SCALE WRAP-UP: THE LONG SCALE

I want to return to 7-note scales for one more exercise before we move on to study chromatic passing notes and bebop vocabulary in the next chapter. This scale exercise is called the long scale exercise, and I think of it as the culmination of all the scale-oriented work we have done in the last two chapters.

Scales appear to be a line moving straight up the piano. Because we can't play them easily all at once (and certainly can't sing them all at once) they appear to be sequential, but they aren't really. A scale is all of the available notes on a given chord: a note set. Sometimes it helps to visualize them more like a bush or a cloud instead of a line. Or a color from a paint brush. Imagine that all the notes that are available to you on the piano for a given chord scale are there in a big thick group and you could pick any note from the group and play it followed by any other note. This is possible to do on the piano, but as I mentioned in the introduction of this book, very hard to do vocally.

So even though we can't randomly jump from note to note in different ranges the way you could do on the piano, **we can experience a little bit of this by starting a scale anywhere on the instrument, let's say the A below middle C on the G-7 chord. Sing the next three notes of the G-7 scale as you play 1, 3 and 7 in your left hand.** Now you should be singing a D. The next chord change is C7, and let's return to the C7 altered scale. **So sing the next note up, using the altered scale, an Eb.** Singing the next three notes of the altered scale gets you to an Ab. The next chord is FMaj7 so continue the scale line upward from A, connecting the notes of the scale. Just as we did with tetrachords, somewhere we'll have to change direction or this quickly becomes an exercise about vocal range. Anyway, **connect all the notes of each scale using four notes for each chord change.** One line you might sing is below.

Just like with tetrachords, I can concoct many different paths through the chord scales of this tune. Here's another:

CHAPTER 7

TRACK 22 and another:

[musical notation: G-7, C7, F∆7, B♭∆7, E-7♭5, A7, D-∆7, D7]

Just like with tetrachords, a valuable next step is to start to vary the order subtly, still moving mostly up the scale, but occasionally adding leaps of a 3rd, and changing directions more often to create melodies. Also, working at a slow tempo, you can try using eighth note subdivisions of the beat instead of the quarter notes we have been using.

TRACK 23

[musical notation: G-7, C7, F∆7, B♭∆7, E-7♭5, A7, D-∆7, D7]

Next, I can add the chromatic approach notes that we used with the tetrachords. I can change the dominant chord scales to Mixolydian and try to incorporate these chromatic approach notes wherever possible.

TRACK 24

[musical notation: G-7, C7, F∆7, B♭∆7, E-7♭5, A7, D-∆7, D7]

TRACK 25 **I can add more changes in direction and skips to these bebop scale lines.**

[musical notation: G-7, C7, F∆7, B♭∆7, E-7♭5, A7, D-∆7, D7]

Once again, keep working on these techniques in the same way we have been doing with all the previous methods. Try composing. Try singing long scales on other tunes.

CHAPTER 7

One last note here. Hopefully, as you practice these different methods, you are getting ideas of your own, things that you might like to try. It goes without saying, that you should try all of these things. (Well, it didn't go without saying, but you certainly should.)

As you can see from the way we are working on these ways of hearing and understanding the harmony better, the process of practicing is about taking some small idea or technique and working with it, experimenting with it, changing it and trying it in different contexts. You never know precisely what you will learn from each new device. You just keep trying them and move on.

CHAPTER 8

Practicing Scatting 5:
Chromatic Approach Note Patterns and Bebop Vocabulary

In the last chapter we touched on a new element of theory that we haven't seen before, chromatic approach notes. We can analyze the harmony of any solo, or indeed any piece of (western) music using three elements: scales (or stepwise movement), arpeggios (or leaps and skips) and chromatic approach notes. We dealt with arpeggios (a bit) in Chapter 4 and scales in most of the subsequent chapters. The chromatic approach notes that we are turning our attention to now are very important to jazz and particularly bebop.

A chromatic approach note is any note that isn't in a particular chord scale, but resolves to a note in that scale. These notes are important for creating tension and resolution within a melodic line. You can demonstrate this to yourself by singing one of the tetrachords we examined in the last chapter. Take the upper tetrachord for CMaj7. First, while playing a CMaj 7 (1, 3 and 7 voicing in the left hand), sing it without a chromatic approach note:

Then sing it with the #5 added:

What is the difference between these two lines? After singing the first line, how does the second line feel?

For me, the addition of chromatic passing notes to a line makes the line feel more **directional.** What I mean by that is, as you sing the G#, we hear a dissonance. It registers on the ear that this note is not in the scale. The next note, A, IS in the scale, so playing it creates a sense of resolution. Lines with chromatic approach notes in them have many of these small tension/resolution patterns within them. For that reason they give a sense of going somewhere that lines that just float aimlessly through the scales don't have.

I found this out for myself when I was just a beginning pianist. I had been studying piano for a while, but I was young and enjoyed hanging out with my friends and playing outside more than practicing. (Weird, huh?) Anyway, I also dabbled in guitar playing but I was more of a folkie on guitar and knew chords and finger picking a little but didn't know where the notes were on the guitar fingerboard. As I became more serious about the piano, I gradually stopped playing the guitar, but every so often I would pick it up and try to play a solo on it, by ear. On the piano, I already knew scales, mostly, and was working on soloing. On the guitar, I would try to play a scale, a line or a melody and would invariably miss by a half step or whole step, not knowing the positions that you use on the guitar as you move up the neck, or which notes were on which strings. Interestingly, my lines on the guitar sounded better to me than my lines on piano. This was because with my near misses and corrections, I was playing chromatic approach notes without realizing it. I was trying to play some bebop (and more modern) influenced music on the piano but it always sounded wrong. The lines were too diatonic sounding and, as one older hard bop player used to say when I was coming on the scene, they "didn't have the right accidentals."

So you need to get the right accidentals. Of course, it's crucially important to listen to players who play the right accidentals, and singers who can sing them. This is what sent me back to working on bebop when I was in my early 20s (before that, I thought I would be the next Keith Jarrett). When I started listening to Bud Powell, Wynton Kelly, and Red Garland again (as well as Keith Jarrett, once I heard him with ears attuned to the use of chromatic approach notes), I realized that there were notes in their solos that I hadn't known were there.

So, you need to listen. Of course, you should listen to Ella Fitzgerald, Sarah Vaughn, Betty Carter, Carmen McCrae, Jon Hendricks and Chet Baker, but also to the instrumentalists that performed with them, influenced them and developed the jazz vocabulary on chord changes: Charlie Parker, Bud Powell, Dizzy Gillespie, Dexter Gordon, Sonny Rollins, Miles Davis.

Listening is a great tool. The great trumpet player and composer Tom Harrell calls it "unconscious practicing." Try and hear as much jazz soloing as you can, focusing on the great players of the 50s and 60s. (Of course, you can listen to any era you are particularly fond of, but most of the vocabulary that defines mainstream improvising developed in the late 40s, 50s and 60s.) Listen to all of the bands of Miles Davis from this period, since very often his bands were among the best.

You should also start transcribing. Transcription is extremely beneficial. Often, I will see a student that suddenly has a musical breakthrough and improves in one big leap, and when I ask him or her what she has been working on, invariably they say they've been transcribing.

The guidelines for transcribing are pretty simple. First, start small. Don't do an extremely difficult transcription right off the bat. Take something that is only a few choruses long. Take something that is at a moderate tempo. Pick something that is central to the musical style you want to understand better. Do a transcription of an instrumentalist at least as often as you do one of a singer.

Here are a few good examples to choose from: Miles Davis soloing on "Freddy Free-

CHAPTER 8

loader" from Kind of Blue (7 choruses of a medium up blues in Bb. Try the first 4); Chet Baker: "It Could Happen to You"; Bud Powell: "Celia"; Sarah Vaughn: "All of Me"; Sonny Rollins; "Blue Seven"; Dexter Gordon: "Cheesecake."

But how do you actually start the process of transcribing? We can break this down into several steps.

1. **Listen to the solo you want to transcribe 100 times before you do anything with it.** (Okay, that may be a little bit of an exaggeration, but not much. If you know the solo well before you begin, it will be much, much easier. Think of this as part of the process of transcribing. Allow as much as possible of the solo to seep into your consciousness before you start working hard on it.)
2. **Try to start singing the solo.** Learn the solo in phrases, don't learn it note by note. Now more than ever, it is possible to transcribe each note separately. All you need is a slow-downer program on your computer, and the music can be slowed down to any tempo and cut into as small a phrase as you like. The problem is, if you tran scribe in this way, you don't internalize the solo. You may get it down on paper, and I've had students who can bring in amazing transcriptions they've done, working dutifully, note by note, but they don't retain what they've transcribed. It doesn't become a part of them. **So, play a few bars of the recording and then sing the solo line. Play the recording. Sing.** Repeat. Sing with the soloist, trying to imitate every nuance of his or her performance. Slow it down, but then speed it up to hear the whole line in the real time it was played in. Going back and forth like this, you can both learn the solo in phrases and check to make sure that you are getting all of the fast notes down correctly.
3. **Learn the solo;** if possible learn the whole thing without writing anything down. Just keep singing and repeating. I'm told that in India, if you want to study an instrument with a master he will play for you and have you imitate what he plays, over and over, phrase by phrase. That's what you do when you transcribe. You are imitating a master.
4. **After you know the solo so that you can sing it perfectly with the soloist, write it down.** Don't worry too much about writing down every rhythm perfectly. Just approximate. If necessary you can write a phrase like "laid back" or "a little late" over a few of the rhythms if they aren't a perfectly mathematical representation of the recording. It's much more important to be able to make the solo feel like it does on the recording than to have it notated absolutely correctly. Still, try for as much precision as you can manage. If you find it difficult to remember the whole solo without writing it down, then write it down in sections, but make sure that you learn each section (4 bars, 8 bars, one chorus, whatever length you can handle) before you write it down.
5. **Make sure that you have all of the melodic embellishments correct in your performance of the solo.** The twists and turns, the chromatic notes, the articulations—getting these things really in tune can be a challenge.

> **6.** Once you have the whole solo written down, memorize anything that you still haven't mastered.
>
> **7. Now analyze the written solo.** Figure out what the chord scales should be for the chords (using the guidelines we've used in earlier chapters) and figure out if the notes of the solo correspond to the scales you think are appropriate for these chords. Figure out where the soloist is using different chord scales. Figure out where the soloist is using chromatic approach notes, and label them as such. Try to understand the thinking behind every note that occurs in the solo, so you can use these same processes when you solo. Your goal is not so much to steal the lines that the soloist is using, but rather, you want to understand how the soloist is thinking about harmony. If you achieve this, you can make lines that are constructed in similar ways, but still are individual to you.

And that's it. For the next few years, it would be great if you were always in the process of working on a solo, either finishing up an old one, or starting something new. This shouldn't take the place of the other things you are working on (piano, second chorus melody practice, theory as applied to lead sheets, scatting practice), but it should be part of your daily practice.

Having a good practice technique always reminds me of the TV dinners I used to see in grocery stores when I was a kid. They had compartments for everything: for the peas, the cherry cobbler dessert, the Salisbury steak and mashed potatoes. Practicing should be like that. There should always be Salisbury steak and cherry cobbler. At least SOME kind of cobbler. Wait a minute...I've lost my point. Oh yes, what I meant was that your practice needs to be compartmentalized. Maybe you have 2 1/2 hours to practice every day. So, 30 minutes or so are transcribing, 30 minutes piano, 30 minutes scatting, 20 minutes melodic analysis of melodies, and the rest of the time you work on your charts. Or maybe one day you concentrate on one or two of these areas, and the next day you do the remaining areas, alternating between the different things you have to do.

So add transcription to your practice list. Of course, like all the other techniques we've been talking about, if you absolutely hate doing it, set it aside for now. But, try it again a few months later. Or try doing a shorter solo. Just one chorus. Or an A section. How about the A section of "Autumn Leaves"?

Maybe you've enjoyed the little vacation this chapter has offered us from the A section of "Autumn Leaves." Let's prolong it by talking about chromatic approach note patterns.

The best description of chromatic approach note patterns I've seen comes from the legendary Boston jazz teacher, Charlie Banacos. Here it is, as I learned it from Charlie.

There are 12 combinations of one and two notes approaching a target pitch by half step:

CHAPTER 8

1 half step below, 1 half step above, 1 half step below and 1 half step above, 1 half step above and 1 half step below, 2 half steps below, 2 half steps above, 2 half steps below and 2 half steps above, 2 half steps above and 2 half steps below, 1 half step above and 2 half steps below, 2 half steps below and 1 half step above, 2 half steps above and 1 half step below, 1 half step below and 2 half steps above.

These are all the possible combinations of 1- and 2-note chromatic approach note patterns if the notes are always approaching the target note (so B, Bb, C is not a possible pattern since the first half step moves away from the target note of C.) These patterns are valuable to work on for a couple of important reasons. One is that when you combine these with scale fragments and arpeggios, you can generate a lot of musical material. As I mentioned above, these chromatic approach notes will make your lines feel more directional and less like floating aimlessly in a scale. A lot of jazz vocabulary and bebop language has to do with these sorts of chromatic approach note patterns, and how to use them rhythmically, generally emphasizing chord tones as target notes on downbeats, or on notes of longer time values. The chromatic approach notes usually occur on the upbeats, leading to the target pitches.

Also, these approach note patterns come under the heading of "common parts of jazz vocabulary that are not easy to sing in tune." In a later chapter we will be doing some interval studies for the same reason. As you try to scat and as you analyze other singers' solos, you need to be aware that there are certain things that are hard to do vocally. When you become aware of one of those "non-vocal" qualities, you want to find a way to break down the difficulty into its components and practice these small parts of the bigger problem. Since jazz solos often make use of chromatic patterns and they are difficult to sing absolutely in tune, we need to find some easy ways to work directly on this problem. If we do so, this will have a big effect on your ability to scat sing in tune.

So, let's start working on these chromatic approach note patterns. The first step is to practice singing each of these patterns to all 12 pitches, starting with C as written above. Practice them starting fairly low in your range. When you begin, play the whole pattern on the piano as you sing it. Then, try and sing the patterns playing the first note of the pattern and then nothing until you finish the pattern

and sing the target pitch. While you are singing the target note, check yourself with the piano to see if you are still in tune. Then play only the target pitch and sing all of the chromatic patterns. Keep working at singing as in tune as you can. After you've done all of the patterns with and without your right hand prompting you, move up a 4th to the next pitch and repeat the process for this new target note. After you've finished the patterns on the next pitch, move up a 4th again. Do all the patterns again and next time go down a 5th to the next target pitch. In this way you work through all of the pitches. Try to cover two octaves (all 12 notes as target pitches in both a lower and higher octave), from low in your range to moderately high in your range, since the implications for intonation are different, depending on where the note is in your range.

Spend time working on these patterns in this way, focusing on intonation issues. Learn all the patterns and try to notice where you have intonation problems. You need to feel pretty comfortable with these patterns and confident of your intonation to move on to the next step.

The next step is hearing these chromatic approach notes over a particular harmony, This step involves a lot of work, so let's break it down into something manageable.

To start, play a CMaj7 in your left hand with the old faithful voicing, 1, 3 and 7. Now play the root in your right hand. Sing each of the chromatic patterns to this target note (C) while sustaining the left hand voicing. Use your right hand to prompt yourself or to check intonation. When you feel fairly comfortable with these patterns approaching the root of the chord, switch to a two-handed voicing, the singer voicing, the singer voicing with a tension or two, or some other voicing of your choice. Repeat the patterns to the root of the chord, this time without prompts. Next, repeat the process with the 3rd of this chord, then the 5th, and finally the 7th. Once you have done all the patterns for the chord tones of this chord, move up a 4th to FMaj7. Do all of the patterns to the root as you sustain the FMaj7 in your left hand, and then over two-handed voicings. Sing all of the patterns to the four chord tones and then repeat this process once more for BbMaj7. At this point, once you've sung all of the chromatic patterns to all of the chord tones for three different major seventh chords, go up a 4th (or down a 5th) to the Eb and play Eb-7. Repeat the process, singing chromatic patterns to each of the chord tones, then move up a fourth to Ab-7, and then Db-7. Once you've sung all the approach note patterns for three minor seventh chords, move up a 4th to a Gb minor seventh flat 5 chord. In this way, do all of the chromatic approach note patterns to minor seventh flat 5 chords, diminished sevenths, minor major sevenths and dominant sevenths. For each quality, sing the patterns to each chord tone, singing over three keys going around the circle of 5ths before switching to another chord quality.

CHAPTER 8

Following this sequence, eventually you will get to all of the chords of every key for every chord quality. Even if you don't finish the whole pattern, you are getting practice at hearing the chromatic pitches as they create temporary dissonances before resolving to the chord tones. This is a long-term project so hang in there and chip away at it steadily, doing some of the whole sequence each day. (Everything is relative. It's not a long-term project in the sense that I think you will be doing it every day for the next five years, but it certainly could occupy you for several months, longer if you feel that it is enjoyable and effective.)

Of course, if you can hear these approach note patterns to each of the chord tones of each chord quality as you work through them, you should also be able to hear these approach note patterns to chords in a chord progression. **So, take a song that you have been working on, such as the A sections of "Autumn Leaves" or something of your own choosing, and (out of time) play each chord and then pick a chord tone and pick one of the 12 chromatic approach note patterns to that chord tone. Then play the next chord, pick a different chord tone and a different pattern and sing that.** If you wish, you can do this mechanically; for example, play the last of the 12 chromatic approach note patterns to the root of the first chord. Now play the next to last of the 12 chromatic approach note patterns to the 3rd of the second change. The next change gets pattern number 10 to the 5th and so forth. The point is simply that you want to develop the ability to sing these chromatic approach note patterns over any chord tone at any time in any progression.

The next step in working on these patterns is to start combining these chromatic approach note patterns with their target pitches into lines. One way of doing this is to simply **write a long string of these patterns over a particular chord, using each of the four chord tones as target notes.** So, the line is comprised entirely of chromatic approach note patterns and (chord tone) target pitches and nothing else. You can arrange these patterns however you want, targeting the 3rd, then the root, back to the 3rd, the 5th, the root, the 7th: any order that you find appealing.

TRACK 27

The above line is written over Bb major7. Compose a similar line of your own and learn to sing it, first over Bb major7 and then transposing it around the circle of 5ths. Eventually you should be able to sing it without right-hand prompts as you play a two-handed voicing of any major seventh. Compose one of these lines for each chord quality: for minor seventh, minor seventh flat 5, minor major seventh, diminished and dominant seventh. Learn to sing each of these lines as you did above with the major seventh line, switching keys and eventually singing over the chord without prompting from your right hand.

At this point you should be extremely familiar with the sound of these chromatic approach note patterns. Try singing them on some other tunes, playing the chords at a very slow tempo and seeing what you can hear on some changes that you haven't been working on as continuously as in "Autumn Leaves."

Another valuable thing to do is to choose several bebop heads to learn. I would suggest "Confirmation" and "Donna Lee," although it doesn't really matter—you can pick any tune you like. (Maybe stay away from rhythm changes for now, since that form has so many different sets of possible changes.) Make sure that you analyze the song thoroughly, noticing where Charlie Parker (or any other bebop composer you like) puts chromatic approach notes, scale fragments and arpeggios. Work on these melodies slowly, employing all of the techniques we have been working on up to this point. Listen to a lot of recordings (many times each) of the tunes you are working on. See if you can sing a few lines from the solos on these recordings without starting a major transcription project.

And that's it for chromatic approach notes. I have had relatively few vocal students work through chromatic approach notes, but I have shown these exercises to many pianists. A talented 15-year-old pianist remarked that after he started working with these chromatic approach note patterns, "it changed his life." (Thanks, Charlie.) I don't know if these will change your life, but I am fairly certain if you work on them seriously and steadily they will radically change your singing, making your lines more interesting and allowing you to hear a lot of notes over the harmony that you are not hearing now. It will help make you a more proactive singer, more in control of your solo. It will make you a scatting force to be reckoned with.

CHROMATIC APPROACH NOTE WRAP-UP

1. Increase the amount of time you spend listening to jazz solos, both instrumental and vocal.
2. Begin transcription project. (One of many..?)
3. Practice the 12 chromatic approach note patterns. Play with right hand alone as you sing, gradually leaving out notes on the piano, using your right hand to prompt you and to check for intonation. Practice all patterns to one target note, fairly low in your range.
4. Repeat step 3 to a target pitch a fourth up and then continue to all 12 pitches. Go through this progression twice, so you have sung the 12 patterns to all 12 pitches in two octaves.
5. Now play CMaj7 in your left hand, 1,3 and 7 voicing. Sing all 12 chromatic approach note patterns to the root of this chord, using your right hand to check for intonation. Now sing all patterns to the 5th of the chord, and finally to the 7th of the chord. Repeat with FMaj7 and BbMaj7.

CHAPTER 8

6. Repeat all the above patterns to each of the chord tones for Eb-7. Repeat for Ab-7 and Db-7.
7. Repeat all of the above patterns to each of the chord tones for F#7. Repeat for B7 and E7.
8. Repeat all of the above patterns to each of the chord tones for A-7b5. Repeat for D-7 b5 and G-7b5.
9. Repeat all of the above patterns to each of the chord tones for C-Maj7. Repeat for F-Maj7 and Bb-Maj7.
10. Repeat all of the above patterns to each of the chord tones for Eb diminished7. Repeat for Ab diminished7 and Db diminished7.
11. Start with major sevenths again, on Gb and continue this drill, doing at least one chord quality daily, until you feel comfortable singing these patterns over any chord, any chord tone.
12. Compose a line over a Bb Major7 comprised entirely of these chromatic approach note patterns to chord tone targets. Make it as melodic and bebop-y sounding as you can. Learn the line and then transpose it, singing it over every major seventh
13. Compose a line similar to the one in step 11 for minor sevenths, dominant sevenths, minor seventh flat 5s, diminished sevenths, minor major sevenths. Memorize each line for each chord quality and sing it in all keys.
14. Learn the melodies of "Donna Lee," "Confirmation" and any other bebop tunes that you like. Analyze these melodies thoroughly, noting how Charlie Parker (or whomever) handles scale fragments, arpeggios and chromatic approach note patterns.

Practicing Scatting 6: Guide Tone Lines

CHAPTER 9

I've had a couple of teaching experiences that led me to writing this book. One of them was with a very experienced teacher and singer (already a good scatter) who took a few lessons from me while I was guest teaching at the college where she teaches. She was feeling stuck, as we all feel from time to time. Over the last few years of teaching, she had been expending most of her energy on her students' musical development and not much on her own.

Listening to her scatting, I was struck by how she sang coherent sensible and lyrical lines, but she didn't stress particularly unusual or interesting notes of the chord change. This is when I started thinking about the reactive nature of a lot of scatting. Not emphasizing unusual or interesting notes, in short, tensions and altered tensions, means there is a better chance of your line fitting with whatever the piano player is comping.

To address the problem of conservative note choice, an exercise that I learned a long time ago from the great alto player, Bob Mover, came to mind. There isn't a lot of information about how Charlie Parker practiced but somewhere he was quoted as saying that he used the upper notes of the chords as "hinge" notes for his lines. This exercise is a way to practice this concept.

So the singing teacher and I did the exercise together, which is to write guide tone lines (notes of long rhythmic duration) over chord progressions, trying to hit as many tensions and altered tensions as possible. The teacher worked on these lines all week, and then returned for another lesson.

The difference in the lines she was singing was remarkable. Interesting notes and colors made her formerly pretty but cautious lines sound brilliant and daring. Once she was empowered to go for more adventurous notes in her scatting, notes that took her away from diatonic common tone note choices, her soloing went from black and white to vivid color.

Since then I have encouraged a lot of singers to try this method because I really believe in it. Although a few singers that I have worked with have dabbled with this approach, no one has worked consistently to develop this skill. So I am hoping that, if it is laid out clearly here, you can employ this system to improve your scatting.

So what is a guide tone line? Sometimes people use this phrase to mean the line that occurs on ii-V-I progressions: the 7 of the ii-7 chord, leading to 3 on the V7 chord, which then becomes a 7 on the major seventh chord (and sometimes moves to 6 after that).

CHAPTER 9

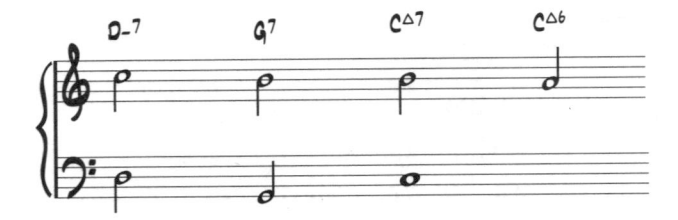

[Musical notation: D-7 | G7 | C△7 | C△6 progression with guide tone line]

This line is so familiar that musicians think the phrase "guide tone" means this particular line. It really doesn't, at least not in the context I wish to use it. The above line is just the most common example of a guide tone line. A guide tone line is a slow moving (notes of long duration), non-bass note line that moves by whole step or half step (meaning smooth voice leading) that can define the harmonic movement (spell out the chord changes) of a progression. In the above line, these long tones show the important notes of the ii-V I progression in such a clear way that even though many notes of the chord are left out, you still have a sense of what the full chords are.

> For our use, the guide tone lines I am interested in will follow these rules:
> 1. Each note of the guide tone line should last as long as each chord lasts, so if the chords are one change per bar the guide tone line should be in whole notes, and if the chords are two changes per bar, the guide tone line should be in half notes.
> 2. Notes should move by whole step or half step.
> 3. You should try to find as many tensions and altered tensions as possible. For variety, and for smooth voice leading, you will always have some chord tones in the lines, more after you have written several of these lines over a particular set of chords and exhausted some possibilities for finding tensions.

So let's return to our old friend, the A sections of "Autumn Leaves." I can write many guide tone lines that satisfy the above conditions. Here is one of them:

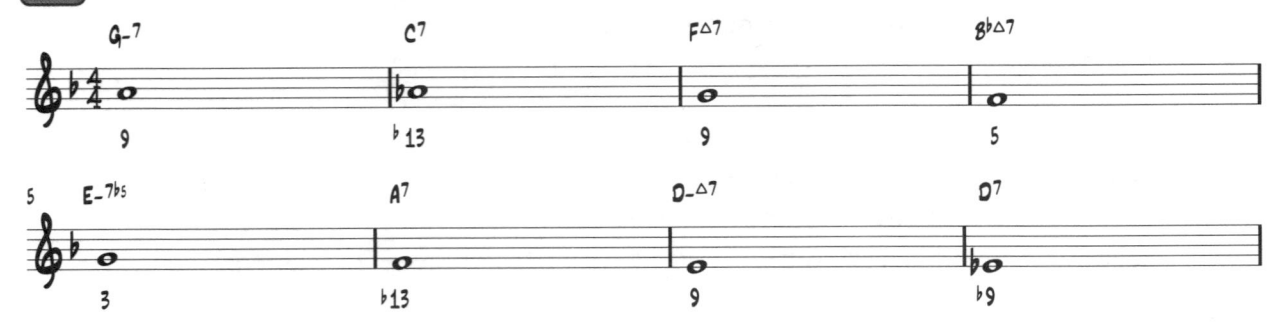

TRACK 28

[Musical notation:
Measure 1: G-7 (9)
Measure 2: C7 (b13)
Measure 3: F△7 (9)
Measure 4: Bb△7 (5)
Measure 5: E-7b5 (3)
Measure 6: A7 (b13)
Measure 7: D-△7 (9)
Measure 8: D7 (b9)]

Sing the line slowly, playing only the roots of the chords. Then sing the line playing full voicings. As you sing the line, sing the number of each note (9, b13, whatever.) You want to try to hear this note, to remember what it feels like against the harmony of the tune. That's all for now, just try to lock in on the sound of these tensions against the underlying harmony. **Memorize the above line, singing it many times.**

Now you have many options of directions that you can go in. Basically, we are interested in adding notes around these guide tones, notes from the chord scale, chord tones, chromatic approach note patterns, anything that sounds good to you. Here are several ideas of things to try but, as always, feel free to reject anything that you don't enjoy doing, and also try to come up with some ideas of your own.

GUIDE TONE LINE EMBELLISHMENT OPTIONS

1. Sing each note of the guide tone line as a half note. Sing the root of each chord after the guide tone note as another half note
2. Sing the root of the chord before the guide tone note.
3. Repeat steps 2 and 3, replacing the root with the 3rd of the chord, the 5th of the chord and the 7th of the chord.
4. Sing each note of the guide tone line as a half note. Sing the root and 3rd of each chord as quarter notes both before the guide tone (on beats 1 and 2 of the bar) and after the guide tone (on beats 3 and 4 of the bar).
5. Repeat step 4, using 3 and 5, 1 and 5, 3 and 7, 5 and 7.
6. Sing each note of the guide tone line as a quarter note. Sing the guide note on beat one of the measure, and then down the appropriate chord scale in quarter notes on beats 2, 3 and 4.
7. Repeat step 6, varying the order of pitches in some way that makes musical sense to you.
8. Sing each note of the guide tone line as a quarter note. Add three other quarter notes, using scale fragments that aren't consecutively connected to the guide tone note, such as 123 and 345.
9. Repeat step 8, varying the order.
10. Use any of the patterns that you came up with in Chapter 6 to add notes to the guide tone line.
11. Improvise added notes to the guide tone line.
12. Compose a chorus based on these embellishment techniques. (Feel free to vary the rhythm however you can to make the composed solo line as interesting as possible.)
13. Compose a second guide tone line and repeat steps 1 through 12.
14. Compose 4 or 5 guide tone lines for each tune you are working on and repeat steps 1 through 12.
15. Repeat Steps 1 through 14 on another tune of your choosing.

CHAPTER 9

Here is an example of my version of step 12, a chorus composed by embellishing the guide tone line I gave you at the beginning of this chapter.

TRACK 29

Since the key to utilizing this guide tone method is the ability to compose good guide tone lines, let's examine a few more guide tone lines for the above progression.

TRACK 30

and

Please notice some of the features that made the line I composed above a good choice. First, I tried to come up with a line that is pleasant to sing, meaning not simply moving up and down over the same few notes. The second line IS a bit repetitive but not as bad as this line:

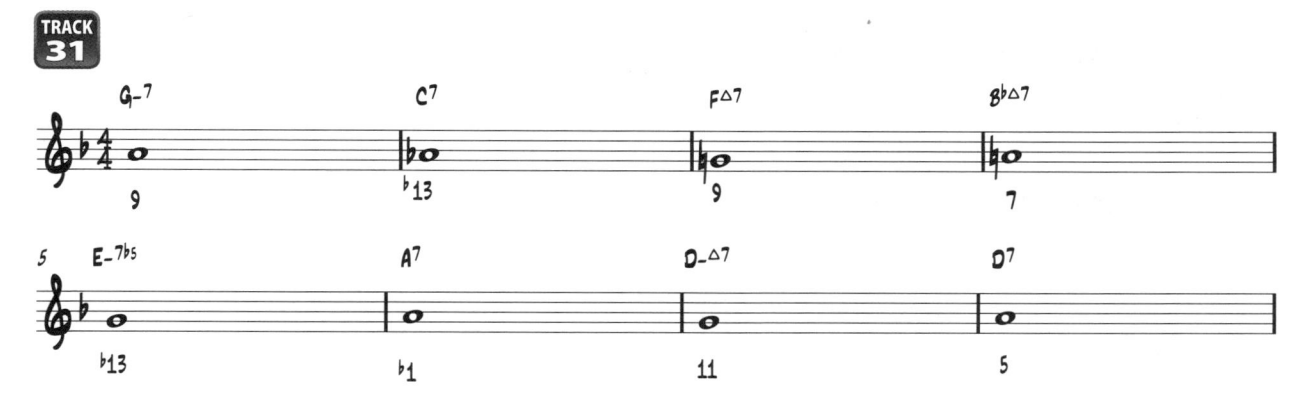

These sorts of repetitive lines are easy to write and should be avoided. Also, the more the line can move by half step instead of whole step, the more enjoyable it will be to sing. It will also lead to your finding nice voice leading relationships between the chords when you start to embellish the line. Still, even the above line is useful—just try to make sure that all the lines you compose aren't quite so repetitive as this one.

Notice also that in all the lines I have given you, I tried to use different tensions in each guide tone line. If I used a 9th for the first chord in the first guide tone line, then I tried not to use it in the second guide tone line. Eventually, when I have used all of the tensions available on each chord more than one time, I will try to get to most of the chord tones on the chords as well. As long as the line is at least half tensions, it will serve my purpose and often the use of some chord tones allows me to create a line with a better melodic flow.

The guide tone method, like the method introduced in the last chapter, very directly addresses an issue that I think is one of the biggest problems in scat solos, namely conservative note choice. Everything that we have been working on up until now is important and will help you improve, but for those with some scatting experience, the material in this chapter and the last one (chromatic approach notes) is extremely important because it specifically addresses this issue.

We are getting to the end of our journey into the world of scat, but there are still a few more things to cover. Next, let's try to use all of our scatting practice techniques over that favorite scat vehicle, the blues.

CHAPTER 10

Practicing Scatting 7: The Blues

I woke up this morning and decided to write a chapter about practicing scatting over the blues. (That's a kind of a joke, because a lot of blues lyrics start with I woke up this...okay, forget it.)

You may be wondering why I have waited so long to introduce the blues. After all, it's the first thing that most singers encounter in their improvisational journey. Often, singers that don't really scat, will scat on blues. There are lots of recordings of singers scatting on blues, instrumentalists blowing on blues, etc. Also, it's a pretty simple form. Everyone has heard it a million times, whether you know it or not. It's everywhere: in commercials (Internet Phone Service is one I've heard lately) TV themes (Batman and Spiderman are among the more well known) wedding band staples (Johnny B. Goode). Also, it's easy to solo over. You don't even have to spell out the underlying harmony because there is something called the blues scale that works over every chord in the progression, so you don't have to learn a bunch of chord scales, one works over everything. In fact, even good singers when singing blues often use this scale compulsively without even knowing it.

Aha. That last feature doesn't sound so helpful in a book about hearing harmonic progressions. And yes, that is the reason I've put off working on the blues, even though it's something that everyone who wants to improvise jazz should spend a lot of time with.

But first, for those of you who don't get out much (and never woke up in the morning with an aching head, cheating wife, man/woman who treats you wrong (or who done treated you wrong) empty pockets or any other blues type of experience), lets define what the blues is.

First and foremost in the world of jazz, blues is a 12-bar progression. At its most basic, the progression (here in the key of F) goes like this:

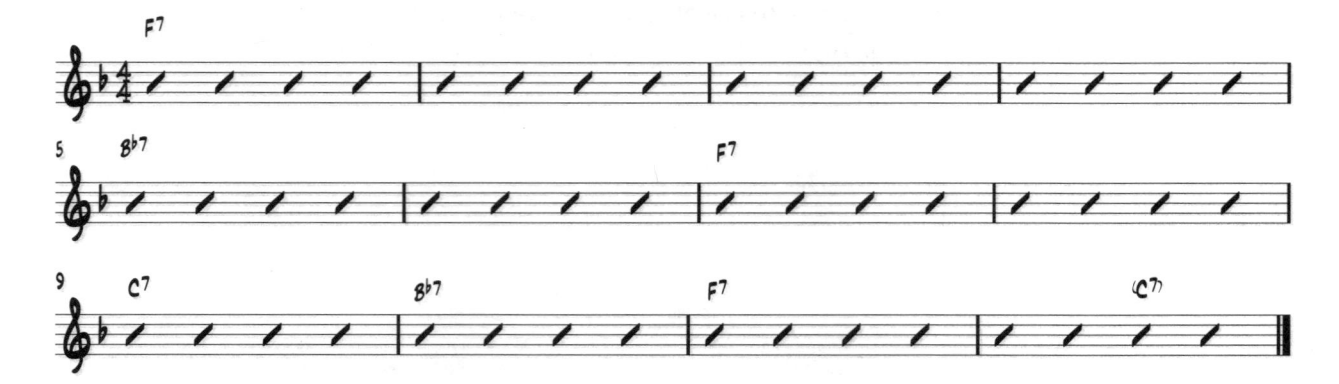

110

CHAPTER 10

There are few things that differentiate this from any of the progressions that we have looked at until now. These are:

1. the I7 chord at the beginning of the progression. In blues the tonic chord is a dominant chord, not a major chord. There are a lot of variations (some of which we will encounter later) that deviate from this, but the standard basic blues usually has this feature.
2. The cadence that brings us back to the I chord in bar 10 is unusual. Actually it is backwards: IV to V to I is a variation of ii V I, but in blues we have the unusual V to IV to I. It's 12 bars. Most standards are built in 8 bar units. Not so for the blues.

Blues is also a scale, as I mentioned earlier. It is a scale that is based on a minor pentatonic (5 note scale) or 1 b3 4 5 b7. To make this minor pentatonic scale into a blues scale you add the #4.

And yes, as I mentioned above, it's true that you can use this scale over all of the chords in the progression. The dissonance that comes from the notes that clash between this scale and the chords of the blues progression (for example the B natural and Ab on the F7 chord, the B natural and Eb on the Bb7 chord, the Ab, B natural and Eb on the C chord) is what gives the blues its melodic tension. It's the feeling of major and minor superimposed over each other. It's bluesy. **Prove this to yourself by playing the chords of the blues in your left hand and playing up and down the blues scale in your right hand. Bluesy, right?**

So, to begin our study of the blues, let's sing the blues scale over the whole form of the basic blues. Keep in mind, the blues scale, like all the other scales you've learned, has kernels of melody buried inside it. Try not to sing straight up and down the scale. Try to find motives that appeal to you. Find the interesting pieces of the scale.

TRACK 32

Blues, of course, is also a genre of music, in addition to being a progression and a scale. The relationship between blues, country, rock and jazz is complex. Where one style ends and another begins is often difficult to say. In general, though, when playing on a basic blues we have two options, whatever style you are performing in. You can play blues scale based melodies or you can play chord tone and chord scale based melodies.

111

CHAPTER 10

Players like B.B. King can concoct a lot of great melodic variations out of relatively simple harmonic material. (That sounds a little bit clinical, especially when considering something that has so much raw emotional power as the blues. I am speaking about what is happening harmonically here. The way harmony is put at the service of feeling, is a little beyond the scope of this book, but it is of central importance for any musical performance, regardless of style.)

In fact, even though the blues scale is available to you for all 12 bars of the progression, a lot of blues vocabulary can be better understood by paying attention to where blues players use the blues scale most in the form. For the first four bars of the form, it's more common to hear chord-tone based melodies. In his book on blues scales, ("The Blues Scales: Essential Tools for Improvisation" Sher Music Publishing) Dan Greenblatt discusses a second "major" blues scale (1, 2, b3, 3, 5, 6), a major pentatonic with a chromatic approach note, that is used in the first four bars of the form.

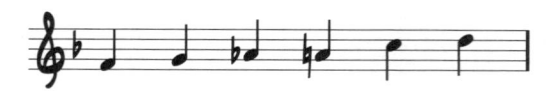

At the four chord, the regular, or in the book's terminology, the "minor," blues scale is used. This is a good way to account for a lot of the vocabulary of blues soloing and those who are interested in looking into this further should get this book.

Suffice it to say that, chord tones get used a lot in the first four bars of the blues. In the fourth bar, the 7 of the dominant seventh is often emphasized. In bars 5 and 6, the blues scale (the traditional one) is a good choice. In this way, your lines will be stronger if you don't indiscriminately use the blues scale everywhere, but rather find the more fitting places for its application.

Playing chord tone based melodies over the basic blues offers a clear demonstration of what I was talking about earlier regarding soloing. Playing the changes means looking for the notes that are changing as we move chord to chord, the new available notes on each chord. In the blues, the 3rd of the I chord is such a note. The A over the F7 changes to an Ab over the Bb7. This is important and many common blues melodies make a lot of this changing note.

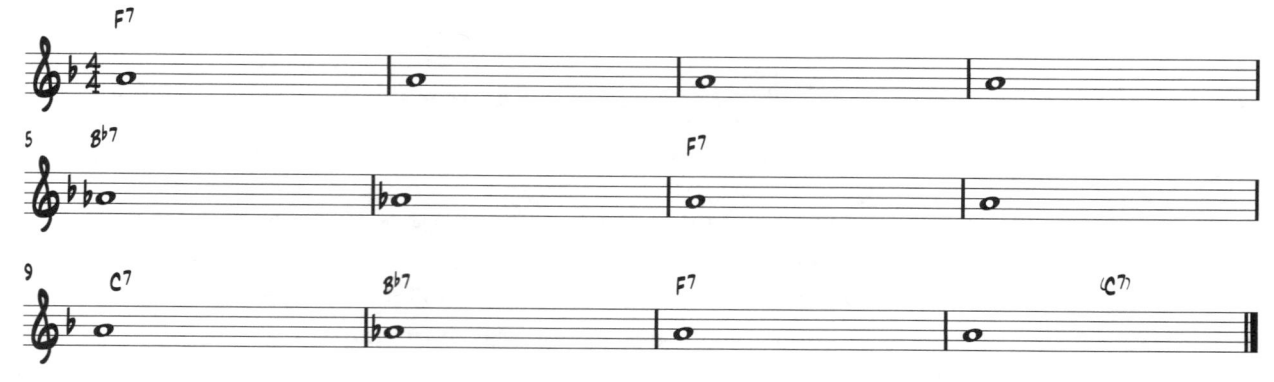

TRACK 33

112

TRACK 34 This note becomes a little like a guide tone line. I can fill in the chords around it and it gives my solo line a sense of direction

So I have two methods for working on the basic blues: playing lines based primarily on chord tones (as above) and soloing with the blues scale motives that we looked at earlier (augmented by the addition of the "major" blues scales on the first four bars of the form, if you prefer).

I was once fortunate enough to be guest teaching a class of jazz students when through a double booking of the school, the great jazz pianist and educator Billy Taylor was also booked. It was really interesting for me, because our approaches were so very different, working with the same group of students. The students were not at a very high level overall and I had been working with them on some very free-oriented exercises, techniques for improvising that weren't very theoretical and allowed everyone to participate, experimenting with improvising without using a lot of complex harmony or chord progressions.

Billy asked them to play a blues. When everyone had taken a couple of choruses, he sighed and then said that none of the students in the class had the slightest idea of what blues melodies ought to sound like. He went on: "There's a vocabulary of blues phrases and a tradition of making melodies over this progression, and unless you spend time listening, imitating, transcribing and...well, in a word, SEARCHING for the way this music is supposed to sound, you'll sound like you can't play, like amateurs, which is what you sound like now." He suggested to these students that they learn as many blues melodies as possible, to get the sound of the blues in their ears, since the melodies of blues are the key to understanding that melodic tradition.

I couldn't have agreed more. It was great for these students (at least, if they took his message to heart) to have Billy Taylor make the case for the importance of checking out the blues tradition and to try and get at the depth of this music.

As a teacher, and a writer, I like to try to solve problems. I like words and writing, and so I enjoy the process of trying to explain how something is put together, whether it's a jazz solo or a compositional technique. But that doesn't change the fact that if you are moved

CHAPTER 10

by jazz or any kind of music, you have to go searching for what makes it sound like that, for what makes it feel so deep and meaningful to you. You can understand a lot of things intellectually, but in the final analysis, that only takes you so far. We can describe common scale choices, or the melodies that people tend to play on the IV chord of a blues, but unless you really HEAR people playing those melodies, or HEAR when a soloist uses an altered chord to lead to the next chord a 4th away, it's all just an academic exercise.

This is something that is missing from some students. I remember clearly the moment when I learned something, the diminished scale for example, and it was a revelation for me. So, that's the sound I have been hearing Herbie Hancock play. (It was an epiphany, one of many in my musical history, whether it was something I figured out myself or something someone showed me: "AHA! So that's how they do it.")

I have two students now: one a tiny Korean girl who hasn't been studying jazz that long, who lives in New York, and the other a very experienced player from Lebanon who is living in Holland; they are both busily transcribing Bud Powell solos. No one told them to do it (or I should say, I had encouraged both of them to check out Bud's playing at some point, but I didn't set them on their current projects), but they both (independently of each other, of course—they don't know each other) decided there was something in Bud's playing that they wanted to understand on a deeper level. Something intrigued them and so they asked, "How does he get the lines to sound like that? The twists and turns, the melodies....how does he do it?" It reminded me of my own searching when I was in my 20s, and then later in my 30s and presently toward the end of my 40s. It's not always Bud; sometimes it's Herbie Hancock or Kenny Kirkland, Brad Mehldau, Keith Jarrett, Tom Harrell, Joe Lovano, Lee Konitz, Danilo Perez, Wayne Shorter. Sometimes it's someone who I am playing with: how does Dick Oatts or Jimmy Greene negotiate that change so effortlessly, build a solo so patiently; how does Lee Konitz make the line feel like that? How does Brian Blade or Nasheet Waits come up with so many different ways of approaching the same tune, making it different and fresh each time? In each case, you have to go looking for something. You have to keep listening to the players that inspire you and try and go after what they are doing, not necessarily in a slavishly imitative way—sometimes you just want to find your way of doing something kind of similar, or something inspired by the way another musician makes you feel. (Sometimes you are hearing something of your own, something that isn't easily traceable to a player/role model. Sometimes it's a feeling—but the common thread is that you have to search a little bit, you have to dig to flesh out what it is you are hearing, whether it's internal or external).

So dig into blues solos from players like Jimmy Smith, Wes Montgomery, Cannonball Adderly, Sonny Stitt, Charlie Parker, Gene Ammonds, John Coltrane, Sarah Vaughn, Billy Holliday, Dakota Staton, B.B. King, Sheila Jordan, Oscar Peterson, Miles Davis, Wynton Kelly, Bobby McFerrin, McCoy Tyner. In short, everybody, because everyone plays the blues, but with special attention to those "bluesy" players that define what it means to play deeply, artistically, in this style.

CHAPTER 10

And as you are listening and wondering how the great blues players get to sound that way, you can also look at the chord scales for the basic blues progression.

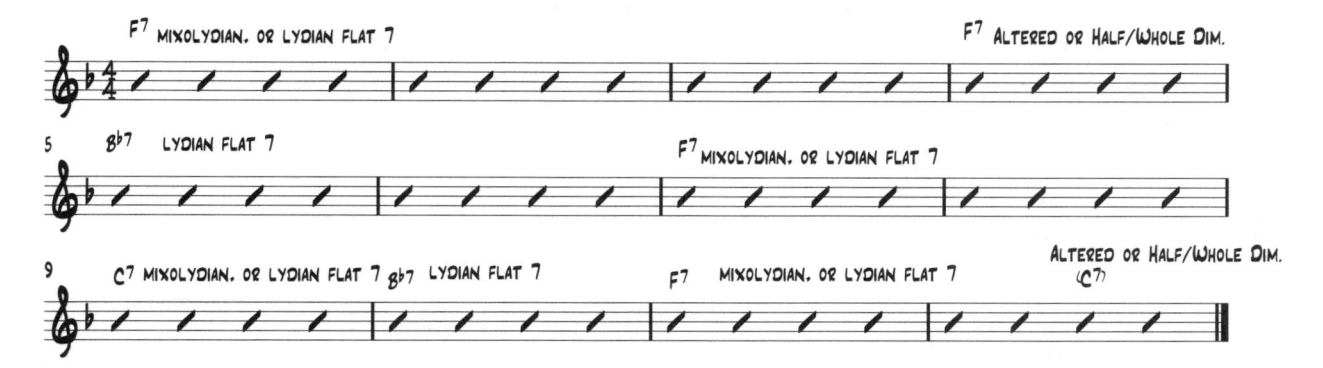

[Musical notation: 12-bar blues progression with chord scales indicated:
- Bar 1: F7 Mixolydian, or Lydian flat 7
- Bar 4: F7 Altered or Half/Whole Dim.
- Bar 5: Bb7 Lydian flat 7
- Bar 7: F7 Mixolydian, or Lydian flat 7
- Bar 9: C7 Mixolydian, or Lydian flat 7
- Bar 10: Bb7 Lydian flat 7
- Bar 11: F7 Mixolydian, or Lydian flat 7
- Bar 12: Altered or Half/Whole Dim. (C7)]

Another way to approach the blues is the same way we would with any tune, all of the techniques we have been looking at throughout the course of this book. **Using the above scales you can practice each chord separately to develop patterns, practice morphing those patterns over the progression, use tetrachords, use tetrachords with chromatic passing notes, use long scale and do everything else we worked through in the chapters devoted to chord scale study.** (If you are foggy on these details, refer to Chapters 5, 6 and 7.

You can also practice singing the chord tones and tensions over the progression (Chapter 4). Start with the roots, then sing 3rds, 5ths, 7ths. Sing different combinations (orders) of the chord tones. Then sing 9ths. Use natural 9 for all the chords except the 4th bar and the last bar second two beats. There you can use altered tensions. Sing #11ths on all chords. Sing natural 13 on all chords except bar 4 and the second half of the last bar where you sing b13. Sing all combinations and orders of notes that you can come up with.

Next, you can use some chromatic approach note patterns (Chapter 8). Use chromatic approach note patterns to target each chord tone. Compose a line made entirely of chromatic approach note patterns and transpose this line over each chord of the blues.

How about transcribing a chorus or two of your favorite scat solos on a basic blues? Or take off a chorus of Cannonball, Wynton Kelly, Miles Davis. Find something that isn't too hard but interests you. Keep listening to other players, and even if you don't transcribe the whole solo, you can always take off a few lines to try to get inside the soloist's head and understand his or her thinking.

Or write a guide tone line over the blues targeting tensions. Write several of these lines and then start embellishing them as we did in Chapter 9.

Now, let's repeat all of these steps over a slightly different blues form: the bebop

CHAPTER 10

blues form. Jazz players, while still occasionally playing the basic blues form above, use a lot of other forms as well. These variations, many of them developed during the bebop period, all add harmony to the blues form to make it more like a standard progression. Some add major seventh chords in place of the I dominant 7. Most of them add ii-7 V7 chords to the form and change the V IV cadence in bars 9 and 10. Below (with slight variations) is the most common form of the blues that jazz players play

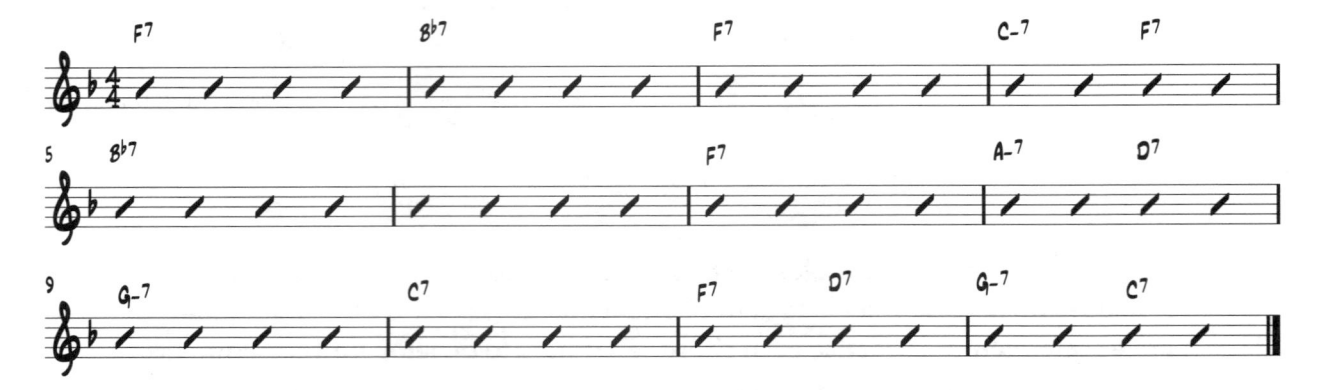

As you can see, there's a lot more harmony in this form. Let's add chord scales. I am adding chord scales using the same guidelines that we developed back in Chapter 5. These guidelines generate the following chord scales.

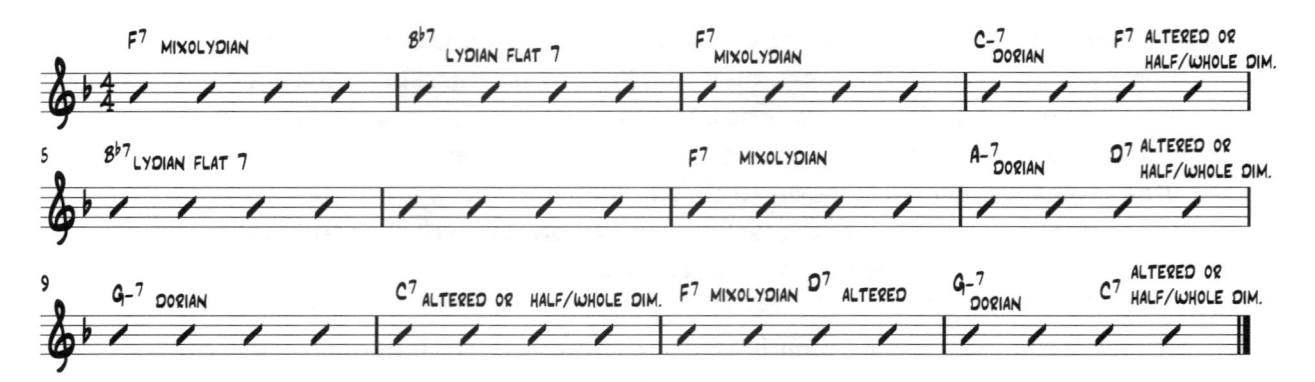

Once again, you can now repeat everything you've done over this new progression: chord scales and patterns, chord tones and tensions (use altered tensions on chords that get the altered scale), chromatic approach note patterns, transcription, guide tone lines. As always, at this or any other point in your practicing process, you can compose a chorus to better understand one of the techniques you are working on.

Finally, you should learn a number of blues melodies. Learn some with words and some that are bebop heads. Since there are blues melodies from every style of jazz, try and find blues melodies that have different feelings associated with them: funky in a traditional way ("Back in the Chicken Shack," "One Mint Julip"), traditional swing ("Frankie and Johnny," "CC Ryder"), compositions by Charlie Parker ("Cheryl," "Billie's Bounce"), Monk ("Blue Monk," "Straight No Chaser"), Bud Powell ("Dance of the Infidels"), modern funky ("The Chicken" by Pee Wee Ellis), open modern, composed by Herbie Hancock ("Eye of the Hurricane"), Ron Carter ("Eighty One"), Ornette Coleman ("When will the Blues Leave," "Blues Connotation"), modern swing ("Blue Tain" by Jeff Watts, "Nothing Personal" by Don Grolnick). The list is almost endless. You can even check out some of mine if you wish ("Creepy," "Blutocracy" and "Triceratops").

Some of the blues compositions mentioned above are minor blues, which is yet another form. Although slightly less common than major blues, this form is also important, and you would do well to repeat all of the above steps over this form as well. The minor blues form has a lot of variations and has similarities to minor tunes such as "Summertime."

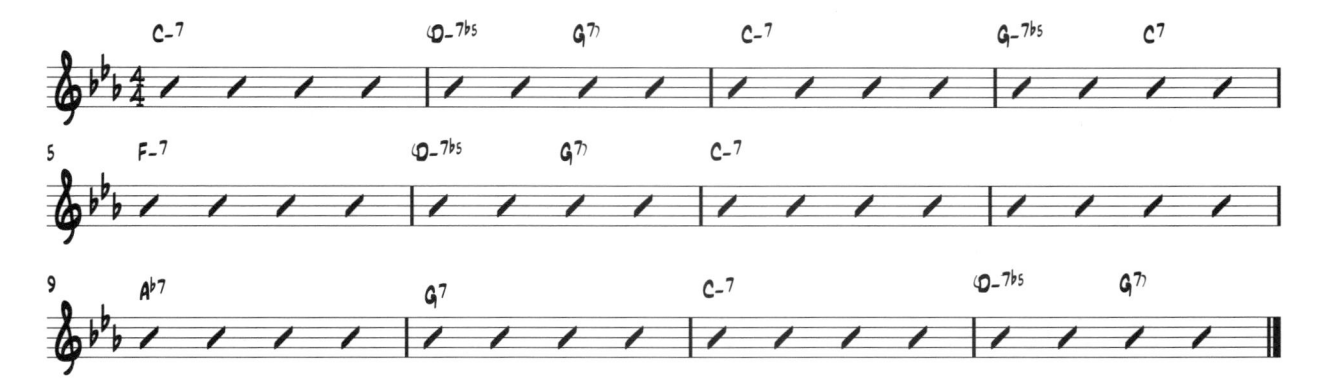

See if you can figure out the chord scales for the minor blues using the guidelines I gave you in Chapter 5.

Specific minor blues melodies that you might check out include "Footprints" (Wayne Shorter), "Mr. P.C." (John Coltrane), "Baltimore Oriole" (Hoagy Carmichael, not exactly a minor blues, but a variation with a more extended form), the theme to the T.V. show "Spiderman" (Robert Harris), "Interplay" (Bill Evans), and "Equinox" (John Coltrane).

So there you have it. Lots of fun activities to do on the blues. As always, keep in mind that having huge lists of possible things to do is not meant to be daunting. It's meant to allow you to pick any one of these things to work on for a while, as long as it interests you. Then you can try something else. Don't worry too much about finishing everything perfectly. You'll never get through the whole list, so work on something that you like until you start to feel less interested in it. Make an effort to be consistent, but don't beat yourself up if you aren't, as long as you keep doing things that engage you. The big list is meant to allow you to decide that a large number of these things aren't for you. You know, perhaps it's part of our American consumer culture to respond to a big bunch of things by assuming that we need to consume the whole lot. Just check out people's behavior at an all-you-can-eat restaurant (Sizzler's Steak House comes to mind). But this isn't like that. You don't need to take the macaroni salad, the potato salad, the pasta salad and the Jell-O salad (Jell-O salad?) just because it's there. (Actually, while we are on this metaphorical aside, the really incredible spot for this sort of

CHAPTER 10

behavior are the wok restaurants where you can take whatever you want and then they cook it for you. The concept there is, take as much as possible of the ingredients you like. I'm not sure, but I think that might not be the technique they are teaching for cooking at the Culinary Institute.) Getting back to your long list of things to try on the blues, you can pass up a whole bunch of things and then come back to them later or for that matter, never. If you find a few things you like to do and then do them repeatedly over different chord progressions, you will have gotten your money's worth out of this book.

Practicing Scatting 5:
Technical Drill

We've almost reached the end of our journey into the world of harmony as applied to the voice. In Chapter 8, I introduced chromatic approach note patterns to you by mentioning that you need to focus on these because they occur very often in jazz solos (and are important for creating a feeling of directionality in a line) and they aren't terribly vocalistic. They are hard to sing in tune so vocalists don't tend to utilize these patterns easily. Because of this, working on chromatic approach notes can be a very powerful tool since they address a fundamental difficulty that goes with the turf of being a scat soloist.

Another "un-vocalistic" qualitiy of jazz soloing is the use of wide intervals. For pianists (as I mentioned earlier) and even more so for guitarists, wide intervals are relatively easy to play. Once we know the available notes of a scale, we can pretty much play them in any octave anywhere on the instrument (of course, there are technical challenges to playing large leaps in a line that is moving quickly, but compared to SINGING these leaping lines, it's child's play.) If you are familiar with Mozart's opera "The Magic Flute" you can probably remember the famous "Queen of the Night" aria with its extremely high and fast arpeggiations. Believe me, that would be a lot easier to play on a piano than to sing.

So interval practice can make your scatting stronger and give you more confidence that you can hit the note precisely when you are singing lines that have a variety of different-sized intervals in them.

So let's start by working on intervals in an atonal context. Play any note and sing up a minor 3rd. Play any note and sing down a minor 3rd. Play any note and sing up a minor 3rd and then up another minor 3rd again. Play another note and sing three minor 3rds up from this note so that you are arpeggiating a diminished seventh chord. Now do the same thing using descending intervals: play any note and sing down two minor 3rds and then play any note and sing down three minor 3rds.

Now let's repeat all of the same steps with major 3rds. Play any note and sing up a major 3rd. Play any note and sing down a major 3rd. Play any note and sing up a major 3rd and then up another major 3rd again so that you are arpeggiating an augmented triad. Play any note and sing down two major 3rds, again arpeggiating an augmented triad, this time descending.

Repeat the above steps for each interval, first practicing each interval alone starting on different random pitches, ascending and descending, and then practicing the interval in combination with other similar intervals. Do this for all intervals (2nds, 3rds, 4ths, tritones, 5ths, 6ths 7ths).

CHAPTER 11

Make a page of random intervals and sing them. (Okay, I'll make the page for you.) You could make many pages like this to give yourself an essentially endless sequence of random pitches. Use intervals larger than an octave if you wish, although I haven't done that here.

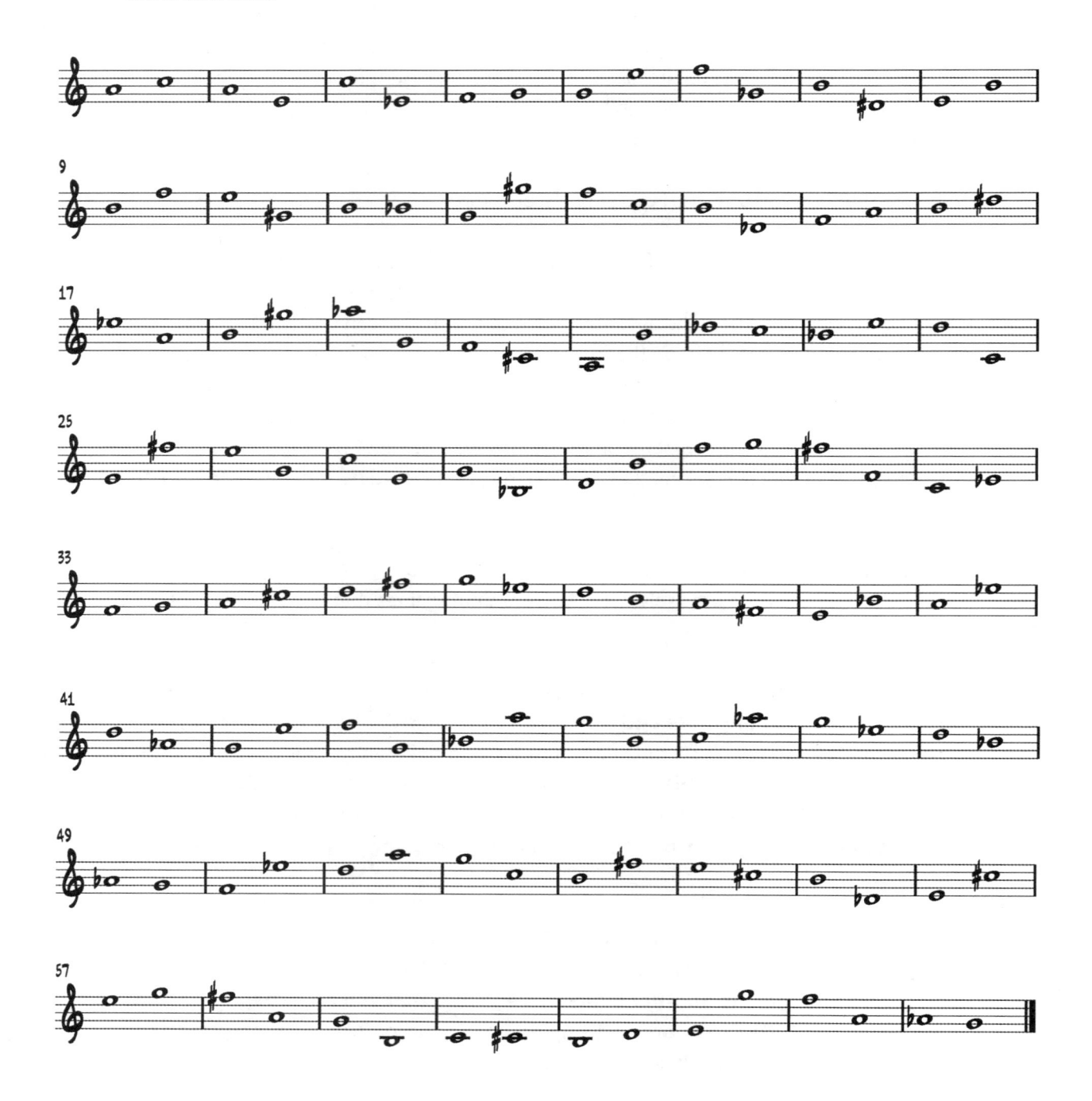

Read through the above interval page many times. You can also read the page upside down and in reverse order for more random intervals.

CHAPTER 11

Another exercise along these lines that I really like is playing air piano. Play a note, say D above middle C. Now, pick another note, let's say an ascending tritone up, so Ab. Just hold your finger above the note and sing it. Pick another interval, say a major 6th down. Sing the B holding your finger above that note. Continue in this manner, picking random intervals and then singing them, following the selected note with your finger above the note, only checking to see if you are right occasionally, perhaps every 4th or 5th note.

You can probably think of many other ways to work on intervals that aren't in a particular key. Doing so really helps you focus on the sound of intervals, since an underlying harmony isn't there (at least, not as much) to complicate what you are hearing. Books such as Modus Novus offer some more possibilities in this area.

Of course, hearing intervals in a key is also important, since you are improvising in a key when you sing over tunes. One way to explore this is by working on scales in different intervals. This is an exercise that I've seen sax players do more than any other instrumentalist, and I am not sure why. Let's start with the major scale. **You can sing it in 3rds.**

TRACK 35

You can sing it in 4ths

TRACK 36 **5ths**

121

CHAPTER 11

6ths

7ths

Please notice that as opposed to the intervals you were singing in an atonal context (not in any key), these intervals will change in order to fit the scale, so when you sing the major scale in 3rds you vary between singing major and minor 3rds; when singing the major scale in 4ths, between 4ths and tritones, when singing the major scale in 5ths, between 5ths and tritones, when singing the major scale in 6ths and 7ths, between major and minor 6ths and 7ths.

Singing the major scale is useful, in that as you get to larger intervals, you can check to see that you are really singing these intervals in tune. However, **much more useful is singing more unusual scales in different intervals.** This will really help you get some of these harder-to-hear scales in your ear, such as **the Locrian scale:**

TRACK 37

THIRDS

FOURTHS

CHAPTER 11

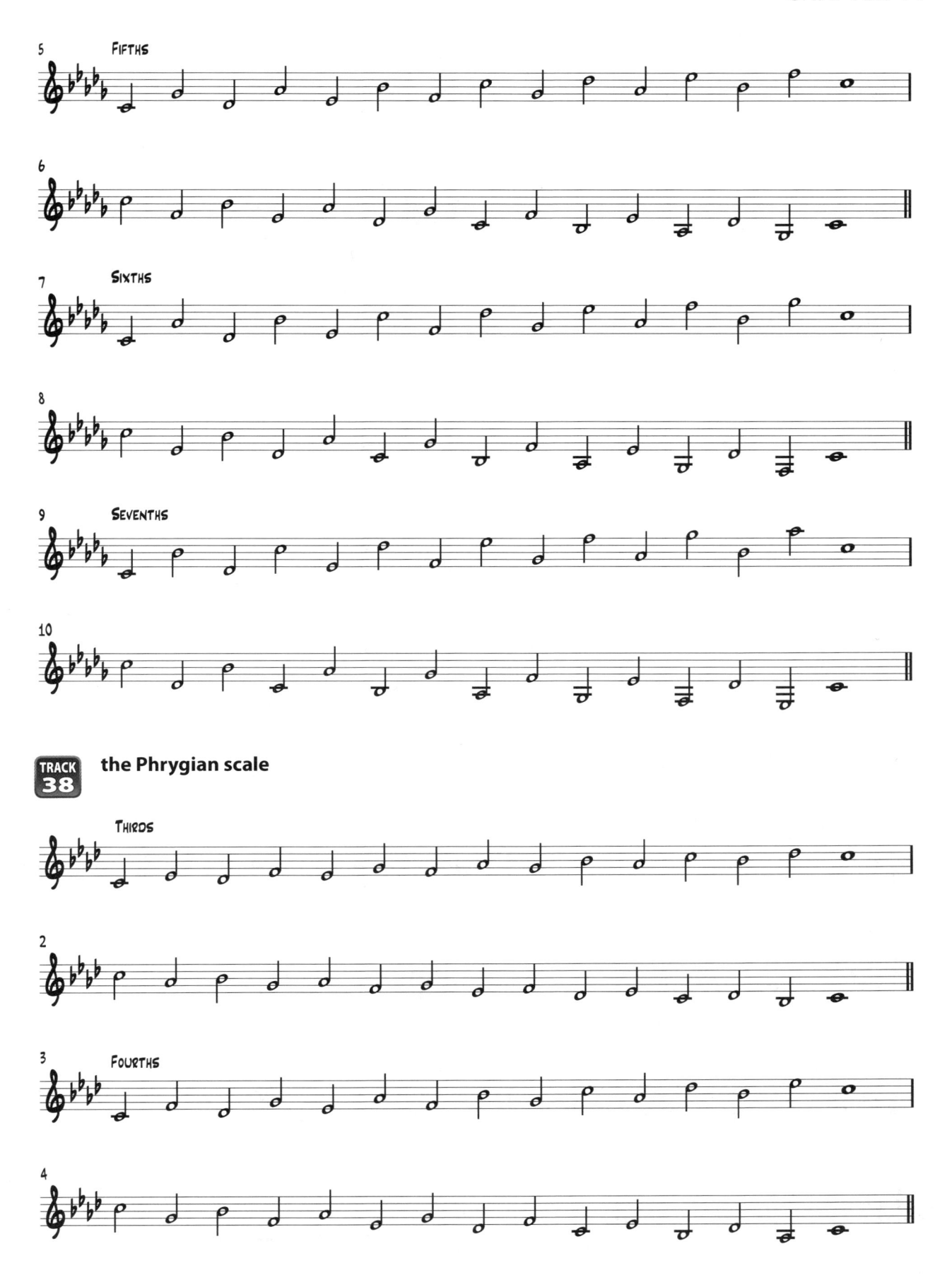

5 Fifths

6

7 Sixths

8

9 Sevenths

10

TRACK 38 — **the Phrygian scale**

1 Thirds

2

3 Fourths

4

CHAPTER 11

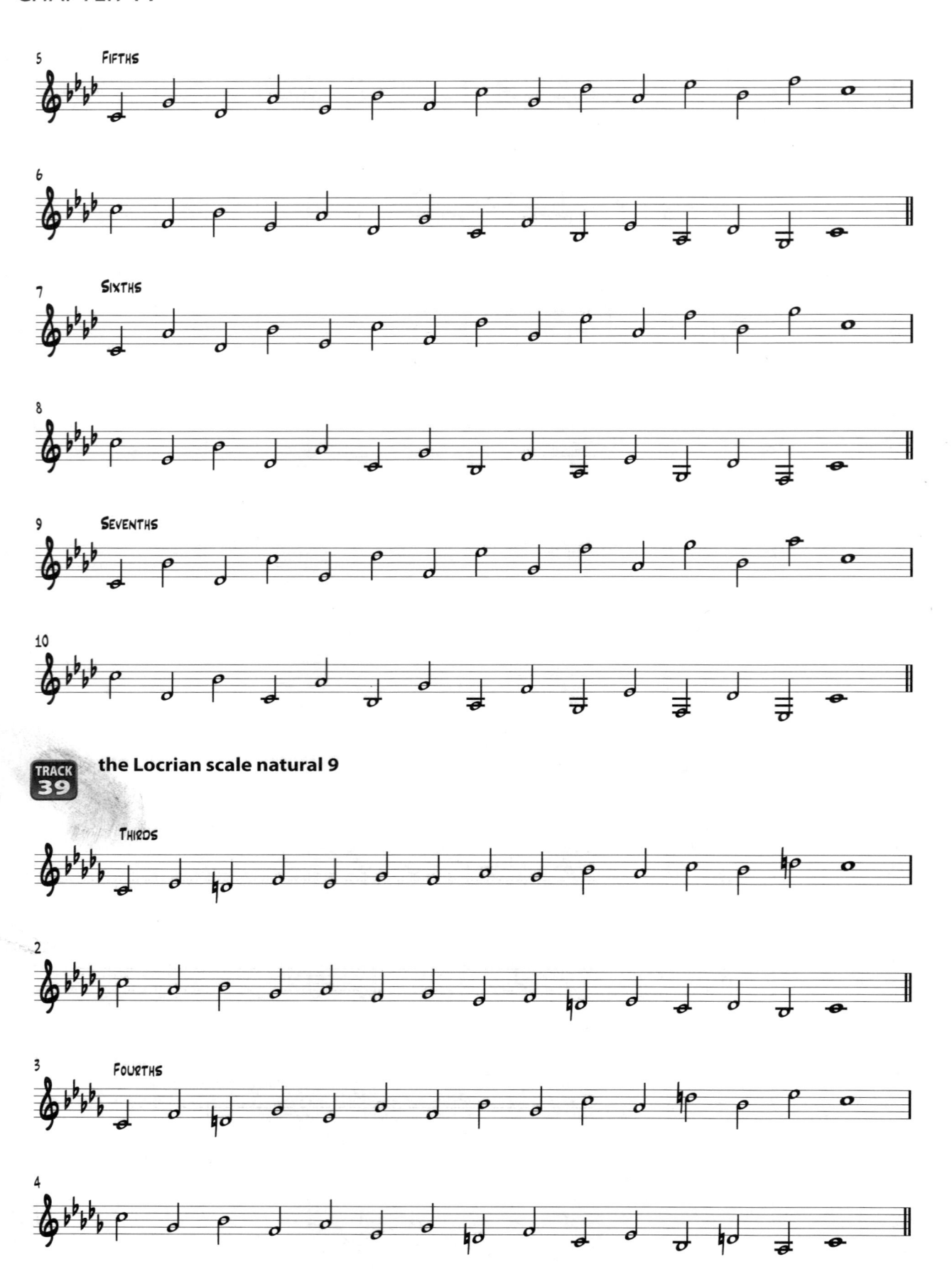

5 FIFTHS

6

7 SIXTHS

8

9 SEVENTHS

10

TRACK 39 — **the Locrian scale natural 9**

1 THIRDS

2

3 FOURTHS

4

CHAPTER 11

5 FIFTHS

6

7 SIXTHS

8

9 SEVENTHS

10

TRACK 40 the diminished scale

MINOR THIRDS

2

3 MAJOR THIRDS AND FOURTHS

4

CHAPTER 11

5 Tritones

6

7 Fifths and minor sixths

8

9 Major sixths

10

11 Minor and major sevenths

12

TRACK 41 — **and the altered scale**

1 Minor thirds

2

3 Major thirds and fourths

4

5 Tritones

6

7 Fifths and minor sixths

8

9 Major sixths

10

11 Minor and major sevenths

12

Doing this kind of practice helps your intonation and scale awareness and will give you a lot more ideas of things to sing over these scales. **After you've worked on these drills carefully, checking intonation frequently with the piano, try improvising freely over the scale and see if you can feel a difference.**

As always, all of these suggestions are just a beginning. If you dive into interval study, as well as all of the other practice techniques in this book, you are on the brink of a new dimension in your musical life. You can really change the amount of harmony you can hear and that will only make your experience of music, whether playing, singing, composing or even just listening, deeper.

CHAPTER 12

Practicing Scatting 9: Additional Forms and Vamps

Now we are all but done. (No, I mean it this time!) In fact, earlier versions of this book ended here, but a student of mine suggested that I include a few examples of common progressions that are useful to work on that aren't based on the progressions that you find in standards.

Actually, the progressions that she was talking about ARE traceable to standards and occur in standards, but she was right that it can be helpful to work on those pieces of progressions that are the most ubiquitous outside of the context of a particular tune. I want to repeat that **you should work with all of the exercises and practice methods in this book over many different progressions and pieces of progressions—practicing an individual chord scale or a 2, 4 or 8 bar section of the progression to gain control of something that you want to work on.**

These "pieces of progressions" should be looped to make short solo forms that you can work on. For example, we worked a lot with the chord changes to the A sections of "Autumn Leaves." I chose that progression because it contains very common harmonic elements, namely, ii-7 V7 IMaj7 in the major key, followed by ii-7b5 V7 i-6 in the relative minor. Of course, it would be extremely helpful to separate out these cadences and work on practicing in all of the ways that we've been doing in preceding chapters over the ii-7 V7 I Major, practicing in all keys:

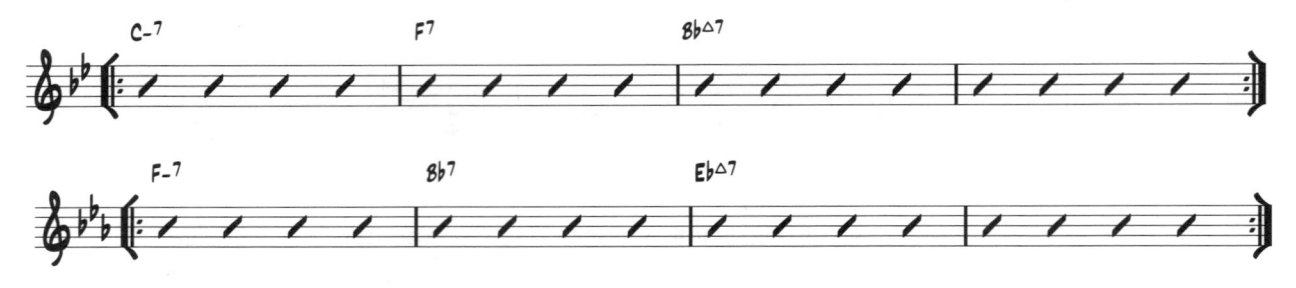

and so forth.

You should also work on the minor ii-7b5 V7 i-6 cadence, practicing THAT progression in all keys:

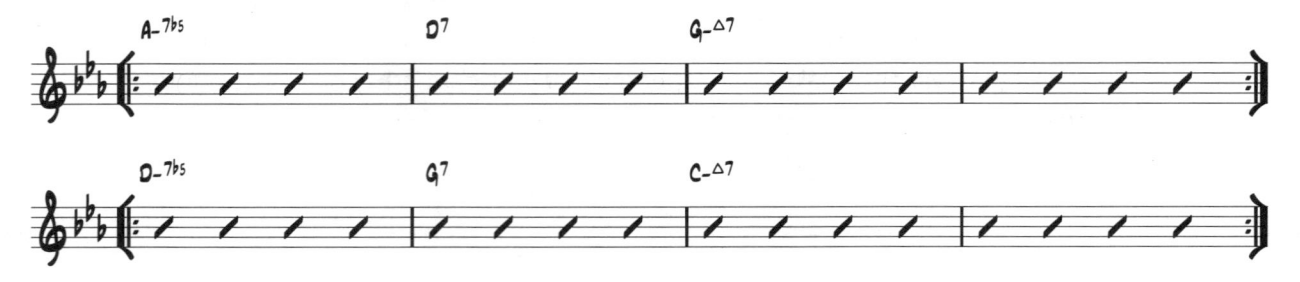

and so forth.

(Make sure that when you practice these progressions, you apply all of the techniques we've worked on to them. Also, make sure you use all of the chord scale options, particularly the dominant seventh chord scales: altered, b9, b13 and half/whole diminished.)

You can also practice ii-7 V7's in all keys:

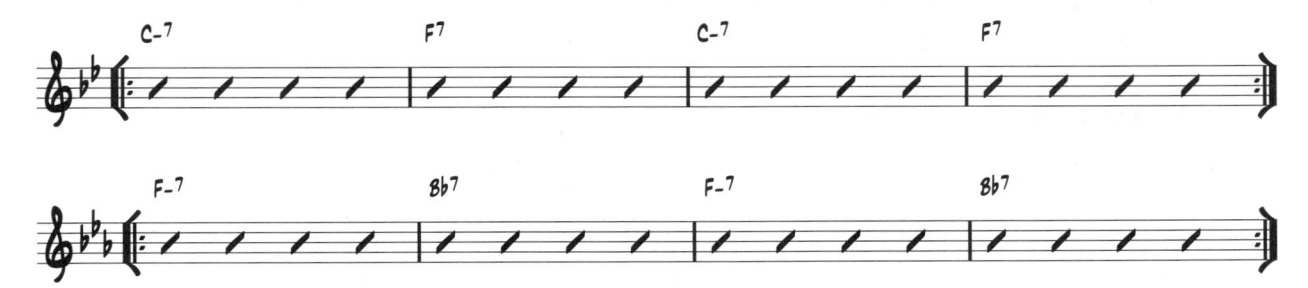

| C-7 | F7 | C-7 | F7 |

| F-7 | Bb7 | F-7 | Bb7 |

and so forth.

Another reason that I wanted to draw your attention to these short chord sequences is that these repeating sections often occur in tunes and arrangements as "vamps." A "vamp" is a short chord progression, often with a repeating rhythmic figure, that allows for extended soloing. It can occur at any point in a tune, but often comes at the beginning as a kind of intro section, or at the end as a kind of "repeat and fade" section.

One reason to work on vamps is that, for many singers, this is the main form that they improvise over. (The static harmony makes soloing easier). Still, there is more than just ease going on here. Vamps can be beautiful to solo over, and many kinds of music (Indian music, salsa and son montuno, modal jazz and funk to name a few) use vamps to great effect. Also, if you are going to spend any time soloing on them, you want to practice them to increase the amount of harmony that you are hearing over them.

Here are some common vamp options. Once again, **these should be practiced in all keys.**

I7 to bVII7 (Killer Joe)

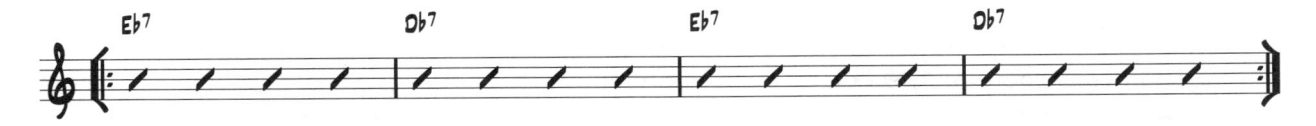

| Eb7 | Db7 | Eb7 | Db7 |

(Try the above progression with Mixolydian and Lydian b7 scales)

| Eb△7 | E△7 | Eb△7 | E△7 |

CHAPTER 12

(Try the above progression with both Ionian and Lydian scales.)

| Bb7sus4 | Bb7 | Bb7sus4 | Bb7 |

(Try the above progression with Mixolydian on the sus4 chord and altered on the dominant seventh chord.

| Bb7sus4b9 (Bδ7/Bb) | Bb7 | Bb7sus4b9 (Bδ7/Bb) | Bb7 |

(Try the above progressions with Bb phrygian on the susb9 chord and altered on the dominant seventh chord.)

In addition to the above vamps, turnarounds often function as vamps at the beginning or ending of tunes. The ii-7 V7 ii- V7 turnaround below is probably the most common way to end a vocal version of a standard.

| F-7 | Bb7 | G-7 | C7 |

It has many common variations:

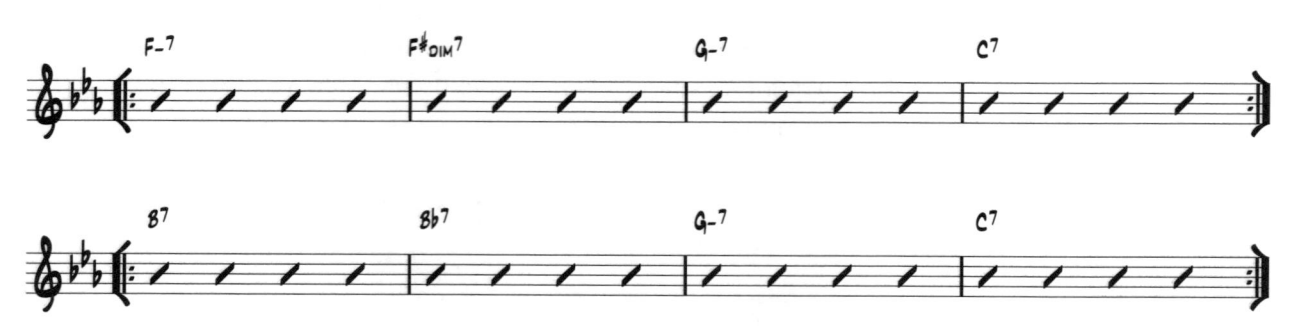

| F-7 | F#dim7 | G-7 | C7 |

| B7 | Bb7 | G-7 | C7 |

These should be familiar to you (or at least, the idea of coming up with variations to a particular chord progression by using tritone substitutes or passing chords should be familiar) from our discussion of turnarounds in Chapter 2. Try and use the rules we discussed in that part of the book to come up with additional variations on the above turnarounds.

Indeed, all of the turnarounds that we looked at earlier should also be looped for drill practice and should be practiced in all keys. For easy reference, here they are again:

CHAPTER 12

| C△7 | | | | D-7 | G7 | C△7 | | | | D-7 | G7 |

(Heart and Soul)

| C△7 | A-7 | D-7 | G7 | C△7 | A-7 | D-7 | G7 |

(Turnaround with secondary dominant, see below)

| C△7 | A7 | D-7 | G7 | C△7 | A7 | D-7 | G7 |

(Walking up and down, diatonic passing chords, se below)

| C△7 | D-7 | E-7 | D-7 | C△7 | D-7 | E-7 | D-7 |

(Turnaround with tritone substitute, see below)

| C△7 | Eb7 | D-7 | G7 | C△7 | Eb7 | D-7 | G7 |

Turnaround with tritone substitute, see below)

| C△7 | Eb7 | Ab7 | G7 | C△7 | Eb7 | Ab7 | G7 |

(Bemsha Swing, tritone substitutes again)

| C△7 | Eb7 | Ab7 | Db7 | C△7 | Eb7 | Ab7 | Db7 |

(C.T.A, bVII7, modal interchange, see below)

| C△7 | Bb7 | Ab7 | G7 | C△7 | Bb7 | Ab7 | G7 |

131

CHAPTER 12

Finally, ii-7 V7's are mixed and matched in different ways. They often move up a minor 3rd

| D-7 | G7 | F-7 | Bb7 |

or down a half step

| Eb-7 | Ab7 | D-7 | G7 |

So, practice the above progressions in many keys, creating harmonic variations by using tritone or other chord substitutes or by varying the harmonic rhythm (one chord per bar as above or changing chords twice as fast--each chord for two beats--or twice as slow--each chord for two bars.) Once again, I urge you to come up with your own progressions to practice over.

And with that brief discussion of vamps we really ARE done.

Conclusion

I hope this book helps you with your practicing, helping to open new musical horizons for you, empowering you to take control of the harmony of tunes to become a better musician. I don't want to be discouraging in any way, but to be absolutely honest, my experience with singers learning to improve their scatting through steady work has not been terribly good. I've seen singers improve, sometimes amazingly so, but in general, most of the singers that I've worked with haven't really made a sustained commitment to improving their scatting or working on harmony in a serious way. I've been trying to figure out why that is, and maybe it's because learning to solo over changes is simply not a high priority for most singers. I hope this is not the case: there are a lot of singers in colleges and jazz programs, and if they aren't there to learn about harmony and improvisation, they are missing a lot of the jazz experience. (One jazz school I know has stopped admitting singers to their graduate program for this reason.) Perhaps an instrumental approach to working on harmony isn't useful or appropriate for singers.

I think there are several other reasons why singers don't practice harmony steadily. One reason is that they don't have a systematic way to approach the material. They aren't sure what they need to do, and they haven't been schooled to connect with the jazz instrumental tradition. They assume that they can't develop the instrumental prowess to deal with hard chord changes, arrangements and singing over complex tunes. That was my real motivation for writing this book, to offer a path, an organized way of developing your inner jazz improvisor. Unlock the scatter within!

Yet another reason that many singers don't seriously work on the ideas in this book is that they think that music is about feeling and that a pragmatic and (perhaps overly) rational examination of the harmonic basis of music takes away some of the mystery or magic of the musical experience.

This is a real fear for some musicians and I DO understand about this one. Music is a complex path and there are a lot of spiritual avenues in it that need to be explored. I've had students who think you can become a great artist by doing a series of mathematical exercises, and I often tell them there's more to it than that. You need to invest more of yourself in it. You can't become a jazz musician in the same way that you can become a bookkeeper (although there may be more magic and spirituality to bookkeeping than I am aware of.) When I was a young jazz player starting out in Cleveland, I was really into Bud Powell's playing, and an older bebop bass player (who was truly out of his mind, but played amazing bebop melodies) said, "Berkman, I don't think you're crazy enough to play like Bud." Which was true up to a point. Over the years I've invested more and more of myself in music: traveling, teaching, writing and "living the life" to the point that I don't think anyone would dispute that I have more than enough of the necessary mental instability to make good music.

However (and in all seriousness), this is what I really want to say to those of you who are afraid to use intellectual approaches for fear of losing something mysterious, musical and magically "you" in your playing.

Don't worry too much about it.

I used to feel somewhat the same way myself, and when I hear tapes of myself from that period, I can't thank my lucky stars enough that I didn't fixate on that level of playing and continued to develop. Even at the risk of using my rational mind to develop aspects of my playing.

Rationality gets a bad rap from certain musicians. While it won't get you to the promised land, it will get you somewhere. You may sound less crazily inspired for a period, but if you stick with it, you will see steady improvement and can eventually find your way back to the magical part of your playing. Rationality and intellectuality, not terribly popular in American society as a whole, have their place in music and music practice, at least so it seems to me. Maybe if we start there, one day these qualities will even seep into our political system.

Of course, people with very few musical skills and a completely intuitive approach to playing often make some pretty great music and the reverse, people who are smart but lack feeling, don't usually do so well, but fortunately in this case, you don't have to choose. I urge you to use all of yourself to make music, from your brains to your heart to whatever other glands and organs you can get involved in the process.

Ultimately the biggest frustration teachers face is the passivity of students. I urge you to go after what you want, as a singer and musician. Practicing is an exploration, and as such it has enriched my life beyond the end result of improving my playing. It has given me a way to break down difficulties. It has taught me how to teach myself, both in the musical and non-musical parts of my life. It has helped me to keep striving to improve. Practicers are all idealists: we think we can always learn something new, we think we can always progress. That's why I am still at it after more than 40 years of playing.

Good luck with your practicing.

David Berkman
July 25, 2008

Sher Music Co. – The finest in Jazz & Latin Publications

THE NEW REAL BOOK SERIES

The Standards Real Book (C, Bb or Eb)

A Beautiful Friendship
A Time For Love
Ain't No Sunshine
Alice In Wonderland
All Of You
Alone Together
At Last
Baltimore Oriole
Bess, You Is My Woman
Bluesette
But Not For Me
Close Enough For Love
Crazy He Calls Me
Dancing In The Dark
Days Of Wine And Roses
Dreamsville
Easy To Love
Embraceable You
Falling In Love With Love
From This Moment On
Give Me The Simple Life
Have You Met Miss Jones?
Hey There
I Can't Get Started
I Concentrate On You
I Cover The Waterfront
I Love You
I Loves You Porgy
I Only Have Eyes For You
I'm A Fool To Want You
Indian Summer
It Ain't Necessarily So
It Never Entered My Mind
It's You Or No One
Just One Of Those Things
Love For Sale
Lover, Come Back To Me
The Man I Love
Mr. Lucky
My Funny Valentine
My Heart Stood Still
My Man's Gone Now
Old Folks
On A Clear Day
Our Love Is Here To Stay
'Round Midnight
Secret Love
September In The Rain
Serenade In Blue
Shiny Stockings
Since I Fell For You
So In Love
So Nice (Summer Samba)
Some Other Time
Stormy Weather
The Summer Knows
Summer Night
Summertime
Teach Me Tonight
That Sunday, That Summer
The Girl From Ipanema
Then I'll Be Tired Of You
There's No You
Time On My Hands
'Tis Autumn
Where Or When
Who Cares?
With A Song In My Heart
You Go To My Head
And Hundreds More!

The New Real Book - Volume 1 (C, Bb or Eb)

Angel Eyes
Anthropology
Autumn Leaves
Beautiful Love
Bernie's Tune
Blue Bossa
Blue Daniel
But Beautiful
Chain Of Fools
Chelsea Bridge
Compared To What
Darn That Dream
Desafinado
Early Autumn
Eighty One
E.S.P.
Everything Happens To Me
Feel Like Makin' Love
Footprints
Four
Four On Six
Gee Baby Ain't I Good To You
Gone With The Wind
Here's That Rainy Day
I Love Lucy
I Mean You
I Should Care
I Thought About You
If I Were A Bell
Imagination
The Island
Jersey Bounce
Joshua
Lady Bird
Like Someone In Love
Little Sunflower
Lush Life
Mercy, Mercy, Mercy
The Midnight Sun
Monk's Mood
Moonlight In Vermont
My Shining Hour
Nature Boy
Nefertiti
Nothing Personal
Oleo
Once I Loved
Out Of This World
Pent Up House
Portrait Of Tracy
Put It Where You Want It
Robbin's Nest
Ruby, My Dear
Satin Doll
Search For Peace
Shaker Song
Skylark
A Sleepin' Bee
Solar
Speak No Evil
St. Thomas
Street Life
Tenderly
These Foolish Things
This Masquerade
Three Views Of A Secret
Waltz For Debby
Willow Weep For Me
And Many More!

The New Real Book Play-Along CDs (For Volume 1)

CD #1 - Jazz Classics - Lady Bird, Bouncin' With Bud, Up Jumped Spring, Monk's Mood, Doors, Very Early, Eighty One, Voyage **& More!**
CD #2 - Choice Standards - Beautiful Love, Darn That Dream, Moonlight In Vermont, Trieste, My Shining Hour, I Should Care **& More!**
CD #3 - Pop-Fusion - Morning Dance, Nothing Personal, La Samba, Hideaway, This Masquerade, Three Views Of A Secret, Rio **& More!**
World-Class Rhythm Sections, featuring Mark Levine, Larry Dunlap, Sky Evergreen, Bob Magnusson, Keith Jones, Vince Lateano & Tom Hayashi

The New Real Book - Volume 2 (C, Bb or Eb)

Afro-Centric
After You've Gone
Along Came Betty
Bessie's Blues
Black Coffee
Blues For Alice
Body And Soul
Bolivia
The Boy Next Door
Bye Bye Blackbird
Cherokee
A Child Is Born
Cold Duck Time
Day By Day
Django
Equinox
Exactly Like You
Falling Grace
Five Hundred Miles High
Freedom Jazz Dance
Giant Steps
Harlem Nocturne
Hi-Fly
Honeysuckle Rose
I Hadn't Anyone 'Til You
I'll Be Around
I'll Get By
Ill Wind
I'm Glad There Is You
Impressions
In Your Own Sweet Way
It's The Talk Of The Town
Jordu
Killer Joe
Lullaby Of The Leaves
Manha De Carneval
The Masquerade Is Over
Memories Of You
Moment's Notice
Mood Indigo
My Ship
Naima
Nica's Dream
Once In A While
Perdido
Rosetta
Sea Journey
Senor Blues
September Song
Seven Steps To Heaven
Silver's Serenade
So Many Stars
Some Other Blues
Song For My Father
Sophisticated Lady
Spain
Stablemates
Stardust
Sweet And Lovely
That's All
There Is No Greater Love
'Til There Was You
Time Remembered
Turn Out The Stars
Unforgettable
While We're Young
Whisper Not
Will You Still Be Mine?
You're Everything
And Many More!

The New Real Book - Volume 3 (C, Bb, Eb or Bass clef)

Actual Proof
Ain't That Peculiar
Almost Like Being In Love
Another Star
Autumn Serenade
Bird Of Beauty
Black Nile
Blue Moon
Butterfly
Caravan
Ceora
Close Your Eyes
Creepin'
Day Dream
Dolphin Dance
Don't Be That Way
Don't Blame Me
Emily
Everything I Have Is Yours
For All We Know
Freedomland
The Gentle Rain
Get Ready
A Ghost Of A Chance
Heat Wave
How Sweet It Is
I Fall In Love Too Easily
I Got It Bad
I Hear A Rhapsody
If You Could See Me Now
In A Mellow Tone
In A Sentimental Mood
Inner Urge
Invitation
The Jitterbug Waltz
Just Friends
Just You, Just Me
Knock On Wood
The Lamp Is Low
Laura
Let's Stay Together
Lonely Woman
Maiden Voyage
Moon And Sand
Moonglow
My Girl
On Green Dolphin Street
Over The Rainbow
Prelude To A Kiss
Respect
Ruby
The Second Time Around
Serenata
The Shadow Of Your Smile
So Near, So Far
Solitude
Speak Like A Child
Spring Is Here
Stairway To The Stars
Star Eyes
Stars Fell On Alabama
Stompin' At The Savoy
Sweet Lorraine
Taking A Chance On Love
This Is New
Too High
(Used To Be A) Cha Cha
When Lights Are Low
You Must Believe In Spring
And Many More!

The All Jazz Real Book

Over 540 pages of tunes as recorded by: Miles, Trane, Bill Evans, Cannonball, Scofield, Brecker, Yellowjackets, Bird, Mulgrew Miller, Kenny Werner, MJQ, McCoy Tyner, Kurt Elling, Brad Mehldau, Don Grolnick, Kenny Garrett, Patitucci, Jerry Bergonzi, Stanley Clarke, Tom Harrell, Herbie Hancock, Horace Silver, Stan Getz, Sonny Rollins, and MORE!

Includes a free CD of many of the melodies (featuring Bob Sheppard & Friends.). $44 list price. Available in C, Bb, Eb

The European Real Book

An amazing collection of some of the greatest jazz compositions ever recorded! Available in C, Bb and Eb. $40

- Over 100 of Europe's best jazz writers.
- 100% accurate, composer-approved charts.
- 400 pages of fresh, exciting sounds from virtually every country in Europe.
- Sher Music's superior legibility and signature calligraphy makes reading the music easy.

Listen to FREE MP3 FILES of many of the songs at www.shermusic.com!

See www.shermusic.com for more information, including a complete list of tunes in all our fake books.
To order, call (800) 444-7437 or fax (707) 763-2038

SHER MUSIC JAZZ PUBLICATIONS

The Real Easy Book Vol. 1
TUNES FOR BEGINNING IMPROVISERS

Published by Sher Music Co. in conjunction with the Stanford Jazz Workshop. $22 list price.

The easiest tunes from Horace Silver, Eddie Harris, Freddie Hubbard, Red Garland, Sonny Rollins, Cedar Walton, Wes Montgomery Cannonball Adderly, etc. Get yourself or your beginning jazz combo sounding good right away with the first fake book ever designed for the beginning improviser.
Available in C, Bb, Eb and Bass Clef.

The Real Easy Book Vol. 2
TUNES FOR INTERMEDIATE IMPROVISERS

Published by Sher Music Co. in conjunction with the Stanford Jazz Workshop. Over 240 pages. $29.

The best intermediate-level tunes by: Charlie Parker, John Coltrane, Miles Davis, John Scofield, Sonny Rollins, Horace Silver, Wes Montgomery, Freddie Hubbard, Cal Tjader, Cannonball Adderly, and more! Both volumes feature instructional material tailored for each tune. Perfect for jazz combos!
Available in C, Bb, Eb and Bass Clef.

The Real Easy Book Vol. 3
A SHORT HISTORY OF JAZZ

Published by Sher Music Co. in conjunction with the Stanford Jazz Workshop. Over 200 pages. $25.

History text and tunes from all eras and styles of jazz. Perfect for classroom use. Available in C, Bb, Eb and Bass Clef versions.

The Best of Sher Music Co. Real Books
100+ TUNES YOU NEED TO KNOW

A collection of the best-known songs from the world leader in jazz fake books – Sher Music Co.!

Includes songs by: Miles Davis, John Coltrane, Bill Evans, Duke Ellington, Antonio Carlos Jobim, Charlie Parker, John Scofield, Michael Brecker, Weather Report, Horace Silver, Freddie Hubbard, Thelonious Monk, Cannonball Adderley, and many more!

$26. Available in C, Bb, Eb and Bass Clef.

The Serious Jazz Book II
THE HARMONIC APPROACH

By Barry Finnerty, Endorsed by: Joe Lovano, Jamey Aebersold, Hubert Laws, Mark Levine, etc.

- A 200 page, exhaustive study of how to master the harmonic content of songs.
- Contains explanations of every possible type of chord that is used in jazz.
- Clear musical examples to help achieve real harmonic control over melodic improvisation.
- For any instrument. $32. Money back gurantee!

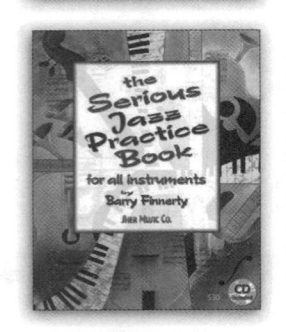

The Serious Jazz Practice Book By Barry Finnerty

A unique and comprehensive plan for mastering the basic building blocks of the jazz language. It takes the most widely-used scales and chords and gives you step-by-step exercises that dissect them into hundreds of cool, useable patterns.
Includes CD - $30 list price.

"The book I've been waiting for!" – Randy Brecker.

"The best book of intervallic studies I've ever seen."
– Mark Levine

The Jazz Theory Book

By Mark Levine, the most comprehensive Jazz Theory book ever published! $38 list price.
- Over 500 pages of text and over 750 musical examples.
- Written in the language of the working jazz musician, this book is easy to read and user-friendly. At the same time, it is the most comprehensive study of jazz harmony and theory ever published.
- Mark Levine has worked with Bobby Hutcherson, Cal Tjader, Joe Henderson, Woody Shaw, and many other jazz greats.

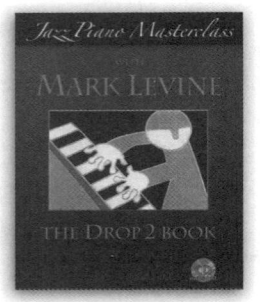

Jazz Piano Masterclass With Mark Levine
"THE DROP 2 BOOK"

The long-awaited book from the author of "The Jazz Piano Book!" A complete study on how to use "drop 2" chord voicings to create jazz piano magic! 68 pages, plus CD of Mark demonstrating each exercise. $19 list.

"Will make you sound like a real jazz piano player in no time." – Jamey Aebersold

Metaphors For The Musician
By Randy Halberstadt

This practical and enlightening book will help any jazz player or vocalist look at music with "new eyes." Designed for any level of player, on any instrument, "Metaphors For The Musician" provides numerous exercises throughout to help the reader turn these concepts into musical reality.

Guaranteed to help you improve your musicianship. 330 pages – $29 list price. Satisfaction guaranteed!

The Jazz Musicians Guide To Creative Practicing
By David Berkman

Finally a book to help musicians use their practice time wisely! Covers tune analysis, breaking hard tunes into easy components, how to swing better, tricks to playing fast bebop lines, and much more! 150+pages, plus CD. $29 list.

"Fun to read and bursting with things to do and ponder." – Bob Mintzer

The 'Real Easy' Ear Training Book
By Roberta Radley

For all musicians, regardless of instrument or experience, this is the most comprehensive book on "hearing the changes" ever published!
- Covers both beginning and intermediate ear training exercises.
- Music Teachers: You will find this book invaluable in teaching ear training to your students.

Book includes 168 pages of instructional text and musical examples, plus two CDs! $29 list price.

The Jazz Singer's Guidebook By David Berkman
A COURSE IN JAZZ HARMONY AND SCAT SINGING FOR THE SERIOUS JAZZ VOCALIST

A clear, step-by-step approach for serious singers who want to improve their grasp of jazz harmony and gain a deeper understanding of music fundamentals.

This book will change how you hear music and make you a better singer, as well as give you the tools to develop your singing in directions you may not have thought possible.

$26 – includes audio CD demonstrating many exercises.

LATIN MUSIC BOOKS, CDs, DVD

The Latin Real Book (C, Bb or Eb)
The only professional-level Latin fake book ever published! Over 570 pages. Detailed transcriptions exactly as recorded by:

Ray Barretto, Eddie Palmieri, Fania All-Stars, Tito Puente, Ruben Blades, Los Van Van, NG La Banda, Irakere, Celia Cruz, Arsenio Rodriguez, Tito Rodriguez, Orquesta Aragon, Beny Moré, Cal Tjader, Andy Narell, Mario Bauza, Dizzy Gilllespie, Mongo Santamaria, Manny Oquendo, Puerto Rico All-Stars, Issac Delgaldo, Ft. Apache Band, Dave Valentin, Paquito D'Rivera, Clare Fischer, Chick Corea, Sergio Mendes, Ivan Lins, Djavan, Tom Jobim, Toninho Horta, Joao Bosco, Milton Nascimento, Leila Pinheiro, Gal Costa, **And Many More!**

The Latin Real Book Sampler CD
12 of the greatest Latin Real Book tunes as played by the original artists: Tito Puente, Ray Barretto, Andy Narell, Puerto Rico Allstars, Bacacoto, etc. $16 list price. Available in U.S.A. only.

The Conga Drummer's Guidebook By Michael Spiro
Includes CD - $28 list price. The only method book specifically designed for the intermediate to advanced conga drummer. It goes behind the superficial licks and explains how to approach any Afro-Latin rhythm with the right feel, so you can create a groove like the pros!.

"This book is awesome. Michael is completely knowledgable about his subject." – Dave Garibaldi

"A breakthrough book for all students of the conga drum." – Karl Perazzo

Introduction to the Conga Drum - DVD
By Michael Spiro

For beginners, or anyone needing a solid foundation in conga drum technique.

Jorge Alabe – "Mike Spiro is a great conga teacher. People can learn real conga technique from this DVD."

John Santos – "A great musician/teacher who's earned his stripes"

1 hour, 55 minutes running time. $25.

Muy Caliente!
Afro-Cuban Play-Along CD and Book
Rebeca Mauleón - Keyboard
Oscar Stagnaro - Bass
Orestes Vilató - Timbales
Carlos Caro - Bongos
Edgardo Cambon - Congas
Over 70 min. of smokin' Latin grooves!
Stereo separation so you can eliminate the bass or piano. Play-along with a rhythm section featuring some of the top Afro-Cuban musicians in the world! $18.

The True Cuban Bass
By Carlos Del Puerto, (bassist with Irakere) and Silvio Vergara, $22.

For acoustic or electric bass; English and Spanish text; Includes CDs of either historic Cuban recordings or Carlos playing each exercise; Many transcriptions of complete bass parts for tunes in different Cuban styles – the roots of Salsa.

101 Montunos
By Rebeca Mauleón

The only comprehensive study of Latin piano playing ever published.

- Bi-lingual text (English/Spanish)
- 2 CDs of the author demonstrating each montuno
- Covers over 100 years of Afro-Cuban styles, including the danzón, guaracha, mambo, merengue and songo—from Peruchin to Eddie Palmieri. $28

The Salsa Guide Book
By Rebeca Mauleón

The only complete method book on salsa ever published! 260 pages. $25.

Carlos Santana – "A true treasure of knowledge and information about Afro-Cuban music."

Mark Levine, author of The Jazz Piano Book. – "This is *the* book on salsa."

Sonny Bravo, pianist with Tito Puente – "This will be the salsa 'bible' for years to come."

Oscar Hernández, pianist with Rubén Blades – "An excellent and much needed resource."

The Brazilian Guitar Book
By Nelson Faria, one of Brazil's best new guitarists.

- Over 140 pages of comping patterns, transcriptions and chord melodies for samba, bossa, baião, etc.
- Complete chord voicings written out for each example.
- Comes with a CD of Nelson playing each example.
- The most complete Brazilian guitar method ever published! $28.

Joe Diorio – "Nelson Faria's book is a welcome addition to the guitar literature. I'm sure those who work with this volume wiill benefit greatly"

Inside The Brazilian Rhythm Section
By Nelson Faria and Cliff Korman

This is the first book/CD package ever published that provides an opportunity for bassists, guitarists, pianists and drummers to interact and play-along with a master Brazilian rhythm section. Perfect for practicing both accompanying and soloing.

$28 list price for book and 2 CDs - including the charts for the CD tracks and sample parts for each instrument, transcribed from the recording.

The Latin Bass Book
A PRACTICAL GUIDE
By Oscar Stagnaro

The only comprehensive book ever published on how to play bass in authentic Afro-Cuban, Brazilian, Caribbean, Latin Jazz & South American styles. $34.

Over 250 pages of transcriptions of Oscar Stagnaro playing each exercise. Learn from the best!

Includes: 3 Play-Along CDs to accompany each exercise, featuring world-class rhythm sections.

Afro-Caribbean Grooves for Drumset
By Jean-Philippe Fanfant, drummer with Andy narell's band, Sakesho.

Covers grooves from 10 Caribbean nations, arranged for drumset.

Endorsed by Peter Erskine, Horacio Hernandez, etc.

CD includes both audio and video files. $25.

MORE JAZZ PUBLICATIONS

The Digital Real Book
On the web

Over 850 downloadable tunes from all the Sher Music Co. fakebooks.

See www.shermusic.com for details.

Jazz Guitar Voicings The Drop 2 Book
By Randy Vincent, Everything you need to know to create full chord melody voicings like Jim Hall, Joe Pass, etc. Luscious voicings for chord melody playing based on the "Drop 2" principle of chord voicings.

You will find that this book covers this essential material in a unique way unlike any other guitar book available.

Endorsed by Julian Lage, John Stowell, Larry Koonse, etc.

$25, includes 2 CDs.

Three-Note Voicings and Beyond
By Randy Vincent, A complete guide to the construction and use of every kind of three-note voicing on guitar.

"Randy Vincent is an extraordinary musician. This book illuminates harmonies in the most sensible and transparent way." – Pat Metheny

"This book is full of essential information for jazz guitarists at any level. Wonderful!" – Mike Stern

194 pages, $28

The Jazz Piano Book
By Mark Levine, Concord recording artist and pianist with Cal Tjader. For beginning to advanced pianists. The only truly comprehensive method ever published! Over 300 pages. $32
Richie Beirach – "The best new method book available."
Hal Galper – "This is a must!"
Jamey Aebersold – "This is an invaluable resource for any pianist."
James Williams – "One of the most complete anthologies on jazz piano."
Also available in Spanish! ¡El Libro del Jazz Piano!

The Blues Scales
ESSENTIAL TOOLS FOR JAZZ IMPROVISATION
By Dan Greenblatt

Great Transcriptions from Miles, Dizzy Gillespie, Lester Young, Oscar Peterson, Dave Sanborn, Michael Brecker and many more, showing how the Blues Scales are actually used in various styles of jazz.

Accompanying CD by author Dan Greenblatt and his swinging quartet of New York jazz musicians shows how each exercise should sound. And it also gives the student numerous play-along tracks to practice with. $22

Forward Motion
FROM BACH TO BEBOP
A Corrective Approach to Jazz Phrasing
By Hal Galper

- Perhaps the most important jazz book in a decade, Foward Motion shows the reader how to create jazz phrases that swing with authentic jazz feeling.
- Hal Galper was pianist with Cannonball Adderley, Phil Woods, Stan Getz, Chet Baker, John Scofield, and many other jazz legends.
- Each exercise available on an interactive website so that the reader can change tempos, loop the exercises, transpose them, etc. $30

Foundation Exercises for Bass
By Chuck Sher

A creative approach for any style of music, any level, acoustic or electric bass. Perfect for bass teachers!

Filled with hundreds of exercises to help you master scales, chords, rhythms, hand positions, ear training, reading music, sample bass grooves, creating bass lines on common chord progressions, and much more.

$24

Walking Bassics: The Fundamentals of Jazz Bass Playing
By swinging NY bassist Ed Fuqua

Includes transcriptions of every bass note on accompanying CD and step-by-step method for constructing solid walking bass lines. $22.

Endorsed by Eddie Gomez, Jimmy Haslip, John Goldsby, etc.

Concepts for Bass Soloing
By Chuck Sher and Marc Johnson, (bassist with Bill Evans, etc.) The only book ever published that is specifically designed to improve your soloing! $26

- Includes two CDs of Marc Johnson soloing on each exercise
- Transcriptions of bass solos by: Eddie Gomez, John Patitucci, Scott LaFaro, Jimmy Haslip, etc.

"It's a pleasure to encounter a Bass Method so well conceived and executed." – Steve Swallow

The Improvisor's Bass Method
By Chuck Sher. A complete method for electric or acoustic bass, plus transcribed solos and bass lines by Mingus, Jaco, Ron Carter, Scott LaFaro, Paul Jackson, Ray Brown, and more! Over 200 pages. $16

International Society of Bassists – "Undoubtedly the finest book of its kind."
Eddie Gomez – "Informative, readily comprehensible and highly imaginative"

Essential Grooves
FOR WRITING, PERFORMING AND PRODUCING CONTEMPORARY MUSIC
By 3 Berklee College professors: Dan Moretti, Matthew Nicholl and Oscar Stagnaro

- 41 different rhythm section grooves used in Soul, Rock, Motown, Funk, Hip-hop, Jazz, Afro-Cuban, Brazilian, music and more!
- Includes CD and multi-track DVD with audio files to create play-alongs, loops, original music, and more.

$24

The World's Greatest Fake Book
Jazz & Fusion Tunes by: Coltrane, Mingus, Jaco, Chick Corea, Bird, Herbie Hancock, Bill Evans, McCoy, Beirach, Ornette, Wayne Shorter, Zawinul, AND MANY MORE! $32

Chick Corea – "Great for any students of jazz.'
Dave Liebman – "The fake book of the 80's."
George Cables – "The most carefully conceived fake book I've ever seen."

THE REAL EASY BOOK, VOL. 2

Now with 3-Horn Arrangements

THE BEST INTERMEDIATE-LEVEL TUNES BY:
Charlie Parker
John Coltrane
Miles Davis
John Scofield
Sonny Rollins
Horace Silver
Cannonball Adderley
AND MORE!

ALSO FEATURING:
Instructional material tailored for each tune. Perfect for Jazz Combos!

Like Vol. 1, extra horn parts make the songs come alive! 8 selected songs

$16 for the digital-only package

AVAILABLE AT SHERMUSIC.COM